BUTTON GWINNETT
America's Accidental Founding Father

BY

MARK J. DI VINCENZO

*For
Jayne
and
Rosie*

Contents

Introduction

You've probably never heard of Button Gwinnett, but if you have, the first time may have been in American history class. I first encountered him there when I was 12, and a few questions immediately popped in my head: Why would anyone name their child Button? How did a British guy get to sign the Declaration of Independence? How did he get himself involved in a duel?

I'm sure I didn't give a thought to trying to find answers to those questions. In fact, I don't remember thinking about him again until about 45 years later when I was on a walking tour in downtown Savannah, Ga., and the guide pointed out a cemetery where Gwinnett "may or may not be buried." *May or may not be buried?* Now *that* was intriguing. I wanted to know more about that, and I ended up with many more questions about a man I found increasingly fascinating. Why did he fail at every business he tried? Why was he chosen to serve in one of the most impactful sessions of Congress in our nation's history? Why is he on every list of America's Founding Fathers? Why do his signatures sell for seven figures?

The quest to answer those questions — as well as the ones that rattled around my 12-year-old brain — led me to this: the first full-length biography of Gwinnett in a century.

This intelligent, confident, selfish and impulsive character has been largely ignored by four generations of historians for two reasons: First, it's very difficult to write a lot about Gwinnett because there is a scant paper trail associated with him, and that's an understatement. During a time when you couldn't email, text or even send someone a telegram, you wrote letters. A lot of letters. But only one personal letter from Gwinnett has surfaced, and it's only two sentences long. No known personal letters *to him* exist. Not from his wife, his parents, his siblings, his daughter or his friends. A lot of people in the 18th century kept diaries, but if Gwinnett had one, it hasn't surfaced. Neither have diaries for anyone who knew him, The second reason he has been ignored is no one has challenged his first biographer's view of him as a patriot and a worthy Founding Father. As a long-time journalist, a history buff and an author, it surprised me that those who are familiar with the historical record would let stand that interpretation of Gwinnett.

I wrote this book because — as we come upon the 250th anniversary of the signing of the Declaration of Independence — I'm making the case that Gwinnett is perhaps the nation's most apathetic and selfish Founding Father, a supremely confident man who craved power and cared much more about himself than about his adopted country. The existing historical record led me to no other interpretation. If you know a little about Gwinnett and you've embraced the narrative that he deserves to be called a Founding Father, you're in for more than a few surprises, but either way I hope you'll consider this the most nuanced and comprehensive telling of his life.

It started in a sleepy English village in the Cotswolds near the Welsh border, and it essentially ended in a cow pasture on the eastern edge of Savannah, Georgia. In between is a wild ride of a life. Amazingly enough, nearly 250 years later, Gwinnett still finds himself in the news. His rare signatures sell for seven figures today, and he has become something of a folk hero, thanks in part to *Hamilton* star Lin-Manuel Miranda's decision to write a rap song about him. (Check out the clever lyrics in the final chapter.)

Whatever you may think of Gwinnett, he lived a tumultuous life and carried strong beliefs. He believed in capitalism. He believed in the philosophy of carpe diem. And most importantly, he believed in himself.

1
A Land of Opportunity

In the insignificant riverfront town of Savannah in the insignificant British colony of Georgia, creamy white flowers from magnolias sweetened the thick air, and across the Savannah River, new green shoots of cordgrass revealed themselves in the dense marsh anchored in the mudflats. Button Gwinnett had no interest in anything happening on that side of the river.

After he tethered his two-masted schooner to a wharf along the river's south side, he walked past the brigantines and the 16 oak-framed warehouses that rose from the shore to the top of a crumbling bluff with a view of the Georgia-South Carolina border. It was early May in 1766. His destination was a cluster of stores called Commerce Row,[1] Savannah's main commercial district, where he entered Read and Mossman's. This dry goods store was owned by two Scots, James Reed and James Mossman, who settled in this remote place named after King George II. Georgia, with only about 10,000 white people and more than 7,800 enslaved men, women and children at the time, was in the middle of nowhere, the south-ernmost of England's 13 American colonies.[2]

Read and Mossman's was a popular shop, where customers could buy thread, padlocks, buckskin gloves, nails, rope, coffee, tea, shoes, candles, beaver hats — just about anything that anyone needed in the out-skirts of 18th-century America.[3]

Gwinnett was a regular there, and its owners knew him by sight — and by number. Shoppers were assigned a number, and Gwinnett's was 309.[4] Everyone who was anyone shopped there, including James Wright, the royal governor, and everyone received a number.[5] If the store was good enough for Savannah's elite, it was good enough for Gwinnett, who stopped in about once a month after he moved to Savannah in 1765. During that trip to the store, he paid 1 British pound, 9 shillings and 11 pence for twine, needles, a pair of buckles, writing paper, pepper, a frock, nails, a pen knife and a silk handkerchief.[6]

Read and Mossman and Savannah's other retailers enticed shoppers with manufactured goods imported from England and Ireland — and enslaved people from the Caribbean and western Africa.

A couple of days after Gwinnett bought his stationery and his silk handkerchief, nine "Negroe boys" were sold there.[7] They went for £30 each, except for one who sold at a discount of £27 and 10 shillings. No reason was given in the store's ledger book for the price reduction. Was he very young? Did he walk with a limp? Was he small for his age? Whatever it was, the person who bought him saw something he didn't like and negotiated the discount. The boys' ages also weren't recorded in the ledger, nor were their names. Enslaved children often didn't get names until they were older. If they were weak and didn't survive, their owners would have wasted their time coming up with names. Whatever they were called at that point didn't matter anyway because more likely than not, their new owners would rename them. Depending on how often they were sold and resold, they could be expected to have more than one first name during their lifetimes, even if their lifetimes ended before their teen years, as they often did.

One of the men who purchased a boy that day at Read and Mossman's was South Carolina-born lawyer Archibald Bulloch,[8] who moved to Savannah in 1764, one year before Gwinnett. He would win election to the colonial legislature before long and become Georgia's first American-born governor in

1777. He would be hailed as one of Georgia's greatest leaders, a patriot and a Founding Father who earned the respect of John Hancock and John Adams.[9] Many years after he died, Bulloch would have a great-great-grandson, Theodore Roosevelt, the 26th President of the United States, and a great-great-great granddaughter, Eleanor Roosevelt, the wife of President Franklin Delano Roosevelt.

Gwinnett would end up with no descendants, and no one who knew him in 1766 would have predicted a bright future for him. He had not attended college or served an apprenticeship, and he had failed in his attempt to become a successful transatlantic merchant. There may have been rumors that he owed a lot of money to a lot of people, but his fellow Georgians couldn't have known then that he had creditors on three continents, and that a ship he owned would soon be seized in the English port city of Bristol and sold to satisfy some of those debts.

His sole focus in Georgia, as it had been since his teen years clerking at a grocery store in England, was to make money. He wanted to make a lot of money. And unlike Bulloch, he wasn't wasting any of his time on public service. Working with others to make laws to improve the lives of other Georgians didn't interest him. Gwinnett believed his big brain and his strong work ethic would lead to a better life for him and his wife and daughter. Nothing else mattered to him.

Like Read and Mossman, Gwinnett also thought Georgia, though small and remote, was a place with a lot of potential, where a man with ambition could become important. And he was convinced his luck was about to change. He believed that even though he shouldn't have. A new opportunity he recently seized would allow him to become that important man he always wanted to be. Or so he thought.

Gwinnett identified Georgia as the perfect place for him to be. What he didn't know when he moved there is that his timing was also perfect.

James Edward Oglethorpe had a reputation for being composed and determined, but as he left England in November 1732 to colonize Georgia, he had reason to worry. About whether his countrymen could survive the heat, the humidity and the mosquitos. About the reaction of Native Americans to their presence. About whether the 113 people who made the trip with him — carpenters, servants, shoemakers, coopers, butchers and others — were up to the task of clearing enough land, growing enough food and building enough houses to survive in a place that was foreign to them in every imaginable way.

But more than anything, Oglethorpe worried about the Spaniards in Florida. When they arrived in

America nearly 200 years earlier, Spain had claimed much of coastal Georgia as its own. So there was no doubt in Oglethorpe's mind that Englishmen and Spaniards eventually would shed blood over that swampy coastline that no one should have wanted badly enough to fight for. To prepare for what he saw as inevitable conflict, he ordered the creation of a fortified outpost called Frederica — protected by a six-foot-high earthen wall, a moat and a cedar palisade — on the coast, about 90 miles southeast of Savannah. The hope was that a small militia stationed there might slow down the Spaniards if they planned to invade Savannah, where the vast majority of these new Georgians lived at the time.

Frederica didn't worry the Spaniards. They had Castillo de San Marcos, in St. Augustine, the capital of East Florida, as it was called then. They built the fort using a masonry compound that required mixing shell, limestone and water. After it hardened, it worked like magic. It could absorb the impact of cannon balls, causing them to sink into the walls rather than shattering them.[10] The fort's walls stood 20 feet tall and were a whopping 14 feet thick at the base and six feet thick at the top. There was a moat on three sides of it, with water depths between 10 feet and 18 feet. If that weren't enough, they planted pine trees around the moat, making it difficult for enemy archers to reach the fort with their arrows. Castillo de San Marcos, which took 23 years to build, was so impenetrable that St. Augustine was often referred to as "the fortified city of St. Augustine."

As early as 1736, Oglethorpe began spying on St. Augustine so he could see the fort, which he heard about from others. He reported what he saw to Parliament and to King George II, and in 1737 returned to England to ask for military support, which he received as well as the title of colonel. Unfortunately for Oglethorpe, the Spaniards knew exactly what he was doing.

In a letter dated March 22, 1737, Manuel de Montiano, the governor of East Florida, asked for money to defend itself "against the premeditated intentions of the English to make themselves masters of it and its Provinces."[11] He continued:

"…the king of Great Britain has (been) submitted in his Parliament by My lord Ogletor, (Oglethorpe) a member of the same, who impressed on it how more useful and convenient would be to G. (Great) Britain this place…. And although the Parliament was opposed to making any irruption during the Peace they agreed to these reports, which have reached me; likewise in Apalache the Cacique Sacafaca of the Pueblo Chalacarliche, who came expressly and voluntarily from those remote Provinces to warn us that the Indians friendly to the English will descend in small bodies to harass these coasts…."

The premediated intentions became premeditated action in the summer of 1740, when Oglethorpe led an attack on St. Augustine. He and his men, about 600 of whom came from the more-established and populated colony of South Carolina, never stood a chance. Their cannon balls did nothing to weaken the fort. "Since the commencement of their fire to this day," Manuel de Montiano wrote on July 6, 1740, "they have showered on us 122 shells of royal size and 31 small ones, from which, glory be to God, we have received no corporeal damage."[12]

Oglethorpe eventually retreated and after he returned, he received a lot of grief from the Carolina House of Assembly. Oglethorpe pushed back, arguing that Carolina also had a lot at stake and should continue to support these efforts. If the Spaniards attacked Georgia, Oglethorpe said South Carolina would be next. He pointed out that most people in South Carolina were enslaved and wouldn't defend the colony even if they were armed. "Carolina has above 40,000 negroes and not 4,000 (Caucasians) that can bear arms," Oglethorpe said. "If they (the Spaniards) remove us (Georgians), all that country is at their pleasure."[13]

The Spaniards, feeling emboldened by their victory in 1740, retaliated in 1742, coming ashore at St. Simons. However, attacking Georgia proved more difficult than defending St. Augustine. Oglethorpe's fledgling militia chased them out of Georgia in what became known as the Battle of the Bloody Marsh. He attacked St. Augustine again, in 1743, and he failed again. After 10 years in Georgia, he returned to England, where he requested a court-martial inquiry to clear his name against accusations brought by South Carolina officers.[14] He was acquitted in 1744.[15] He never returned to America.

Just as his arrival changed Georgia forever, so did his departure. In the years after he left, the colony's demographics changed, and so did its economy. All because of slavery.

Oglethorpe wouldn't allow it in Georgia when he was in charge mainly for two reasons: First, Parliament intended for the development of Georgia to be somewhat of a social experiment. Unlike the other British colonies in America, the plan was for white Englishmen — not enslaved people — to clear the forests to make room for towns and farm fields. However, Oglethorpe underestimated how difficult that would be for the relatively few men who initially settled in Georgia, and he overestimated how many of those men would be willing to put in the enormous amount of work to make this experiment a success. And second, Spain promised freedom to runaway slaves who reached Florida and became Catholics. The caveat: Those freed slaves would be required to help fight against English militias.[16]

Oglethorpe reasoned that if there were no enslaved people in Georgia, then he didn't have to worry about anyone fleeing to Florida and later teaming up with the Spaniards to disrupt what England was trying to accomplish in Georgia.

Although he was on the right side of history, morally speaking, his insistence that Georgia ban slavery stunted its economy during a time when it would have benefited from that growth.

With Oglethorpe gone, Georgia found itself without a strong anti-slavery voice, and slaves trickled into the colony, dozens at a time, starting in the mid-1740s. Savannah-based merchants imported them from the Caribbean, landing them in Charleston, S.C., where they briefly stayed before they were shipped to Savannah and sold to planters. The influx of slaves was slow. By 1750, about 3,000 people lived in Georgia, and less than 500 were enslaved.[17]

James Habersham, an English-born Georgia who would become a leader in the colony, lamented what he viewed as a shortage of enslaved people then. "I suppose we shall hardly make Rice this year sufficient to Load a Ship of 500 barrels to London, and if a Small Portion of our hands were Employed in the Cultivation of Indigo, it wou'd go but a little way in Loading a Ship."[18] What went unsaid is that year South Carolina exported 54,745 barrels of rice, and that was a down year for rice production there.[19]

On the first day of 1751, slavery was officially instituted by royal decree in Georgia — the last of England's American colonies to allow it — and a slave ship arrived in 1752, bringing 20 enslaved Jamaicans to Savannah.[20] By then, South Carolina had an 82-year head start importing enslaved people. In fact, by 1708, they outnumbered white people in South Carolina,[21] turning it into an agricultural powerhouse. Slavery not only enriched the planters who needed them to work their fields but the merchants who found markets for those crops and transported them. Not long after slavery was instituted in Georgia, merchants from England and Scotland, such as James Read and James Mossman, began arriving in Savannah, steering the colony's economy by importing increasing numbers of enslaved people from the Caribbean and manufactured goods from Great Britain.

If Georgia followed South Carolina's lead and used slave labor to produce crops, these merchants assumed the economy would grow, and they would prosper. They assumed correctly, and they were in a great position to succeed. Merchants in Georgia then possessed a retail know-how, access to investment capital in London and strategic connections with merchants and wholesalers in England and the Caribbean.[22] In 1753, the number of merchants in Savannah doubled from about five or six to 10 or 12.[23] While that might not represent a stampede, so many ships were bringing goods to the city's port that an inn reserved for mercantile crews opened that year in Savannah. (That building, known today as The Pirates House, has survived devastating fires and powerful hurricanes and still stands two blocks from the Savannah River waterfront — believed to be the second oldest existing structure in Georgia.)

Around the time the inn opened for business, about 7,900 people lived in Georgia, many in and around Savannah.[24] Population estimates, which came from the British Board of Trade before there was such a thing as a U.S. census, didn't include Native Americans, but they did include enslaved people. About four out of 10 people who lived in Georgia when Button Gwinnett arrived in 1765, were enslaved.

By then, most enslaved people came from Caribbean nations, but 1766 — the first full year that Button Gwinnett worked as a planter — marked the year of the earliest direct shipment of West Africans to Georgia. The Liverpool-based sloop *Mary Brow* landed in Savannah on July 26 with 78 enslaved people that embarked at Saint-Louis, Senegal, a major slave trade port.[25]

Transatlantic voyages from West Africa to Savannah in the latter half of the 18th century lasted between two and six months, depending on routes, winds and storms. They were hell on earth for enslaved people, who were jammed into a ship's lower deck often with fewer than 18 inches of headroom and shackled to each other, sometimes lying on their backs or sides to maximize space. Slave ship captains called this "tight packing" — like sardines in a can — and it was done for one reason: to increase slave traders' profit margins.

There was no such thing as sanitation on these ships. Urine, feces, vomit and blood pooled on the floor, causing crew members who entered the lower decks to hold strips of vinegar-soaked cloth to their faces to curb the stench. Dysentery, smallpox and scurvy were rampant. There wasn't enough food and fresh water aboard, leading to malnourishment and dehydration, and some enslaved people protested their conditions by refusing to eat. If so, they would be force fed, beaten and whipped, and crew members sometimes raped the women and girls. Resisting a beating could lead to torture.

Survivors described the experience as soul-crushing. One man, Olaudah Equiano from what is now Nigeria, wrote of the conditions he endured in his 1789 autobiography *The Interesting Narrative*.[26]

> *"The shrieks of the women, and the groans of the dying, rendered the whole a scene of horror almost inconceivable. ...The stench of the hold while we were on the coast was so intolerably loathsome... that it was dangerous to remain there for any time... The closeness of the place,*

and the heat of the climate, added to the number in the ship, which was so crowded that each had scarcely room to turn himself, almost suffocated us. ...I now wished for the last friend, death, to relieve me; but soon, to my grief, two of the white men offered me eatables... and one of them held me fast by the hands, and laid me across I suppose the windlass, and tied my feet, while the other flogged me severely."

Slave traders bought insurance on enslaved people as if they were sacks of sugar or tobacco. These policies covered losses due to disease, insurrection or "perils of the sea," which included shipwrecks, storms or accidental deaths. The policies rarely covered deaths from abuse or neglect, such as beatings, starvation or dehydration, but a ship captain could claim someone who was beaten to death died of a disease, and only those on the ship would know the truth because the deceased were thrown overboard. Live people also were sometimes dumped into the sea. The owners of the British slave ship *Zong*, for example, told their insurer that their crew needed to throw overboard 132 live slaves for the "preservation of the ship."[27] An additional 100 enslaved people aboard *Zong* died during that journey before disembarking in Jamaica.

As brutal as these transatlantic voyages were, somehow 85 percent to 90 percent of enslaved people survived them,[28] though only 74 percent of those aboard *Mary Brow* made it to Savannah in 1766.[29]

When enslaved people reached their destinations, they, of course, were weak and susceptible to infectious diseases, if they weren't already sick.

In 1767, two years after Button Gwinnett made Georgia his home, a two-story, 1,600-square-foot masonry warehouse — known as Lazaretto, Italian for pest house — was built on the west end of Tybee Island, about 15 miles east of Savannah.[30] It amounted to a staging area for enslaved people. While there, most were separated from their family members and examined. If a doctor determined they were disease free, they were washed — and sometimes oiled to make them look healthier — and then shipped to Savannah, via the Savannah River. If not, they stayed put and either recovered or died. The bodies of the dead were thrown in mass graves in Tybee's sandy soil. (A bit of cruel irony: Jim Crow laws prevented Blacks from strolling or sunbathing on the beach at Tybee until October 1963.)

Despite everything they endured, the Caribbeans and Africans brought to America were strong and resilient, and as population estimates make clear, tens of thousands of them made it to Savannah during the 1760s and 1770s. The 78 men, women and children aboard *Mary Brow*, all shackled, were brought to the mercantile firm of Broughton and Smith, where they were sold. As it turned out, *Mary Brow* was the first of six British slave ships that transported Africans to Savannah in 1766.[31]

This was good news for Button Gwinnett, whose plantation required a regular supply of slave labor. As a newcomer to Georgia, Gwinnett might have assumed enslaved people outnumbered white people in the colony, as they did at the time in South Carolina. The *Georgia Gazette*'s inside pages were always crammed with advertisements for slave sales and reward notices for runaway slaves. The space devoted to these ads and notices reflected the importance of enslaved people on the colony's economy. A typical ad:

RUN AWAY,

Two Negroes, a fellow and a wench. The fellow is named PETER, country born, black, very sensible, about five feet ten inches high, has lost one of his little toes and half of one of his fore teeth, square made, a jobbing carpenter. The wench is named DAPHNE, black, country born, sensible, has one of her legs larger than the other, about five feet five or six inches high. Any person delivering said Negroes to the gaoler (jailer) in Savannah shall receive three guineas for each; and I hereby offer a reward of ten guineas to any person that will prove their being harboured by a white person, and the harbourer may depend on being handled as severely as the law will permit. THOMAS CATER.

Runaway slaves were a persistent problem for planters and others who owned them, and most Georgians had no patience with white people who sympathized with them enough to help them evade their masters.

In 1765, state lawmakers, fearing the growing number of enslaved people would revolt, passed a "patrol law." It established groups of white people between the ages of 16 and 60 who inspected plantations to make sure slaves were where they were supposed to be.[32] The law required patrol members to carry loaded pistols or rifles, and they could be fined for refusing to participate. When they arrived, slaves had to show them the "passes" or "tickets" given to them by their owners. Enslaved people who didn't have the proper paperwork often were whipped, and the person with the whip decided how long the punishment would last. The patrol groups also had the authority to enter slave quarters to search for "offensive weapons."[33] Slaves who weren't where they were supposed to be were sent to the nearest jail, where the jailer put them to work. When they weren't working, they were shackled and whipped if the jailer thought they deserved it.[34] Their presence in jail would be reported in the *Georgia Gazette* so their owners would know where to retrieve them. If they went unclaimed for 18 months, the jailer sold them and kept the money to reimburse himself for room and board.

Georgia wasn't breaking new ground with these slave patrols. South Carolina started them in 1704, when its leaders, realizing that enslaved people were about to outnumber white people there, feared widespread rebellions and decided they needed to come up with an organized form of intimidation. South Carolina's patrol law created what amounted to America's first police force, existing only to reinforce dominance over people with brown and black skin.

Just two years before Gwinnett settled in Savannah, two events occurred that greatly impacted Georgians.

The French and Indian War, known globally as the Seven Years' War, ended. The spoils of the war — a power struggle between Great Britain and France — were spelled out in the Treaty of Paris of 1763. England's victory made it a global power. In the New World, France and Spain relinquished claims to North America, leaving much of the eastern half of the continent to England.[35]

According to Hugh McCall, Georgia's first historian, this was significant because the French often served as instigators, pitting Native Americans against American colonists, particularly in Georgia and the Carolinas.

"France added fuel to the flame by telling them (Native Americans) that the English intended to kill all their men, and make slaves of their wives and children; they instigated them to bloodshed, and furnished them with arms and ammunition. The scattered families on the frontiers of Georgia, lay much exposed to the tomahawk and scalping knife of these savages, who commonly make no distinction of age or sex, but pour an indiscriminate vengeance upon the innocent and guilty.

"... The soldiers as usual making excursions into the woods, to hunt for fresh provisions, were attacked and some of them killed: from this time such dangers threatened the garrison, that every one was confined within the small boundaries of the fort; all communication with the distant settlement, from which they received supplies being cut off, and the garrison being but poorly provisioned, had no other prospects but those of famine or death. Parties of Indians took the field, rushed down among the settlements, and murdered and scalped a number of people on the frontiers."

The Treaty of Paris also moved Georgia's western border from the Altamaha River, about 60 miles southwest of Savannah, all the way to the Mississippi River, about 500 miles west of Savannah. France relinquishing its claims east of the Mississippi River reduced threats to Georgians from the west, and Spain ceding Florida to England removed a major rival from the south. While England's European rivals evacuated much of eastern North America, royal Gov. James Wright dealt with Georgia's other rivals: Native Americans. A treaty he signed with them brought an additional layer of peace to the most populated parts of Georgia, primarily from Augusta to the Atlantic coast.

These two milestone events — the peace treaty and the end of the French and Indian War — generally came as a huge relief to Georgians, who no longer had to worry about the Spaniards and the French encroaching on their borders and had to worry a lot less about Native Americans attacking them from within their borders.

The combination of this peace and the steady importation of enslaved people into Georgia led to prosperity in Georgia, and Savannah was at the center of an economic boom.

A visitor to the city then wrote, "...much building has been going on ...there are about 200 houses, three brick and the rest are wood and painted in shades of blue and red."[36] Gov. Wright, who once served as the crown-appointed attorney general in South Carolina, had come to Georgia with the goal of increasing the colony's population and supercharging its economy. His efforts were paying off. At around this time, he reported back home to England that Georgia was "in a very thriving condition, our Trade considerably increased."[37]

Proof of the economic good times could be seen at the ports. In 1761, Georgia exported £13,140 of deer hides, nearly all through the port in Savannah.[38] As relations with Native Americans improved, Savannah-based fur traders paid them more for these hides than did Charleston's merchants,[39] and by 1768, Georgia exported £306,510 — more than any other British colony in North America.[40] Georgia also became a major exporter of lumber, shipping three times more than South Carolina by 1765. South Carolina's 82-year head start with slavery meant it still exported much more rice and other crops than Georgia then, but those with the means to buy large tracts of land were moving to Georgia, betting, as the merchants did more than a decade earlier, that the colony was on the move.

This was the Georgia that Button Gwinnett moved to in 1765, and it was the Georgia he knew well by 1766, when he bought his needles, nails and silk handkerchief at Read and Mossman that day in May.

Georgia was a land of opportunity. That much was clear to him.

2

A Man Who Married Well

Aseries of unrelated events occurred in England in 1735 that showed the nation was modernizing and revealing its ambition to evolve from a European power to a global power.

Parliament passed the Witchcraft Act of 1735 to abolish the hunting and killing of people who identified as witches.[1] George Hadley, an English lawyer and amateur meteorologist, became the first person in the world to accurately explain trade winds, the understanding of which would help European ships more efficiently reach North American shores, and return home.[2] And King George II gave his permission for the first copyright protection laws to take effect.

George II was also intent on developing and strengthening his North American colonies, and tens of thousands of British citizens who sought adventure and new lives relocated across the Atlantic. Theologian John Wesley, the founder of the Methodist Church, was one of them. In 1735, Wesley left England to accept an invitation from Georgia founder James Oglethorpe to lead a congregation in Savannah. And dozens of Scotsmen — described as some of the world's best fighting men — were preparing to leave the Highlands in 1735 and set sail for a swampy, alligator-infested and densely wooded area near the Georgia coast that no one, including Native Americans, had ever attempted to settle.

Unrelated to all of these developments, in early March of 1735 in the English village of Down Hatherley in the county of Gloucestershire in the Cotswold region near Wales, Button Gwinnett came into this world.[3]

The village is about 110 miles northwest of London, which at the time was developing into a financial and cultural capitol. Jobs lured thousands of people from the English countryside to London starting in the early 1700s, and this influx led to urban growing pains, such as crime, pollution and a housing shortage. London was an exciting place to be, however, and the arts were flourishing. The city's first Royal Opera House was newly built, and about a month after Gwinnett was born, the composer George Frideric Handel premiered *Alcina*, his first Italian opera, there.

In 1735, Gloucestershire, Gwinnett's home county, also was in the midst of a growth spurt, becoming a center of wool production in England. It was a place of striking contrasts in many ways when Gwinnett became its newest resident. Its people ranged from wealthy landowners, wool merchants and clothiers to laborers, tenant farmers and paupers. Sheep far outnumbered people there, and the wool trade clothed, fed and housed its residents. Tall, ornate "wool churches" were built from the profits of the wool industry, as were grand manor houses in the Tudor and early Georgian styles. Simple, timber-framed cottages and Cotswold stone houses and barns, all with stone-tiled or thatched roofs and small windows, lined the streets of the villages and dotted the Gloucestershire hillsides. Those who didn't own sheep bought finished wool from clothiers, made their own clothes, grew much of their own food and often bartered with neighbors for what they needed and wanted. The landscape ranged from evergreen valleys to rolling, limestone-pocked hills to dense, old-growth forests of oak, elm and beech.

Despite the region's growth, Gloucestershire in the 1730s — in fact, throughout the 18th century

— experienced high infant mortality rates and low life expectancy because most medicine was ineffective and medical knowledge elementary. Faced with frequent deaths, families clung to religion for comfort, community and hope. The Church of England, also known as the Anglican Church, dominated the religious landscape there. At the center of Down Hatherley and other Gloucestershire villages stood a parish church, built of Cotswold limestone with a stout tower and clear glass windows. Inside, plain, whitewashed walls greeted congregants, who sat on pews made of local hardwoods. Life revolved around the seasons and the church calendar, and because religion was central to community life, clergy were viewed as leaders in their villages as well as in their congregations.

Many residents of Gloucestershire knew Button Gwinnett's father, the Reverand Samuel Gwinnett, a university-educated Anglican vicar whose ancestors lived in Wales and at various times spelled their surname Gwinneth, Gwynedd or Gwynnett.[4] Samuel Gwinnett, who earned a master of arts degree from Glasgow University, oversaw two local parishes and occasionally delivered sermons at other churches in the county, receiving the paltry fee of one guinea per engagement — less than $1.50 today.

He and his wife Anne, who married in 1728, had seven children[5]: Anna Maria, who died before her

15th birthday; Samuel Jr.; Button; Thomas, who died as an infant in 1736; Robert, who also died soon after he was born, in 1738; John, about whom nothing is known; and Emilia, who lived her entire life either with her parents or with Samuel Jr.

In Gloucestershire in the 18th century, children in middle-class families, like the Gwinnetts, typically received home schooling that included basic reading, writing and mathematics. Some boys attended small schools while girls stayed at home and learned how to make and repair clothes and quilts, garden, cook, bake and do needlework that — if good enough — might be hung on the walls. Children were expected to obey their parents without question, and those who didn't felt the sting of paddles and switches. In their free time, they played with dolls, hoops, balls and carved whistles. In the days before child labor laws in England, many boys and girls, some as young as 7 or 8, worked in the county's sheep farming, wool processing and cheese making industries.[6]

As the son of a respected minister, Button Gwinnett's childhood work most likely amounted to no more than household chores, but what he was doing, thinking, feeling, saying, coveting, avoiding, loving, hating and fearing during the first 14 years of his life is anyone's guess. If he or any of his family members wrote about his childhood, letters or diaries have never surfaced. All that is known today about young

Button's life is when and where he was baptized, who his siblings were, and where he went to school.

His school, located in a single classroom at Gloucester Cathedral, offered a relatively challenging academic curriculum that prepared college-bound students for higher levels of rigor. The Gwinnett name came from the northwest Welsh county of Gwynedd,[7] and that side of the family valued education, so it's safe to assume that Samuel Sr. and Anne's dream for Button and their other surviving sons involved a university and a career behind a desk rather than a trade that could be physically demanding and unstable.

Whether Button mastered the curriculum at his school or struggled with it is a mystery. For whatever reason, his parents did not view him as college material, while his eldest brother, Samuel Jr., attended the same school, matriculated to Oriel College at Oxford University and became an Anglican minister, like their father. If Button dreamed of attending a university, there is no record of it, but if he did — and if he mentioned it in a letter or a diary — it would have been a moot point. That was his parents' decision to make, and they made it sometime before he turned 14.

None of this is to say that Button was unintelligent. He valued books, and as an adult, he owned them and kept some of them, unlike many people in the 18th century. An inventory from his estate, taken soon after he died, listed three general dictionaries, one law dictionary, a spelling book, a grammar book, two books on agriculture and six others.[8] It's difficult to draw conclusions about his level of intelligence based solely on the fact that he valued books enough to keep them, but his writings from later in his life make it clear he possessed the vocabulary of an educated person.

Unfortunately for him, his parents' decision to remove him from a college track set him on a course that led to financial uncertainty and instability. He never broke free of that. At some point after that decision was made, he began working for an uncle, William Gwinnett, a former transatlantic merchant who then made his living as a grocer.[9] It's safe to assume his parents sent Button to work with a relative because they viewed that as the best option for him at the time. This job amounted to an unofficial apprenticeship.

In 18th-century England, a person couldn't set up a trade without completing an official apprenticeship, which typically would last seven years and sometimes longer. England was the only country in Europe at that time that legislated apprenticeships, and that length of time — the equivalent of a medical school and a residency program for a doctor today — reflected the importance of experience and expertise.[10]

During an apprenticeship, marriage was prohibited, forcing young men and women to focus on their chosen fields rather than courtships. The agreement between the apprentice and the master involved more than a time commitment and a personal sacrifice: There was a significant financial commitment on behalf of a teen's parents, who paid the master — an artisan or a craftsman — the equivalent of tuition and room-and-board for several years. In return, the apprentice received the insights he or she needed to know to make it in the working world. That was the hope anyway. Some masters treated their apprentices more like indentured servants, doling out only menial tasks and never teaching them the skills they needed to get long-term jobs or start their own businesses.[11] Yet others were cruel to their apprentices, causing them to run away and abandon their professional dreams.

Not only that, but apprenticeship contracts could be difficult to break, so if Button Gwinnett's parents were unsure in which career he would shine, they would have been unwise to make this sort of financial commitment and force their son to make a lengthy time commitment. Why not expose Button to the life of a grocer, who happens to be a relative, and see what he thinks about that? If that lit a fire under him, great. If not, his parents could expose him to other opportunities.

He most likely started working with his uncle in 1750 in Bristol, a port city across the Avon River from Cardiff, Wales. Bristol is synonymous with adventure, a launching pad for explorers well before it received city status in 1542. In 1480 and 1481, two different groups left from there in a search for a place called Hy-Brasil, which turned out to be a non-existent island thought to be somewhere west of Ireland. In 1497, the Italian explorer Giavanni Caboto, better known by his anglicized name of John Cabot, departed Bristol on a Henry VII-funded voyage to India, but landed a month later in Newfoundland — long thought to be the first time a European set foot in Canada. Upon his return to England, he reported, among other things, massive schools of cod that could be caught simply by lowering baskets into the water.

Cabot didn't discover Canada — Norse Vikings from Iceland and Greenland beat him to it by about 500 years — but his voyage caused Britain for the first time to see North America as a potential goldmine. This view held true 250 years later when Button Gwinnett was in Bristol, trying to figure out what to do with his life.

By the time he started working with his uncle, Bristol had a large port, a destination for ships from all over the world. The city's many "sugar houses" processed sugar from Jamaica,[12] and the cocoa that arrived there from West African nations turned the city into a center for chocolate making. Europeans also craved tobacco, most of which came from the British colonies of Virginia and North Carolina, and entrepreneurs in Bristol processed tobacco. Like many large ports then, Bristol was also known for its slave trade. During the 18th century, as many as 500,000 enslaved Africans arrived at and disembarked from there enroute to Caribbean and North American colonies.[13]

There is no record that Button's uncle bought and sold slaves during his time as a transatlantic merchant, but while in Bristol, Button almost certainly got the bug to follow in his uncle's footsteps. As part of this unofficial, four-year apprenticeship, William would have taught his nephew what he needed to know about buying and selling in wholesale and retail markets, negotiating, staffing, managing employees, budgeting, and bookkeeping. He also would have told his nephew about the growing American port cities of Philadelphia, New York, Boston, Newport, R.I., and Charleston, S.C., and about the people who lived there — what they ate and drank and how they dressed, spoke, sang, looked and behaved.

But Button had to shelve that dream because in 1754, when he was 19, this unofficial apprenticeship ended and another one began, this one in Wolverhampton with an ironmonger named John Weston Smith. (This apprenticeship was off the books because masters who used apprentices had to pay taxes, and records show that Weston Smith didn't begin paying these taxes until 1757, when he oversaw an apprentice named John Pershouse.[14] In subsequent years, he paid taxes on two other apprentices, neither of whom were Gwinnett.) Ironmongers — the hardware store owners of their time — sold household items such as pots and pans, locks and keys, and candlesticks and lanterns as well as tools for tradesmen and farmers such as hammers, chisels, nails, rivets and screws, saws, ploughshares and hoes.

Wolverhampton — in central England, just northwest of Birmingham — was home to about 8,000 people in the mid-1750s, making it a mid-sized market town. But it felt larger because it was on the main road from London to Holyhead, a coastal village in Wales where travelers would go to catch ferry boats to Dublin and other ports along the east coast of Ireland. Many people on horseback or in coaches passed through Wolverhampton, and Weston Smith catered to their needs, selling them items such as horseshoes, tacks and axles and other iron parts for carts and wagons.

Less than a year into Gwinnett's employment with Weston Smith, Gwinnett's godmother, Barbara Button — the source of his first name — died.[15] Barbara, a first cousin of Button's mother, never married, and at some point, she inherited a sprawling estate that included a large house. Her will describes Button as her "God Son" and designates £100 to him[16] — or about \$35,000 today — an inheritance that a 20-year-old working-class man must have welcomed. She also left money to Button's mother and to his siblings, but most of her estate went to a niece, Emilia,[17] who later married Button's older brother, Samuel Gwinnett, Jr. That inheritance provided them with a comfortable life.

Button Gwinnett was born in Down Hatherley, spent his teenage years working in Bristol, and married in Wolverhampton.

There is no evidence that Button was jealous of Emilia's good fortune, but it would have been human nature if he felt slighted by his share of the inheritance. An unmarried or widowed lady with no children during this period very often left the bulk of her estate to a nephew or other male relative. A woman in Barbara Button's position may have given her assets to a godson, but she didn't do that. This also begs a series of questions that cannot be answered: Did Samuel and Anne Gwinnett make it clear to Barbara Button that their son Button was not to be trusted with overseeing and maintaining an estate? If Button felt disrespected and cheated out of a life-changing inheritance, did it motivate him to prove to his family that he could become a wealthy man by his own smarts and his own sweat? Did Barbara Button's decision fuel the perseverance that Button showed the rest of his life?

These questions can be answered only with assumptions and theories, but it's clear that Gwinnett did not fall in love with the hardware business. He may have fallen in love with a lady in Wolverhampton because his employment with the ironmonger ended after three years, in 1757, when he applied for a marriage license.

Just eight days later, on April 19, he married Ann Bourne, who was identified on the marriage certificate as "Spinster aged 22."[18] They were married in The Collegiate Church of St. Peter, where Ann's parents were married 25 years earlier. Ann's father, Aaron, was a successful grocer in Wolverhampton, and the journalists of the day must have considered the marriage an event worthy of a brief story because it was published in a few local newspapers.

This version appeared in the Gwinnetts' hometown newspaper, *Gloucester County News:*[19]

> *Country News, Glocefester, May 13th. A few days ago, Mr. Button Gwinnett, son of Rev. Mr. Gwinnett, Rector of St Nicholas in this fair City, was married to Mifs Bourne Daughter of Mr. Aaron Bourne, an eminent Grocer of Wolverhampton in Staffordshire, a most agreeable lady with a fortune of 10000L.*

This begs yet other questions: Did Ann Bourne Gwinnett bring a 10,000-pound dowry — roughly the equivalent to $3 million in purchasing power in 1757 — to the marriage? A Gloucester newspaper would have received that information from the Gwinnett side of the family, who lived there, and the family would have given their local newspaper the "facts" that they wanted members of their community to know. Gloucester and Wolverhampton are 65 miles apart, and a newspaperman in Gloucester was not going to brave pitted and muddy roads and travel to Wolverhampton to confirm that he received accurate information from the Gwinnetts.

Could the newspaperman who penned the story meant to write £1,000? Perhaps. A dowry of £1,000 in 1757 was still enormous. A newspaper reporter living in England in the 18th century certainly would have considered £1,000 a "fortune," as would other working-class Englishmen. In 1755, a domestic servant could expect to earn as little as five pounds per year, plus room and board and work-related clothing. An experienced housekeeper might make £15 annually. A coachman, £25. Artisans, between £30 and £40 a year.[20]

Even if the size of the dowry was exaggerated by the Gwinnetts, another obvious question comes to mind: Did Gwinnett marry for money, or was love his primary motivation? No love letters — or letters of any kind — written by Button to Ann, or vice versa, have surfaced. Their relationship might have been love at first sight, but if it wasn't — if he did marry for money — that was very common in the 18th century. Button's mother, after all, married Button's father, a prominent clergyman, less than two years after the death of her father, who financially supported her. In 18th-century England — and just about everywhere else in the world — marital decisions were at least partially based on what brides and grooms could financially contribute to the union. If Ann's dowry attracted Button as much or more than her personality, her intelligence or her appearance, marrying her would have been a practical thing to do. A sizable dowry, however large it was, would allow him to pursue his professional dreams — or at the very least help provide for Ann and their future children.

After experiencing the excitement of bustling Bristol and hearing about America from his uncle, Gwinnett would have wanted to see America's eastern port cities, from Canada to the Caribbean. Working as an ironmonger and a grocer, while noble and stable professions, would not allow him to see those and other places, and they didn't have the earning potential of a merchant.

He wanted to be a transatlantic merchant. The fact that Gwinnett chose that as his first career speaks to his confidence, his intelligence and his ambition. As his uncle would have told him, being a successful transatlantic merchant required a mastery of its myriad logistics. He needed to figure out the best places to buy wholesale goods in England, how to pay for them, where to store them, how to transport them from a warehouse to a port, how to ship them to America, how many crew members he needed for the voyage, how much and what kind of ballast to use to ensure the vessel was properly balanced, where in America to take the goods, and who would buy them at American ports. And that was just half the battle. For the return trip, he needed to do all those things all over again to get American goods to market in

England, arguably a more difficult undertaking given his unfamiliarity with America and those who operated its warehouses and ports.

And another thing: In 1757, he was just 22 years old.

Planning and executing all of this would take time, so he didn't leave England right away. He was a newlywed after all, and 1757 was turning out to be a great year for him. That year he left a job for which he had no passion, married into a well-to-do family, and began working a stable job with his successful father-in-law, a grocer, in preparation for what he hoped would be a lucrative career.

He also became a Freeman in Gloucester that year.[21] Freeman status was important in 18th-century England. It allowed a man the full privileges in a town, city or trade guild. No one could carry out business or own property unless he was a Freeman, and that included craftsmen, shopkeepers and merchants.[22] Freeman membership could be obtained by birth, apprenticeship, gift or purchase. The document where his membership is documented doesn't mention that he completed an apprenticeship or that he was gifted this membership or that he paid to become a Freeman. It only points out that he is the son of Samuel, a Freeman himself.[23] So he gained entry because of nepotism, the easiest way for him to enter this important businessmen's club. And becoming a Freeman in Gloucestershire would make it easier to become a Freeman wherever he lived in England in the future.

In 1758, just a few months after he became a Freeman, he became a father. Ann gave birth to a daughter, Amelia, almost exactly nine months after she and Button married. While Amelia's date of birth is unclear, she was baptized on February 27, 1758,[24] and it was customary in the Anglican Church to baptize healthy children about one month after they were born, so Amelia probably was born in late January or early February.

He continued to work for his father-in-law that year, and a little more than a year later, a second daughter, Ann, was born, probably in April 1759 because she was baptized on May 14 of that year.[25] However, Ann didn't make it to her first birthday. She died in December in Wolverhampton.[26] Around this time, Gwinnett was likely close to leaving England. The death of his second daughter wouldn't keep him from doing that. It wouldn't keep him from pursuing his dream. At some point, he left his wife in England to deal with that grief alone.

To be successful, he was convinced he needed to do business in America, and nothing would keep him from reaching it.

3

An Ambitious Man

During the time when Button Gwinnett decided to embark on a career as a transatlantic merchant, some of the wealthiest men on both sides of the Atlantic were making their living doing just that. Robert Morris, a signer of the Declaration of Independence who oversaw the financing of the Revolutionary War, was thought to be the wealthiest person in America in the mid-1770s. Fellow signer John Hancock, who inherited a shipping fortune and had one of the largest personal libraries in America, was not far behind.

In England, merchants represented "the life, spring and motion of the trading world," and their role was never more vital than it was in the 18th century.[1]

Many of the most successful merchants in England and elsewhere did more than wholesale trading in distant markets. They lent money because they had so much of it, and they bought and sold currencies and gold and silver for clients, who paid them hefty fees. Some merchants were also considered financial experts who employed "stockjobbers," the equivalent today of stock brokers or financial advisors.[2]

Eighteenth-century merchants often specialized in order to build a brand for themselves. Some focused on dry goods, such as textiles and clothing, while others bought and sold rum, molasses, coffee and other "wet goods." American colonists, many of whom came from England, Ireland and Scotland or had roots there, craved goods that they could only get from Great Britain and mainland Europe. And British residents and other Europeans wanted a lot of what the North American colonies and Caribbean nations had to offer. In order to give their customers what they desired, English merchants shipped textiles, pottery, glass, silk handkerchiefs and luxury items to America. While their ships were in America and the Caribbean, they were loaded with lumber, rice, tobacco, tea, coffee, chocolate, indigo, sugar, molasses, dried fish and many other items that were shipped to London, Bristol, Liverpool and Glasgow, the largest port cities in 18th-century Great Britain.

This trading back and forth across the Atlantic made North America the fastest growing part of the British economy. Consumers in America and in Europe paid a premium for this imported cargo, and merchants who knew how to locate the best markets, control expenses and maximize profits became very wealthy.

Button Gwinnett aspired to be one of those people, someday overseeing a thriving import-export empire from behind a desk in Bristol or Liverpool, and employing the ship captains and crew members who crossed the Atlantic and did the hard work that would make him wealthy. He surely wanted to show his family that he didn't need a college degree to become successful, and he didn't need a large inheritance to become wealthy. He would make his parents as proud as they were of his brother Samuel, who had earned a degree, led a congregation and married into money.

Speaking of money, Gwinnett was going to need a lot of it to pursue his professional dreams. At some point after he got married, he realized his wife's dowry — whatever it was — wasn't available to him or wasn't as much as he needed.

Fortunately, a fledgling merchant in the 18th century had many ways of financing his business: He could go to established merchants, who often lent to one of their own if they had reason to believe they would get a decent return on their money. He could borrow from banks that not only lent money but sometimes bought shares in voyages. He could find a team of individual investors who would finance these voyages and share in the profits. He could borrow against his house, his land and his ship — if he owned those things — to raise money. He also could buy on credit, which would have to be repaid as soon as possible after the goods were sold overseas. A lender might have to wait nine months to a year to be repaid, so cash-starved merchants who bought on credit typically paid steep interest rates. Early in his career, Gwinnett took the latter route.

He turned to a well-established merchant, Thomas Pennington of Bristol,[3] who sold him goods on credit and, records show, later hounded him for what he owed. Pennington was a slave trader in the 1730s and 1740s who also lent money to people in England and America. (In 1765, he even lent money to Ann Gwinnett and charged it to her husband's account — a clear sign that either the 10,000-pound dowry was much smaller than reported, or she didn't have control over it, or it was gone by then.) Pennington did not forgive debts. New Jersey Historical Society records show that in exchange for unpaid debts and interest, he received mortgages for several tracts of land in Bergen and Morris counties in 1766 as well as for a New Jersey mining operation in 1769.[4]

Gwinnett would come to realize that Pennington was no different from other lenders when it came to collecting money owed to them. They had the means and connections to doggedly pursue it, and they did so, even if their borrowers lived on the other side of the Atlantic.

Gwinnett also did business with Bentley & Boardman of Liverpool.[5] Thomas Bentley, the agent and manufacturer for the acclaimed ceramic artist Josiah Wedgwood, got his start apprenticing in a warehouse to learn the wool and cotton trades and later went into business with James Boardman, about whom little is known. Other businessmen also lent Gwinnett money or sold him goods on credit during this early phase of his career. He was indebted to flax merchants William Shepperd, Thomas Langston and John Birley,[6] who owned multiple warehouses in northern England, and to the firm of Durand & Phillips,[6] which exported massive amounts of sugar in the 18th century from the Danish colony of St. Croix in the Caribbean to the American colonies and to England.

Gwinnett was doing business by at least 1761. In April of that year, soon after he turned 26, he shipped goods to Philadelphia on the *Polly*, and shortly after that to New York City using the *New Grace*.[7] In August, he used the *Bristol Packet* to ship goods to Philadelphia, and in March 1762, the *Garland* took some of his cargo to New York.[8] He owned none of these ships so he had to pay to use them, and during this time, he often paid for goods on credit.[9]

The earliest known document that shows Gwinnett doing business in America is a receipt he wrote and signed in 1762 and handed to ship Capt. Benjamin Davis of New York. It reads:[10]

Rec'd Oct 12, 1762
£107
14 shillings
7 pence
in Ballance
New York

By this time, Elizabeth "Betsy" Gwinnett, Button and Ann's third daughter, was born in England.[11] The wonderful news of her birth in December 1761 was dampened by the death of 3-year-old Amelia, their first born, just three months later.[12] With her husband gone, Ann leaned on her parents. Not only would they have provided emotional support, but they would have been able to afford the best medical care available in Wolverhampton, though that wasn't saying much.

The deaths of children, regardless of how much money their families had, were common in England in the 18th century.[13] In London, where the best medical care could be found, infant and child mortality peaked in the middle of the 18th century. Nearly two-thirds of all children died before their fifth birth-days.[14] And there wasn't much difference in mortality rates between the rich and the poor, a clear sign that doctors were no match for the deadliest diseases of the day: cholera, smallpox and typhus fever. Button and Ann Gwinnett's personal experience — losing two of their three children — mirrored the mortality statistics in 18th-century England, though records do not the list the cause of their daughters' deaths.

Gwinnett, meanwhile, continued plugging away, trying to become an established and successful merchant. He sued someone named John Keating for an unspecified amount of money in the New York Supreme Court of Judicature in 1763.[15] It's unclear if he prevailed, but around that time he acquired an ownership stake in a ship called *Recovery*, which was registered in Barbados on January 20, 1764. Records show that the ship, with a five-member crew, weighed 60 tons and carried ballast from Havana to Bridgetown, Barbados. All ships carry ballast — under the water line — to bring them stability. It's possible that the ballast was cargo, but if it was only stones, bricks, gravel and sand, as was common in the 18th century, Gwinnett may have been struggling to find goods to buy and sell in American port cities.

The historical record provides no further information about his mercantile work until September 1765, when Button Gwinnett "of Savannah" — the first known reference to an American residence — was listed as the sole owner of *Nancy*, a 60-ton brigantine with a crew of eight. The ship, which was registered in Barbados, traveled from Pensacola, on the west coast of Florida, to Savannah, carrying non-perishable food, tobacco, medicine and saddles, among many other things. Bentley & Boardman, one of Gwinnett's creditors, owned a quarter of that cargo.

Gwinnett's ownership of *Nancy* was ending soon, whether he knew it or not. When she returned to England, after a trip from Savannah to Antigua with a cargo of timber, *Nancy* was seized by the sheriff while in the port at Bristol and sold to settle debts Gwinnett owed to Thomas Pennington, one of his creditors. The seizure more likely than not surprised Gwinnett. Had he seen it coming, he would have been wise to sell the lumber elsewhere and the ship before it arrived in Bristol. By then, he was done with transatlantic trading, and *Nancy* no longer mattered to him other than how much he could get for her. He had moved on.

By the late summer of 1765, he decided to stay in Savannah, and he had to have been pleased with how things started out there. September 1765 was a very busy month for him. He signed as a witness to the sale of a boat called *Dolphin*, docked in the port in Savannah.[16] The fact that he also wrote the bill of sale means he may have brokered the deal and earned a sales commission. He needed a place to sell the cargo he picked up in Pensacola, so that month he bought a general store from Dora Wylly, a recent widow in Savannah. In the sales agreement, dated September 23, 1765, she wrote: "Be it known that I Dora Wylly do agree to sell all interest in General Store of deceased J.M. Wylly to Button Gwinnett for the sum of £125, buyer in good faith agrees to pay full amount of any agreement in ninety days."

Gwinnett wasted no time trying to sell the Pensacola cargo as well as the store's existing inventory. Even before he entered into the sales agreement with Wylly, he bought an advertisement in the *Georgia Gazette* and listed what was for sale "on the most reasonable terms, by BUTTON GWINNETT, at the store lately occupied by Messrs. Johnson and Wylly."[17] A partial list includes "Rhubarb, Turlington's balsam of life, Dr. James's powders for fevers, salts, Florence oil, mustard, tinware, ironmongery, plain silver, gold laced hats, breeches, silk, earthenware, mould candles, fine beer, glass, shoes, sheeting, canvas, Irish linens, paint, cheese, butter, nails, cider, Scots barley, English manufactured tobacco, vinegar, bed furniture ...and many other articles too tedious to insert."

This eclectic mix of products would have been in demand anywhere in the American colonies — let alone in Georgia, the most remote colony — and he should have been able to sell it for a hefty profit. But when Gwinnett arrived in Georgia, he may not have known how sparsely populated it was and how few Georgians had money to spend. He also may not have been aware of his competition: retailers who had established themselves in Savannah and who had better connections in Great Britain and elsewhere to capital and goods. Gwinnett's newspaper advertisement may have given the impression that his store could satisfy anyone's needs and wants, but in the same month his store began doing business, he shopped at Read and Mossman's store.[18] As his inventory shrunk, his store quickly became an afterthought — not only for other Savannahians, but for him — and there's no evidence that it provided him with a reliable source of income as he tried to establish himself in Georgia.

Just about the time his store opened, something else caught his eye: this 40-word advertisement in the October 10, 1765, issue of the *Georgia Gazette*.[19]

"To be Leased for a Number of Years, THE VALUABLE ISLAND of ST. CATHERINE, with the STOCK and CATTLE, and USE of the TIMBER. — For particulars enquire of the Rev. Mr. Bosomworth on the said island, or of GREY ELLIOTT."

To say that Gwinnett's life took a turn when he saw that brief ad would be a huge understatement. If he hadn't seen it, nothing that happened to him after that point would have happened. No one would have heard of him, remembered him or cared about him. Royal Gov. James Wright wouldn't have given him the time of day, let alone several land grants and two government appointments. Gwinnett probably wouldn't have met Lyman Hall, his friend and mentor and a leader of the independence movement in Georgia. He wouldn't have rubbed shoulders with the men who signed the Declaration of Independence. John Adams wouldn't have mentioned him in his autobiography. John Hancock wouldn't have received letters from his widow. George Washington's colleague Gen. Lachlan McIntosh wouldn't have insulted him, and, well, Gwinnett might have lived a lot longer than he did.

If he hadn't seen that newspaper ad, Button Gwinnett would have been a nobody.

4

A Major Pivot

St. Catherines is a manatee-shaped sea island about 40 miles southeast of Savannah, between the mouths of the Santee River in coastal South Carolina and the St. Johns River in northeast Florida. The island stretches along the Georgia coast for slightly more than 10 miles, and its westernmost edge is only about three miles from the Atlantic Ocean. It measures 22,265 acres, roughly the same size as the Caribbean nation of Anguilla. More than half of its land mass consists of salt marsh, meadows and freshwater ponds. Live oak and pine forests make up the remainder, except for slivers of white sandy beaches, which line the eastern, northern and southern sides of the island.[1]

St. Catherines is full of life. White-tail deer shelter in the island's tall marshes, loggerhead sea turtles nest on its 11 miles of beaches, gopher tortoises prefer the pastures in the northern part of the island, armadillos reside in the inland areas, and wild hogs roam its dense forests, foraging for everything from roots, acorns and berries to worms, snails and the eggs of nesting birds.

Archaeological excavations show that Native Americans have lived there since at least 2,000 B.C., and they had the place to themselves until 1587, when Jesuit missionaries established Mission Santa Catalina de Guale. The center of Spain's world in North America was St. Augustine, Florida, but it considered this island to be among the northernmost part of its territory. In 1597, Native Americans killed two Franciscan friars there, not in a rebellion against the Spaniards or Catholicism but because of tensions between indigenous Georgia chiefdoms.[2] The murders didn't chase off the Spaniards, who remained there until 1680, when Englishmen from Charleston, S.C. — with the help of Native Americans — forced them south to Florida. With the Spaniards gone, Santa Catalina became St. Catherines.[3]

Fast forward to 1717, when Robert Montgomery, a British nobleman, received a land grant that included much of what lies between the Savannah and Altamaha rivers, including St. Catherines. After a visit, he decided it was too wonderful for Native Americans to enjoy for themselves. In fact, he didn't think they should be there at all. He viewed himself, among other things, as a developer, and he envisioned the island as a great place for Brits in South Carolina or England to live.

The development, which he called Margravate of Azilia, was featured in a booklet with the wordy and most optimistic title: "A Discourse Concerning the design'd Establishment Of a New Colony To The South of Carolina, in the Most delightful Country of the Universe." In it, Montgomery explains that his desire to develop the land comes not from "a Sudden Motive," but from "a strong Bent of Genius I inherit from my Ancestors."[4]

In short, his booklet marketed St. Catherines as a utopia — with mining.

"It abounds with Rivers, Woods, and Meadows. Its gentle Hills are full of Mines, Lead, Copper, Iron and even some Silver; 'Tis beautiful with odoriferous Plants, green all the Year. The Air is healthy, and the Soil is general fruitful. ...The many Lakes, and pretty Rivulets throughout the Province, breed a Multitude of Geese, and other Water Fowl. ...The River Banks are covered with a strange Variety of lovely Trees."[5]

All of this came with an attractive financial enticement for buyers: Pay nothing "until 3 years after arrival."[6] Despite the creative content in this marketing booklet, Montgomery's development lured no one to St. Catherines, and Native Americans continued using it for hunting and fishing, as their ancestors had done for centuries.

In 1733, when James Oglethorpe and 113 other adventurous Brits arrived to colonize Georgia, England considered St. Catherines and the other sea islands to be part of the colony. Oglethorpe, who was ahead of his time in many ways, saw the advantages of cozying up to Native Americans, and he never tried to displace them. Rather, he managed to convince them that the British had a lot to offer.

In a meeting with 50 chiefs, "Oglethorpe represented to them the great power, wisdom and wealth of the English nation, and the many advantages that would accrue to the Indians in general, from a connection and friendship with them; and as they had plenty of lands, he hoped they would freely resign a share of them to his people, who were come to settle amongst them, for their benefit and instruction."[7]

It didn't take long for Oglethorpe's diplomacy to win them over. Creek Chief Tomochichi, with whom Oglethorpe had an especially close relationship, gave him a present. "...a buffalo skin adorned on the inside with the head and feathers of an eagle, which I desire you to accept, because the eagle is an emblem of speed, and the buffalo of strength: the English are swift as the bird, and strong as the beast, since like the former, they flew over vast seas to the uttermost parts of the earth; and like the latter, they are so strong that nothing can withstand them: the feathers of the eagle are soft, and signify love; the buffalo skin is warm, and signifies protection; therefore, I hope the English will love and protect their little families."[8]

His good relationships with Native American chiefs were in part due to the woman who became his primary interpreter, Mary Musgrove, the daughter of a Creek Indian mother and an English trader father who lived near Charleston.[9] Musgrove, whose Creek name was Coosaponakeesa, lived as a Native American when she was with her mother and as an American colonist when she was with her father, giving her a foothold in both cultures. She understood the Creeks and spoke their language, Muscogee, as well as she understood the British and spoke English. Her English last name came from her husband, John Musgrove, whose trading post she helped operate. She contributed to the success of the business, which for a time was the center of deerskin trading between the English and Native Americans in coastal Georgia and southeast South Carolina.[10]

Mary Musgrove played an increasingly important role as a liaison between the English and the Native Americans because her husband, who was also a translator, often overindulged in alcohol. He once gave a Native American so much alcohol that the man died, and his frequent drunkenness sometimes postponed trade talks. During a period when women did not work with men — let alone perform important jobs — Musgrove provided a reliable plan B when her husband was unavailable, and Georgia's leaders occasionally paid her bonuses. Because of her husband's unreliability, she eventually replaced him as Georgia's most coveted translator and was so valued that Georgia's trustees fretted when she informed them in the summer of 1737 that she might move to South Carolina.

If that had happened, Georgia trustee John Earl Perceval wrote, "(That) would be a great loss to Georgia, by reason of her being our best interpreter with the Indians, and having great influence over them. We replied that we knew Mrs. Musgrove's usefulness, and the consequence of disobliging her on account of the Indians, and (if she stayed) the Trustees (would be) well disposed to favour her in all they can do consistent with the good of the Colony."

Musgrove's sneaky plan to increase her wages ended after Oglethorpe informed the trustees that she was unlikely to move to Carolina because she owed someone there £1,000. He was right. She lived the rest of her life in Georgia, and she not only served as a translator, but as a negotiator and a mediator,[11] further cementing her importance as an important link between British leaders and Native American chiefs. John Musgrove died, as did her second husband, before she married Thomas Bosomworth, a Christian missionary who in 1743 was commissioned to "perform all religious and ecclesiastical affairs in Georgia."[12]

That year, after Oglethorpe lost another battle with the Spaniards and he left Georgia for good, about 10 Native American families lived on St. Catherines, where they grew corn and hunted game.[13] With Oglethorpe gone, Mary Musgrove continued to ensure that the Creeks and the British had a good working relationship. In appreciation for her role, Malatchi, chief of the Lower Creeks, gave the St. Catherines, Sapelo and Ossabaw sea islands to "our beloved man Thomas Bosomworth and our sister Mary, his wife."

After Mary and Thomas began living on St. Catherines, the British nullified the gift, saying tribes could give land only to other tribes. Mary responded by claiming to be a Creek princess, but that did not persuade the British. After years of contentious disputes and legal battles between Mary and Thomas and the British authorities, Henry Ellis, the royal governor at the time, thought it was in the best interest of Georgia to end this legal tussle, and he suggested a compromise: Give the Bosomworths St. Catherines

Island and as much as £2,100 in proceeds from the sale of Sapelo and Ossabaw islands.[14] They ended up with £2,050, and on June 13, 1760, they signed the deed to St. Catherines,[15] making Mary the female with the most land in Georgia. The couple lived there until 1765, when Mary died in her sleep. She was about 65.

Thomas wasted no time remarrying, but his new wife, who had served as Mary's chambermaid, may have associated the island with Mary and did not want to live there, so Thomas agreed to lease St. Catherines.

Enter Button Gwinnett. On October 30, 1765, three weeks after Gwinnett saw the advertisement in the *Georgia Gazette* that St. Catherines was available, Bosomworth leased 6,200 acres of the island to "Button Gwinnett of Savannah, Merchant."[15] Merchant? By then, trading was in his past, but the Bosomworths probably didn't know that. His decision to pivot and try to become a planter was bold, considering he had never owned land before and had no knowledge of how to operate a farm or a plantation. He was starting from scratch, but he was confident, and he convinced the Bosomworths that he could be a successful planter and could fulfill the agreement.

At the time of the transaction, the brigantine *Nancy* had not yet been seized, and Gwinnett almost certainly had the paperwork to prove he owned it. He also owned the general store in Savannah and its inventory, and the Bosomworths may have seen his advertisements for the store in the *Georgia Gazette*. On paper, he appeared established, successful and solvent, and that had to have given the Bosomworths confidence.

Gwinnett negotiated a shrewd deal, giving the Bosomworths relatively little money at the time of the transaction. He paid them £1,000 for about 600 heads of cattle and hogs and a 20-foot-long boat.[16] He also made a lot of financial promises: He pledged a bond of £500 to repay within five months, and a bond of £3,000 that essentially served as an annuity for Thomas Bosomworth.[17] Gwinnett agreed to make monthly payments over four years to pay the £3,000 note. Besides the cattle, hogs and boat, he received a house, outhouses, barns, stables, and an unconditional use of the land to monetize in any way he could, whether that included harvesting timber, growing crops or fishing.[18]

Gwinnett first settled in Savannah, then moved to
St. Catherines Island. He spent a lot of time in Sunbury.

What Gwinnett told them about his ability to fulfill
these financial pledges and what he knew to be true
had to be two different things. At around the time
he bought the lease, his wife, who was in England,
was borrowing money to pay the bills. But give him
credit: He was good at identifying lucrative careers,
even if he didn't possess the business acumen to succeed at them. His merchant career had fizzled, but
St. Catherines gave him the opportunity to become

wealthy as planter and land owner. He knew from his time as a merchant that American timber was prized in the Caribbean as well as in England, and he knew from his brief time living in Savannah that enslaved people allowed planters to clear more land and grow more crops on it.

Georgia planters who knew what they were doing became incredibly wealthy. If they could do it, Gwinnett reasoned, so could he. He may never have given any thought to growing crops until now, but he never lacked for confidence.

With that revenue potential staring him in the face, Gwinnett had to deal with a British land-use policy that he found onerous and complained about for years to come. It required anyone who owned more than 100 acres of land to "improve it" by having one person on the land for every 50 acres of farmland and for every 100 acres of timberland.[19] Gov. Wright and the king's council reasoned that this would encourage landowners to do something with their land — whether that be harvesting its timber or growing crops on it — with the end goal of stimulating Georgia's economy.

England wanted its colonies to be economic juggernauts, and it was Wright's job to make that a reality in Georgia. When it came to land use, he led by example. Wright, one of the largest landowners in the South, didn't acquire land just to sell it for a profit in the future. He worked it.[20] Or rather, enslaved people did. At one point, he owned more than 2,000 of them.

The "person" who worked farmland or timberland in Georgia didn't have to be enslaved. He could be a member of the landowner's family or a hired hand, but Georgia's population was so small in the 1760s that someone with a lot of land would need to buy enslaved people — and a lot of them — to fulfill the requirement to staff land.

In the fall of 1765, when Gwinnett took control of St. Catherines, his immediate family consisted of his wife and their 4-year-old daughter, who were in England, so he had no choice but to begin buying enslaved people. As the years went on, he owned more and more of them, many of whom came by birth from the enslaved men and women he had. At the time of his death, he owned 61 enslaved people, 30 of whom were children born into slavery.[21]

The land use plan was new to Gwinnett, but it wasn't new to Georgia. From its start as a British colony, its trustees had made it clear that they expected land grantees to use the land they were given in some income-producing way. The trustees decreed, "If any of the Land so granted shall not be cultivated, planted, cleared, improved or fenced ... during the Space of Ten Years ... then ... every part thereof not cultivated ... shall belong to the Trust."

Many Georgians grumbled that the sparsely populated colony could not reach its agricultural potential without enslaved people.

"That Negroes are not only much fitter than White Servants; for Hott (sic) Climates, but they are likewise much cheaper, and more beneficiall (sic) to the Planter in ever'y respect," Peter Gordon, chief bailiff of Savannah, wrote in his diary in 1733. "Nay it is Morrally (sic) Impossible: That the People of Georgia, can ever gett (sic) forward in Their Setlements (sic), or even be a degree above common Slaves, without the help and assistance of Negroes. Because the People of Carolina, Who are remarkable for Their Industry, and who inhabite (sic) a Country equally as fine, and productive as Georgia, will at all times, by the help of Their Negroes be able to Undersell the People of Georgia, in any commoditie they can possibly raise, at any market in Europe."[22]

A South Carolinian named Samuel Eveleigh, who moved to Georgia to grow rice, realized he couldn't grow nearly as much as he wanted there and returned to South Carolina in 1735, the year the British House of Commons officially banned slavery in Georgia. Without slavery, Eveleigh predicted Georgia "will never prove considerable by reason the heat of the climate will not permit white men to labour as the negroes do, especially in raising rice, nor can they endure the wet season when rice is to be gathered in."[23]

In 1739, a group of settlers near the Ogeechee River wrote to the trustees that they couldn't make it work. "We have received a Letter signed by your Secretary, of the 25th March last … in which we set forth that we had abandoned our Settlements upon the Ogeeche (sic) River … because you [Trustees] would not allow black Servants to cultivate your Lands."[24]

Even after slavery became legal in Georgia in 1751, many planters couldn't import enough slaves as they needed because growing and harvesting rice was so labor intensive.

Starting in 1766 — the year Gwinnett began his planting career — slave traders began bringing slaves to Georgia from northwest Africa, specifically the nations of Sierra Leone, Senegal and Gambia. Those nations grew rice, and the people who had worked in rice fields in Africa and were forced into slavery in Georgia and South Carolina were known as rice slaves. They fetched higher prices at slave auctions because of their knowledge and experience.

Although rice can be grown in higher ground, the vast majority of it grows near sea level. This back-breaking work starts with clearing and leveling the land, loosening the soil, then digging trenches and levees to dike nearby marshes in order to flood the fields. This labor, done by male slaves, happened as often as six times a year during an era when machines didn't exist to help with that work.

Enslaved people were "put to moving mud in the malarial swamps; and people who would not voluntarily have spent years moving mud — for every winter the embankments had to be repaired, and the canals and ditches cleared — could be forced to do so,"[25]according to one account.

While men were leveling and shaping the land, women and children grew rice in seedbeds, and after a few weeks uprooted and transplanted them one at a time to flooded fields in straight rows. The men had to understand the ebbs and flows of the rivers so they could know how much water to release and when to keep the fields flooded. Women and children stood barefoot in ankle- or knee-deep water to weed between the plants, exposing themselves to snakes and mosquitos. When stalks turned golden in three to six months, male slaves slowly drained the fields, cut the stalks with sickles, bundled them and let them dry. Women and children then threshed the dry stalks to remove the grains and the chaff. Then they separated the grains from the chaff and used mortars to mill the grains.

This time-consuming and grueling work wore them down physically, as did their poor diet and exposure to dysentery, yellow fever and other diseases. Most enslaved children in America didn't make it to their 16th birthdays,[26] and the early deaths only increased the demand for more slave labor. Eighteenth-century population figures were nothing more than rough estimates in the days before the U.S. Census Bureau began counting people, and that was especially true of enslaved people, but their numbers in Georgia grew from about 7,500 in 1760 to 15,000 in 1773.[27]

Because growing rice required so many people, the vast majority of Georgia's enslaved population in the 18th century worked in coastal counties and along the Savannah, Ogeechee, Altamaha, Satilla and St. Mary's rivers, the so-called "rice rivers," where rice growing continued until after the Civil War.

In Button Gwinnett's time, Georgia planters supplemented their rice and timber exports with indigo, the highly prized source of blue dye. The bulk of the production in America shifted from Louisiana to South Carolina, which first shipped "Carolina indigo" to England in 1744. It arrived there at a time when the textile industry was growing fast, and demand for it was great.[28] England also bought indigo from French and Spanish colonies, but tensions with France and Spain made those supplies unreliable, so it counted on Carolina indigo, providing more incentive for planters there to grow it. In 1747, South Carolina exported £138,300 of indigo, and in 1755, more than £200,000. Georgia's planters never approached that level, exporting only £4,500 of it in 1755 and never more than £20,000 a year.[28]

Gwinnett had a lot to learn about indigo and rice if he hoped to become a successful planter. He also needed to learn how to manage slave labor, and find markets for his crops and timber. He owned at least two books on agriculture that shed light on how coastal Georgia's subtropical climate allowed farmers and planters to grow crops nearly year-round.[29]

His lack of knowledge and experience — and the British land-use requirements that he staff his land — weren't his only obstacles to success. Unbeknown to him, when he began living on St. Catherines, the island was quasi-public. While the Bosomworths lived there, the land was used for hunting and fishing, apparently with no consequences. Gwinnett wanted to put a stop to that, so he bought a two-sentence, 175-word public notice in the September 10 and 17, 1766, editions of the *Georgia Gazette* to make it clear that the island was off-limits to hunters and fishermen — and to those who wanted to steal his cattle and hogs.[30]

"All persons whatever are hereby prohibited from hunting and shooting upon the Island of St. Catherine's, or carelessly landing upon the same, or fishing on the shore or beach, or in any of the creeks thereunto belonging, as such trespassers, when known, will be prosecuted without distinction to the utmost rigour of

the law. And whereas loose and disorderly people have frequently killed and carried off from the said island hogs and cattle to the great loss of the subscriber, to prevent such practices for the future, I do hereby offer a reward of twenty pounds ...to any person or persons who shall discover any person who has been or may hereafter be guilty thereof, to be paid upon the conviction of the offender; and if any person, who may have been concerned, or hereafter may be concerned, in such practices, will discover and give evidence against his accomplice or accomplices, such person shall be entitled to and receive the same award from BUTTON GWINNETT."

The *Georgia Gazette* was a must-read starting with its first issue in 1763, and buying an advertisement or public notice was guaranteeing your message would receive a lot of attention. Of course, Gwinnett's warning wasn't read by the Native Americans who still fished and hunted on the island — and may have helped themselves to a few of his cows and hogs — but it may have done the trick because he never paid the newspaper to publish another notice of that kind.

If Button and Ann Gwinnett missed each other during this time, no letters have surfaced to prove that, but their long-distance relationship ended, at least temporarily, on January 8, 1767, about one year after he started his career as a planter. Ann's arrival in Savannah — her first trip to America — merited a mention in the January 14, 1767, issue of the *Georgia Gazette,* which reported that "Mrs. Gwinnett, the wife of Mr. Button Gwinnett" arrived on the brigantine *Diana* along with Nancy Wright, one of royal Gov. James Wright's daughters.[31]

It was a difficult voyage, as all transatlantic crossings were then. For one thing, brigantines, while larger than schooners, were smaller than brigs, which offered a smoother, safer and roomier ride. Brigantines going from England to America in the 18th century were often owned by merchants and loaded with textiles, ceramics and household goods. They were packed in nearly every nook of these boats to make the best use of space. So there wasn't a lot of room for passengers. Storms and wind patterns were always a major concern, and transatlantic crossings, when possible, were timed for the spring and early summer, when weather conditions made safer voyages more likely. *Diana's* crossing occurred in the fall and early winter.

Passengers aboard these ships experienced cramped quarters, stale and sometimes rotten food, rat bites, lice infestations, a lack of privacy, a shortage of fresh water, stomach-churning seas, and bumps and bruises from frequent collisions with door jambs, railings and short ceilings. Females sometimes endured advances from crew members who went long periods without seeing women. And that wasn't the worst of it. Illnesses, such as dysentery and typhus, spread quickly aboard these ships, and medical care was non-existent. Monotony, boredom and isolation sometimes led to bouts of depression and anxiety.

Abigail Adams, the wife of the American Founding Father John Adams, didn't enjoy her voyage from London to Boston aboard the brigantine *Lucretia*:[32]

"The wind with which we sailed scarcely lasted us 5 hours, but we continued our course until Monday Evening when it blew such a gale that we were driven back and very glad to get into Portland (Maine) Harbour. … I think that God will suit the wind to the shorn Lamb, that we may be carried through our difficulties better than my apprehensions. … Want of Sleep is the greatest inconvenience I have yet suffered but I shall not escape so. … The confinement of a Ship is tedious and I am fully of the mind I was when I came over that I will never again try the Sea."

The day-to-day discomfort associated with a transatlantic crossing in the 18th century paled in comparison with the worst-case, most-feared scenario — shipwrecks. Any number of things could cause ships to run aground or sink, including storms, navigation errors, damaged hulls or pirate attacks. Shipwrecks in the Atlantic Ocean during the 18th century were not rare. Although ships were more seaworthy than those made in the 17th century, for every 150 or so transatlantic voyages in the 1760s and 1770s, one was "foundered," "lost," or "wrecked."[33]

During the latter quarter of the 18th century, Thomas Lynch Jr., a signer of the Declaration of Independence, Scottish poet William Falconer, and Henry Vansittart, a member of British Parliament, died in transatlantic shipwrecks. And in 1763, Gov. James Wright's wife Sarah and daughter Mary died in a shipwreck in the Atlantic Ocean, the details of which were never recorded. This had to haunt Nancy Wright as she traveled to Georgia aboard *Diana*. Regardless of the hardships she endured during the voyage, imagine her relief at reaching the port of Savannah on January 8, 1767. She might have wanted to kiss the wharf where her feet first touched down.

Because brigantines that crossed the Atlantic in the 18th century typically carried few, if any, passengers, it is entirely possible that she and Ann Gwinnett were the only passengers aboard *Diana*. The *Georgia Gazette* notice of their arrival made no mention of anyone else, including Elizabeth Gwinnett, Button and Ann's only surviving daughter. Elizabeth was five years old then, and the hardships associated with transatlantic travel would have been even more miserable for her than it was for her mother.

After they disembarked in Savannah, Nancy Wright and Ann Gwinnett would have had very different experiences in Georgia.

Wright stayed with her father in a relatively new, "proper and convenient dwelling-House" for "the present and every future (royal) governor of Georgia," on St. James Square in downtown Savannah.[34] (The lot where the governor's residence was built later became the site of Telfair Academy, an art museum, on what is now Telfair Square.) Nancy would have eaten at formal dinner parties and ridden in comfortable coaches around town. By that point, Gov. Wright had not yet received the nobility title of sir, as he would six years later, but she would have been treated like royalty by Savannahians who wanted to curry favor with him. In 1767, that would have included just about everyone in Georgia.

Ann Gwinnett, who enjoyed a relatively comfortable life in central England thanks to the success of her father's grocery business, stayed with her husband in a house on St. Catherines Island that was most likely smaller than any she lived in before, not to mention chilly, wet and drafty in the winter and hot and humid most of the rest of the year.

Eighteenth-century plantation houses looked nothing like the tall, stately plantation houses built in the 19th century throughout the South. The first floors typically included no more than a few rooms, and the second floors, often accessible by a ladder, had a room or two just below a pitched roof. (A larger house on St. Catherines today is called the Button Gwinnett House, but the house he lived in no longer exists.)[35] Gwinnett's house would have been framed with wood and covered with a type of concrete made by burning oyster shells to create lime, then mixing it with water, sand, ash and broken shells. Sixteenth-century Spanish explorers brought with them to Florida this recipe for "tapia," roughly translated to mud wall. Spaniards used tabby, as it was called in America, in St. Augustine, where Oglethorpe, Georgia's founder, first saw it, and introduced "Oglethorpe tabby" to Georgia.[36]

It's unclear what role Ann Gwinnett played on the plantation, which she must have viewed as foreign in every way. Its many hogs, sheep and cattle far outnumbered her and Button and the 14 enslaved people who worked there in 1767. Her husband may have assigned an enslaved woman or a girl — if she could be spared — to tend to Ann's needs at St. Catherines at certain times in much the same way that a wealthy lady in a large house in England would have relied on servants.

Wolverhampton, her hometown, and Savannah were roughly the same size then, and she would have traveled to Savannah from time to time to shop, as her husband did.[37] She also would have made the shorter trip by boat across St. Catherines Sound and up the Midway River to visit nearby Sunbury, smaller than Savannah but with a bustling port. Button told Ann about his financial struggles and complained to her about British land-use policies that burdened him.[38] He would have justified using slave labor by pointing out — accurately — that Georgia didn't have nearly enough able-bodied white men for hire in the 1760s and 1770s.

The only other mention of Ann Gwinnett in the *Georgia Gazette* was a single sentence that she returned to England. Whether she was homesick for England, missed Elizabeth and her parents, became frustrated with St. Catherines, or all of the above, the newspaper simply reported in its January 20, 1768, edition that "Mrs. Gwinnett, the wife of Mr. Button Gwinnett," set sail for London on the merchant ship *Polly* on an undisclosed date in January 1768, one year to the month after she arrived.[39]

Upon her return to England, she would have told her family — and written to Button's family — about the growing port cities of Savannah and Sunbury, and her husband's vast island plantation, stocked with hogs and cattle and the 20-foot-long boat and the barns and the stables. It's less likely that she would have said much about the simple tabby house that came with the plantation and the growing number of slaves her husband owned. The house might not have given her side of the family confidence that Button was a good provider, and his side of the family — with his clergyman father and clergyman older brother — would not have approved that the laborers on his plantation were overworked, unpaid and stripped of all freedoms. For what it's worth, Gwinnett never bought an ad in the *Georgia Gazette* about a runaway slave, so perhaps he treated his enslaved workers better than his peers, or maybe they felt trapped on the island plantation.

There is no record of Ann meeting Lyman Hall, her husband's good friend in Georgia, but she almost certainly did. Button would have wanted her to meet Hall. By all accounts, he was an intelligent and friendly doctor and planter who was popular in Sunbury and well known from there to Savannah. Like many Georgia residents in the 1760s, Hall came from somewhere else.

He was born in 1724 in Wallingford, Conn., just north of New Haven and Long Island Sound. Like Button, he was the son of a minister. Unlike Button, he followed in his father's footsteps and led a congregation in what is now Bridgeport. After two years on the job, the bachelor clergyman's "moral character" was called into question.[40] It's unclear what he did that concerned his congregants, but there reportedly was proof, and he confessed to having sinned.[41]

Lyman Hall

Despite this indiscretion, Hall filled in when needed at the pulpit, but he shifted his focus to teaching school and studying medicine.[42] Someone who wanted to become a doctor in 18th-century America could accomplish that in one of four ways: Attend medical school, learn medical skills during military service, serve as an apprentice to a doctor, or show up in a community that didn't have a doctor and volunteer to fill that role. Although Hall completed "a thorough preliminary course,"[43] he falls into the latter category. The workings of the human body were much more of a mystery in the 18th century than they are today, and anyone with even a little knowledge of anatomy was welcome to try his best to heal a community's ills.

Hall, who had large brown eyes and a straight nose, married Abigail Burr in 1752. She died the next year. Four years after becoming a widower, he married Mary Osborne and moved to Dorchester, S.C., near Charleston, in a community settled 60 years earlier by Puritans from Dorchester, Mass. Starting in 1752 and continuing until 1771, many of the Dorchester South Carolinians resettled to the Georgia coast in an area called Midway, in St. John Parish. It took that name because of its proximity to the Midway River and because it was roughly midway between the established towns of Savannah and Darien.

Midway residents referred to themselves as Congregationalists — descendants of Puritans — and like Puritans, had a reputation for being rigid and morally upright, but they were largely ambivalent about slavery. They knew they couldn't grow large quantities of rice and other cash crops without slave labor, so they viewed enslaved people as necessary to their success.

The first Puritans who came to America generally accepted slavery and used biblical references to rationalize owning other people. In a sermon called "A Good Master Well Served," the New England Puritan clergyman, author and slaveowner Cotton Mather said:[44]

"Give Ear, ye pitied Blacks, Give Ear! … It is allowed in the Scriptures … yet they may aspire to be 'Freemen of the Lord' after death: 'It will be but a little, a little, a little while, and all your pains will end in everlasting joys.'"

By the 18th century, especially in the South, planters who considered themselves religious rationalized slavery as God's will. To justify their use of slave labor, some slave owners baptized enslaved people, provided them with regular religious instruction and sometimes condemned slave owners who mistreated enslaved people more than they did. But they didn't condemn the *institution* of slavery because it served their interests. They depended on slave labor as much as farmers today depend on tractors, seeders and harvesters.

There actually were rules for treating slaves in 18th-century Georgia. Four years after the colony formally instituted slavery, its trustees ratified the Slave Code of 1755, the first law in Georgia that governed how slaves were to be treated. It was patterned after the 1690 Carolina Slave Code, also known as the "Act for the Better Ordering of Slaves." Georgia's law sought to keep enslaved people "in due Subjection and Obedience" and to prevent masters "from exercising too great Rigour and Cruelty," such as castrating, blinding and killing them.[45]

The law made whipping and imprisonment the preferred forms of punishment, required slave owners to provide enslaved people with a minimum amount of food and clothing, and permitted them to establish a work day of as many as 16 hours a day.[46] It encouraged masters — but didn't require them — to implement a six-day work week to respect the Sabbath, but slave owners were not required to provide religious instruction to enslaved people on Sunday or any other day of the week. Some did, but many more believed religion might give enslaved people the impression that God loved them as much as He loved their masters and other white people. If they believed that, the masters reasoned, they might also believe they were equal to white people, and that could lead to rebellion.[47]

In 1770, about 350 whites and 1,500 enslaved people lived in Midway.[48] One of the biggest problems associated with living and working in a swampy area is that mosquitoes thrive there. No one knew this then, but female mosquitoes were Midway residents' worst enemies because they feed on blood and some of them transfer the parasite that causes malaria.

"After the rice swamps were opened and cultivated in Midway settlement in the parish of St. John's, it was soon ascertained that a residence on the sea-shore proved more healthy than on the in land swamps, particularly during the summer and autumnal months," wrote Hugh McCall, Georgia's first historian.

Africans, some of whom came from malaria-endemic regions, possessed some genetic resistance and survived malaria at a greater rate than did Europeans.[49]

Malaria, which brought fever, chills and weakness, often was referred to as "intermittent fever" or "malignant fever," and the first Europeans who settled in Georgia knew about it. Samuel Núñez, a Sephardic Jewish physician who came to Savannah in July 1733, used Peruvian bark to treat these fevers, and after his supply ran out, he used local barks that he hoped would work. The bark was mashed into a powder and mixed with water, or syrup to curb its bitterness. Peruvian bark was the preferred medicine to treat malaria when the British arrived in Georgia, and in later years, Georgia's leaders created a medicinal garden where it was grown.

Enslaved people and Native Americans also used herbal remedies to try to combat malaria. This bark-based medicine generally came to be known as quinine and was used in one form or the other to treat malaria into the 20th century. Quinine was expensive and usually in short supply in 18th-century Georgia, and doctors — even those who received medical education and training — didn't always administer it properly, and it did not always cure their malaria patients.

Lyman Hall's desire to want to help white people suffering from malaria and other illnesses and diseases endeared him to Midway residents.

"His reputation as a successful planter and sympathizing friend was most enviable," Charles C. Jones, Jr., a 19th-century historian, wrote. "...His polite address, literary attainments, public spirit, social habits, thoughtful views and well-rounded character united in rendering him popular and influential with the inhabitants of St. John Parish."[50]

Hall was also a successful planter, one of many who lived in St. John Parish. In fact, the enormous amount of rice grown there necessitated a port, which was built in 1761 and 1762 in Sunbury.[51] The town, which stood on a bluff overlooking the Midway Rive, also became something of a vacation destination.

William Bartram, a Philadelphia-based botanist who traveled through Georgia and the Carolinas in 1773, wrote this about Sunbury: "There are about one hundred houses in the town neatly built of wood frame having pleasant Piasas [sic] around them. The inhabitants are genteel and wealthy, either Merchants or Planters from the Country who resort here in the Summer and Autumn, to partake of the Salubrious Sea breeze, Bathing & sporting on the Sea Islands."[52] McCall, Georgia's first historian, wrote: "...the entire exposure of this place is above the horizon. Soon after its settlement and organization as a town, it rose into considerable commercial importance: emigrants came from different quarters to this healthy maritime port,..."

By 1770, Sunbury's port rivaled Savannah's in terms of economic importance. Rice, corn, peas, indigo, lumber and livestock left the port for Caribbean nations and the northern colonies.[53] McCall wrote that, "Seven square rigged vessels have been known to enter the port of Sunbury in one day,… In this prosperous state it continued with very little interruption, until the war commenced between Great Britain and America." In the early 1770s, Sunbury's port employed packers, cullers and inspectors of lumber, hemp, flax, wheat flour and tanned leather as well as a comptroller and a tax collector.[54]

Sunbury's waterfront, with its wharves, shipyard, warehouses and large houses, projected wealth. Rice, more than anything else, made many people there rich, so much so that Midway residents possessed nearly one-third of the aggravate wealth of the Georgia colony in 1770. And as one historian reported, "…its citizens were remarkable for their thrift, courage, honesty, and determination."[55]

The success of the port at Sunbury was a point of pride for royal Gov. James Wright, who had pledged to grow the economy in Georgia when he arrived in October 1760. In a letter to the Earl of Halifax, also an early advocate of encouraging commerce in America, Wright took full credit for building a port in Sunbury:[56]

"I judged it necessary for his Majesty's service that Sunbury, a well settled place having an exceedingly good harbour and inlet from the sea, should be made a port of entry.... There are 80 dwelling houses in the place. There are considerable merchant stores for supplying the town and the planters in the neighborhood with all kind (sic) of necessary goods; and around it, for about 15 miles, is one of the best settled parts of the country."

What Wright didn't realize — or wouldn't admit to the Earl of Halifax — is the residents of Sunbury and the rest of St. John Parish began growing weary of British rule, and some resented and even despised it. Before residents in other parts of Georgia tired of British occupation, these folks wanted nothing to do it, and St. John's Parish became a bellwether for Georgia's independence movement.

"Of all the parishes composing the province none was more patriotic or resolute, none more public spirited or anxious to form a league against British oppression, than the parish of St. John," Jones, wrote.[57]

Gwinnett's friend Lyman Hall would become a face of the independence movement, not only in St. John, but throughout Georgia. It's unclear when Hall and Gwinnett met, but it would have made sense if Thomas Bosomworth, who sold the lease to St. Catherines to Gwinnett, introduced them to each other. Bosomworth turned to Hall to be a witness on the deed of trust that secured St. Catherines for him and his then-wife Mary in 1760. When Thomas

Bosomworth and his new wife, Sarah, sold the lease to Gwinnett, they wanted him to be a successful planter because that would allow him to more easily meet his financial obligations to them. They should have wanted to introduce Gwinnett to successful planters such as Hall, who grew rice and indigo on his 2,000-acre plantation, known as Hall's Knoll, 11 miles inland from Sunbury.

In fact, Sunbury, a brief boat ride from St. Catherines Island, became Gwinnett's home away from home, and he was often seen with Hall. "…all of his public and much of his private business was there transacted," Jones wrote of Gwinnett's time in Sunbury. "He was constantly seen in the streets."[58] He and Hall "constantly exchanged social courtesies."

Hall was 11 years older than Gwinnett and served as his mentor as well as his friend. He was the perfect person to introduce Gwinnett to anyone he wanted to meet and to advise Gwinnett on how to make his plantation successful. He was the best friend Gwinnett could have had, and thanks in large part to Hall, Gwinnett's name would be known in Georgia and throughout America until long after Gwinnett died.

5

A Judge and a State Lawmaker

In 18th-century America, owning land made many people wealthy and gave them status and respect. The more land, the more status and respect. In Georgia, for example, a man with at least 50 acres could vote and a man with 500 acres or more could be elected to the state legislature.

Land wasn't always something someone had to buy. England's desire to turn Georgia into an economic powerhouse meant it was willing to give land grants to men and women — yes, women received about 67,000 acres of land in the colony between 1755 and 1775[1] — who wanted to monetize land by selling crops and timber.

That excited Button Gwinnett, who wanted as much free land as he could get. His purchase of the St.

Catherines lease made him a somebody, but he wasn't satisfied with those 6,200 acres, so he petitioned the Governor's Council for more land in 1767, and royal Gov. James Wright gave him 1,000 acres near the Sapelo River, a tract south of St. Catherines Island that was almost completely forested. Harvesting and selling its timber could be very lucrative.

After he received those 1,000 acres, he asked for another. And another. And another. In all, he was granted 3,750 acres,[2] and he didn't have to pay anything for it besides survey and administrative fees.[3] That still wasn't enough for Gwinnett. In the late 1760s, most likely 1768, he acquired the Barber Islands, named after John Barber, who was granted them in 1767 and lived there until he died.[4] In all, Gwinnett controlled more than 11,000 acres. Not bad for a guy who failed as a transatlantic merchant.

If he could handle the responsibility of all that acreage, he could become a public official. That was the prevailing opinion anyway in colonial America. Owning a lot of land led to opportunities that were unavailable to others.

In Gwinnett's case, it led to his appointment as a commissioner for regulating navigation in the waterways near St. Catherines and the Midway River.[5] Commissioners in 18th-century America collected taxes, ensured regulations were followed and earned fees. In Georgia, commissioner jobs went to merchants, lawyers and planters who Gov. Wright trusted. And it couldn't have hurt that Gwinnett was also British.

Shortly afterward, Wright named him one of His Majesty's justices of the peace for the rural parishes of St. John and St. Mary. The *Georgia Gazette* published this news in its February 24 and March 3 editions in 1768, along with the appointments of justices in Georgia's other parishes.[6] Justice of the peace positions were rarely declined because they came with a fair amount of prestige.[7] Unlike today, justices of the peace heard a wide range of cases — sometimes with a jury of 12 men — but these men didn't have to know the law.[8] The governors who appointed them counted on them to possess common sense and good judgment, to fear God, and to "not neglect the public for private employment or ease."[9]

In Georgia, these courts were formally called Courts of Conscience and informally called Inferior Courts.[10] General Courts, run by judges who studied law and worked as lawyers, were known as Superior Courts. But because the colonies valued the Courts of Conscience, governors sometimes appointed lawyers and judges as justices of the peace. By 1776, there were 81 justices of the peace in Georgia. Of those, 65 were legal layman, 11 worked as lawyers, two were assistant judges, one was the colony's chief justice, one was its attorney general, and one served as the superintendent of Indian Affairs.[11]

Although most of the justices of the peace in Georgia hadn't studied law, the vast majority of them owned a lot of land. One of those justices was Lachlan McIntosh, a Scotsman who served as justice of the peace in St. Mary and St. James parishes while Gwinnett served in St. Mary and St. John.

McIntosh arrived in America on January 10, 1736, as a 10-year-old, with his father, John McIntosh Mohr, his mother, Marjory, his siblings, William, John, Phineas, Lewis and Janet, and about 170 other men, women and children who had lived near Inverness in the Scottish Highlands.[12] (Lachlan's other siblings, Anne and George, were born in Georgia in 1737 and 1739, respectively.) The clan, led by Lachlan's father, came to Georgia after accepting an invitation from the colony's founder James Oglethorpe, who wanted the clan to protect Georgians from the Spaniards in St. Augustine, Florida.

These Scots were stellar soldiers, "... men of good character, and they were carefully selected for their military qualities."[13] They carved their settlement out of a dense forest — about 60 miles south of Savannah and 120 miles north of St. Augustine — along the Altamaha River in coastal Georgia. Their settlement, initially called New Inverness, was later renamed Darien, in memory of a failed 17th-century Scottish settlement in Panama that was abandoned in 1700.[14]

Before they arrived, the Creek tribe managed the land with controlled burns and cuts. It was otherwise untouched by man. White oaks, bald cypress, black gums and a variety of pines dominated the forest, where a vast number of animals and birds lived, including white-tailed deer, black bears, bobcats, red wolves, foxes, beavers, otters, raccoons, squirrels, rabbits, alligators, rattlesnakes, turtles, wild turkeys, woodpeckers, owls, hawks and bald eagles.

This cornucopia of flora and fauna provided much of what the clan needed, but they still depended on supplies from Savannah that sometimes didn't arrive on time.[15] Before long, the Scots built a guard house, a store, a chapel and crude houses, which they called huts.[16] The children viewed the forest as an exhilarating playground, but it could be a dangerous place, as Lachlan discovered when an alligator mauled his brother Lewis and "carried him quite off" while his siblings were swimming in the Altamaha River.[17]

Before long, Lachlan's father became the leader of this self-sufficient clan. "Many of these new Emigrants, being all together, never learned the English language," one historian wrote, "and the whole lived in the greatest simplicity and harmony, having neither Lawyers nor Courts, but their differences all amicably settled by the decisions of their good old Captain (John McIntosh Mohr)."[18]

Because the Scottish Highlanders served as a buffer between the British in Savannah and the Spaniards in Florida and because England and Spain both claimed

Georgia's coastal region as their own, Lachlan grew up during a time when the clan was always either preparing to fight or fighting. Warfare was in the clan's blood, so it was in his blood, too.

After his father was captured by the Spaniards during Oglethorpe's 1740 attack on St. Augustine, Lachlan lived in an orphanage south of Savannah to ease the parenting burden on his mother. After two years there, Oglethorpe sent him to serve as a military cadet at Fort Frederica on St. Simons Island, about 90 miles southeast of Savannah.[19] He was 17 years old when he arrived there in 1743, the year of a second failed British attack on St. Augustine.

In 1748, after tensions between the British and the Spaniards cooled, Lachlan, who had reunited with his family, moved to Charleston, where he eventually worked in the administrative office of a business operated by Henry Laurens, a partner in the largest slave trading firm in North America. In the 1750s and 1760s, Laurens viewed slavery as a means to make agriculture a thriving industry in the South.

In a 1755 letter to his partners at Austin & Laurens, Laurens described the enslaved people he preferred to buy and sell:[20] "Very likely healthy People, Two thirds at least Men from 18–25 Years old, the other young Women from 14–18... Gold Coast and Gambias are best... our people like tall Slaves best for our business and strong withall... Such as small, meager or other ways ordinary won't sell better here than with you." The slave trade enriched Laurens, but his feelings toward it changed, according to a letter he sent to his son John in 1776:[21] "You know, my dear son, I abhor slavery… I am devising means for man-umitting many of them, and for cutting off the entail of slavery. Great powers oppose me—the laws and customs of my country… my own and the avarice of my countrymen."

Lachlan McIntosh

Unlike slavery, his feelings for Lachlan McIntosh never changed. Laurens, who succeeded John Hancock as president of the Second Continental Congress in 1778, served as McIntosh's mentor, friend and business partner, advising and helping him until Laurens' death in 1792.

McIntosh lacked a formal education, but thanks to his military training and exposure to educated people such as Oglethorpe and Laurens, he was articulate and had impeccable manners, which served him well. William Bartram, a Philadelphia-based botanist who once visited Savannah, described him as a smiling, friendly and generous man with "grace and dignity peculiar to himself." In a travel memoir, Bartram wrote that McIntosh initially greeted him with these words: "Friend Bartram, come under my roof, and I desire you to make my house your home, as long as it's convenient to yourself; remember from this moment, you are part of my family, and on my part, I shall endeavor to make it agreeable."[22]

His polished manners matched his distinguished appearance, with a long face, steely eyes and a widow's peak. He was tall for his time, and a friend described him as the "handsomest man he had ever seen."[23] In short, he was a catch, and on the first day of 1756, he married Sarah Threadcraft. Not long afterward, he returned to Georgia, where he acquired land in the

Altamaha River delta — near where he grew up —
and partnered with Laurens to grow rice.

Like other Georgia planters during this time,
McIntosh's success depended on slave labor, a reality
that must have disappointed his father, who frowned
on slavery.[24] In fact, McIntosh's name appears for the
first time in the *Georgia Gazette* on June 16, 1763,
in this public notice:[25] "Brought to the Savannah jail
the 3rd of June instant, A Negroe man named Jemmy,
speaks proper English, and says his master's name is
Lachlan McIntosh of Darien."

In Georgia during the second half of the 18th century,
there was an understanding between slave owners
and other white people that runaway slaves should be
detained and taken to the nearest jail. They had value
to the person who apprehended them, like finding a
wallet and knowing for certain that the owner would
provide a reward for returning it. A slave owner
always made sure the person who returned his runaway slave was paid for his efforts.

McIntosh and Button Gwinnett, each of whom
owned dozens of slaves by the late 1760s, probably
didn't know each other before 1768, when they began
serving together in the justice of the peace court in
St. Mary Parish. That courthouse is where they would
have had the most interactions and where they would
have decided if they liked and respected each other,

or not. Justices often worked as pairs, and although other men were assigned to that parish, Gwinnett and McIntosh almost certainly shared the bench from time to time. Like any workplace, they were not required to get along, but Gov. James Wright, who appointed them, counted on these men to work together and meter out justice fairly.

Wright served as a powerful executive who controlled nearly all aspects of the colony, not unlike a modern CEO with a passive board of directors. He called the shots, and his authority went beyond appointing justices of the peace and judges. The Governor's Council, Wright's cabinet, advised him and made recommendations to him on matters such as approving land grant requests, for example, but Wright essentially did as he pleased. He informed the British Board of Trade about the colony's census and commerce, and he wrote letters to high-ranking British officials, but he reported only to the king.

Wright wanted Savannah to be Georgia's capitol, and very soon after he became governor in 1760, the colony's legislature, the Commons House of Assembly, authorized the creation of a governor's residence in Savannah.[26] During the early and mid-1760s, the Assembly was largely under Wright's thumb. It made the laws, but many were recommended by him, and if the Assembly members passed a law he didn't like, he would veto it, or the king would. What's more, Wright could adjourn a legislative session whenever he pleased and for whatever reason he chose.

As the years passed, Wright clashed more and more with the Assembly. For example, he ended the 1768 legislative session early after the legislators chose Noble Wimberly Jones as its speaker. Wright considered this an act of defiance because Jones, unlike his loyalist father, didn't respect the monarchy or crown-appointed authority and advocated for expanding the rights of American colonists.

To be elected to the Assembly, you had to own a lot of land, and throughout the 18th century, there weren't many of those men to choose from in rural Georgia, where very few people lived. By 1770, only about 1,000 white people lived in St. John's Parish, and its relatively few voters — white males who owned at least 50 acres of land — sent Button Gwinnett and two others to the Assembly to represent their interests for a two-year term starting in 1770. The 1770-71 session promised to be exciting. Gwinnett would have known beforehand about the power struggle between Wright and the Assembly over Noble Wimberly Jones being chosen as speaker. He could have weighed in on this challenge to British authority, but he didn't care enough to want to be there.

Gwinnett didn't show up on the first day of the session in 1770 or on the second day or on the third day. He didn't show up the first week at all. On November 6, the first day of the second week, the Assembly messenger was ordered to take Gwinnett into custody and escort him to the session.[27] Eight days later, the messenger showed up with Gwinnett, who blamed his absence on "a Severe fit of Sickness."[28] He must have recovered because later that day he "proved himself duely (sic) Qualified to serve as a Representative" and was sworn in to office.[29]

Besides the ongoing power struggle with Wright, the Assembly debated a law to prevent the stealing of horses and "neat cattle" and to come up with effective punishments for thieves. Given Gwinnett's personal experience with hog and cattle bandits on his plantation on St. Catherines, this should have piqued his interest, but when it was discussed on January 9-11, 1770, his name doesn't appear in a summary of the *Journal of the Commons House of Assembly*. In fact, it's not clear if he was still in Savannah then or had returned to his plantation. The Assembly's detailed meeting minutes from the first part of the 1770-71 session don't mention his name beyond his tardiness.

The second leg of the session began on October 29, 1770, but again, Gwinnett couldn't be bothered to attend. He didn't show up by the first of November or by the first of December. Unlike his first session, when Noble Wimberly Jones, the Assembly speaker, sought Gwinnett's appearance not long after the session began, this time Jones waited until December 14, 1770, to say "the House requires Button Gwinnett's immediate Attention."[30] Gwinnett still didn't show up, and that may not have mattered to anyone in the legislature because Jones waited another two months, until February 20, 1771, before he ordered the Assembly messenger to take Gwinnett into custody "for absenting himself from his Duty in Assembly."[31] Two days later, Gov. Wright flexed his muscles and abruptly ended the session as a reaction to the Assembly re-electing Jones as its speaker.[32]

This was a turning point in Wright's dealings with the Assembly. From that point on, the relationship was doomed, whether or not Wright realized it at the time.

The *Journal of the Commons House of Assembly* doesn't record the date the messenger brought Gwinnett to Savannah, but he fulfilled his duty because he requested a fee of six pounds and 19 shillings "for his trouble in fetching Button Gwinnett, Esq. p(er). warrant."[33] Gwinnett, whose attendance record shows he had no interest in public service, couldn't have been upset to learn that Wright had suspended the legislative session. Not only didn't he have to waste his time serving his constituents, but he didn't have to face the legislators who took their responsibilities seriously enough to attend the legislative sessions.

The men who would become the leaders of Georgia's independence movement — Noble Wimberly Jones, Archibald Bulloch and John Houstoun, to name a few — served in the Assembly then. The historical record sheds no light on what they thought of Gwinnett, but it's safe to assume they didn't admire him.

During the next five years, Gwinnett had no role in government in Georgia and mostly spent time on his plantation and in nearby Sunbury. That's not to say he was idle. He had many pressing matters that required his attention.

6
A Tangled Mess, Part 1

During his lifetime and after his death, Button Gwinnett was called a lot of things: a scoundrel and a lying rascal, "the Lord of the Earth," a con man, a rogue, and a demagogue. He was also called intelligent, spirited, very firm, a Founding Father and a patriot. Of all those descriptors, he can accurately be called intelligent, but there isn't enough evidence in the historical record to definitively say that any of the other labels — the compliments or the insults — are true.

What is true is that his extreme confidence led him to believe — and allowed him to convince others — that he had the ability to successfully carry out his plans. Whether it was transatlantic trading or operating a store or running a plantation, he would make it work. He told people that. He believed that, and many others did, too.

Because he always needed money, he had to convince lenders that he would repay what he borrowed. The record shows he borrowed compulsively, often from people who were unaware that they shouldn't do business with him. Fortunately for him and unfortunately for others, credit agencies didn't exist, and lenders didn't do their due diligence as thoroughly as they should have. Gwinnett was able to borrow as much as he did for as long as he did because he owned so much land — more than 10,000 acres, or nearly 16 square miles. Because he owned that much land, lenders assumed he must be successful. He must be responsible. He must be able to repay the money he borrowed. In the 18th-century South, land and enslaved people were the best collateral, and he owned a lot of both.

Gwinnett also knew how to say the right things in the right way to people who he believed could help him. Hugh McCall, Georgia's first historian, wrote that Gwinnett's "language was mild & persuasive but not eloquent. His manners were polite and his deportment graceful."[1] Persuasiveness is the only social skill he may have needed to convince wealthy men to loan him money or allow him to buy goods on credit, and it didn't hurt that he also could be polite and graceful.

There is only a scant paper trail associated with Gwinnett's life, but it makes this much clear: He didn't have a head for business. His expenses always exceeded his revenue. And his creditors were dogged and protected their financial interests by doing everything in their power to collect what he owed them. Many of the financial documents that exist refer to bonds, which required borrowers to make pledges to repay debts in the future in exchange for receiving something in the present. These bond agreements allowed lenders to seize borrowers' land or other assets if the debts weren't repaid.

Gwinnett failed as a transatlantic merchant. A general store he bought in Savannah quickly went out of business. And his plantation wasn't making enough money. In fact, existing records show his career as a planter was in trouble shortly after it began. The first evidence that the plantation was struggling financially became clear on January 6, 1768, the date he signed a bond agreement — the first known bond since he purchased the lease at St. Catherines — associated with a loan from Noble Jones, the father of Assembly speaker Noble Wimberly Jones.[2] Noble Jones, an English-born carpenter who arrived in Georgia with its founder James Oglethorpe in February 1733, became a surveyor and a close aide to Oglethorpe. Jones, unlike his son, was a British loyalist, and he aligned himself with royal Gov. James Wright. Jones loaned Gwinnett £180, 18 shillings and eight pence, and the bond stipulated that Gwinnett would give him six slaves if he didn't repay the loan plus interest.

Gwinnett must have had a similar agreement with James Read, the co-owner of Read & Mossman, the store where Gwinnett frequently shopped in Savannah. Not long after he signed the bond agreement with Jones, Gwinnett gave Read seven enslaved women and two enslaved children to satisfy the terms of a loan.

The dry goods store he bought from the widow Dora Wylly was still open in 1768,[3] but it probably wasn't worth much because lenders never used it as collateral, and there is no evidence that it lasted beyond that year.

On March 16, 1770, at a time when Gwinnett was supposed to be serving as a colonial legislator, he signed another bond agreement related to a loan from Savannah brothers Mordecai and Levi Sheftall.[4] Mordecai was one of the first white people born in Georgia, and his bar mitzvah in 1748 is the first recorded observance of this Jewish rite in America.[5] He was a cattle farmer and a merchant, and by 1760, he owned a warehouse and a wharf on the Savannah River. Levi, four years younger, worked as a butcher and is best known for re-establishing Congregation Mikveh Israel — the third oldest Jewish congregation in America — which their father, Benjamin, founded in 1735. (Seven years after Gwinnett signed the bond to the Sheftalls — and one day after Gwinnett wrote his will — he signed over a mortgage to the Sheftalls for his land on St. Catherines Island.[6])

If it's fair to call Gwinnett a con man, it has to do with land he sold in 1768 and reportedly tried to sell again in 1770, when he no longer owned it. In April of 1770, as his first Commons House of Assembly session was winding down, this public notice appeared in two editions of the *Georgia Gazette*:[7]

> *Notice is given the publick that, in case, Button Gwinnett, Esquire, offers for sale, the islands known under the denomination of Barber Islands; I hereby protest against it, said Button Gwinnett having sold me the islands two years ago, and having received from me the whole amount of the purchase money: But whereas he ever since was dilatory in giving me the title of said islands, under frivolous excuses, I understand, that, taking advantage of my present misfortunes, he talks of no less of selling said islands again, I therefore caution any such persons against such an unjust purchase, unless they choose to put themselves to unavoidable inconveniences, since I am determined to lay my just claims to said islands in any court, even of equity, whenever, in better times, I'll be able to ascertain my unquestionable rights.*

> *Sunbury, April 3, 1770.*

ANTHONY LAMOTTE.

Lamotte, a merchant, accused Gwinnett of taking his money for the land, keeping the title and trying to sell the same land again, in 1770. Lamotte warned anyone who bought it that he would would go to court to protect his property.

If he intended to expose and humiliate Gwinnett, his timing couldn't have been better. It's unlikely Gwinnett was still in Savannah to finish his first session in the Commons House of Assembly, but the Assembly was still in session, and many of Georgia's most influential leaders were in town. At a time when the *Georgia Gazette* and gossip were the only sources of news in Savannah, these men would have read Lamotte's sternly worded notice or heard about it from someone who did. There is no record of this accusation leading to a civil lawsuit, so the notice may have put an end to a plan Gwinnett had to resell the islands that he had already sold to Lamotte. If Lamotte was being truthful, Gwinnett was desperate to raise money in 1770. This accusation not only soiled his reputation, but it may have contributed to his decision to stay on his island plantation, far from the colony's most influential leaders, many of whom lived in Savannah.

In the same month Lamotte's notice appeared in the *Georgia Gazette*, Edward Mease, a Florida-based merchant and lawyer who invested in *Nancy*'s trip from Pensacola to Savannah in 1765, made a claim on St. Catherines Island.[8]

This was the beginning of a years-long legal battle over the control of the island plantation that included Thomas and Sarah Bosomworth, the Sheftalls, Mease and other creditors. By the time Mease took this action, Ann Gwinnett had returned to Georgia, this time with their daughter Elizabeth. Their presence had to be a comfort to Button, whose creditors were breathing down his neck.

The paper trail dries up until February 1773, when a meeting of some of Gwinnett's other creditors led to a slew of documents that shed additional light on his financial problems. On the fifth of that month, Gwinnett signed three documents: one regarding the sale of St. Catherines Island to merchant Robert Porteous, a creditor, for £5,250; a second attesting that he was indebted to Porteous and merchant Alexander Rose, another creditor; and a third transferring cattle, hogs and Gwinnett's 20-foot-long boat to Porteous and Rose for £250 — £750 less than he paid the Bosomworths for all of that in 1765.[9] By the time he signed these papers, his debt totaled £6,267 — the equivalent of about $1.6 million in 1773.

In a letter written right after he signed the documents, a representative for Porteous informed Mease's lawyer that they "are on the point of Settling Matters with

Mr(.) Gwinnett." He wrote that Porteous pledged a bond to acquire St. Catherines Island. Knowing that Mease was also trying to collect from Gwinnett, the representative said Porteous would compensate him by offering Mease "wines to the amount if you think you can run them off at any rate, they may remain in your hands till we can contrive to pay the Debt." On March 11, 1773, Gwinnett signed a receipt for land sold to Porteous and Rose.[10] (Porteous and Rose were British loyalists whose real estate and enslaved people were seized during the Revolutionary War. After the war, they were permitted to stay in Georgia but couldn't work in a government office or vote for 14 years.[11] They asked the British government to compensate them for their losses, including debts they were not allowed to collect. Britain's finances were a mess after the war, and claimants such as Porteous and Rose are believed to have received only a small fraction of what they requested.)

Not long after Gwinnett signed the receipt on March 11, Mease stopped in Savannah on his way to England and wrote that Gwinnett was "considerably indebted" to him personally as well as to his merchant clients in northern England: Thomas Bentley and Samuel Boardman of Liverpool as well as William Shepherd, Thomas Langston and John Birley of Kirkham, northwest of Manchester. Gwinnett borrowed money from all of these men during his time as a transatlantic merchant. In three bonds, Mease detailed the terms that he and his clients were prepared to offer to get a share of what Gwinnett owed them.[12]

There's more.

The following year, Gwinnett appeared to want to narrow his list of creditors by taking out a massive loan — £7,182 and 10 shillings, roughly equivalent to $1.8 million — presumably to pay off his other creditors. The loan was in the form of three bonds, two signed on July 8, 1774, and one on October 9 of that year. The lender, John Neufville, was a major player. He was a successful Charleston-based merchant who also served as a South Carolina legislator and the commissioner of loans in that colony. He lent money to individuals in the American colonies and in Portugal and England.

Gwinnett might have heard of him from Thomas Savage III, a merchant friend of his who operated in the same financial circles as Neufville in Charleston. Neufville was so wealthy at the time he did business with Gwinnett that he was in the position a few years later to loan money to the South Carolina government to help it fund expenses associated with the Revolutionary War. He also loaned money to merchants in Bristol, England, where Gwinnett worked with his uncle as a teenager, but it's unclear how Gwinnett had heard of him. If Neufville asked Savage about Gwinnett, Savage must not have volunteered that his friend was deep in debt. (Unfortunately for Neufville, he lost most of his money during the war because many of his debtors didn't repay him, though Gwinnett's estate made him whole.)

Gwinnett's financial paper trail ends with Neufville — at least until after Gwinnett died. The good news for Gwinnett is that his creditors, as aggressive as they were, allowed him and his wife and daughter to live on St. Catherines Island along with his slaves. He could stay on as they cultivated and harvested crops, allowing Gwinnett to earn an income, however small.

And Gwinnett waited — for what, he didn't know. But he hoped something good would happen.

7

A Revolution Brewing

During the early 1770s, as Gwinnett struggled financially, Georgia looked to be doing well. The colony's population and economy were growing, and many Georgians seemed content. Georgia remained more dependent than any other colony on England for trade and protection, and Parliament believed that dependence made it unlikely to join the growing independence movement in its other North American colonies.

Much of the credit for this surface-level contentment went to royal Gov. James Wright, who was widely viewed as competent, reasonable and relatively popular, unlike past governors.[1]

Born in England in 1716, he moved with his family in 1730 to South Carolina, where his father, Robert, was the colony's monarch-appointed chief justice. James came to know South Carolinians' customs, traditions and values, and this understanding helped him when he arrived in Georgia in 1760 to govern the colony. South Carolina was a larger, more prosperous and more established colony, but South Carolinians and Georgians had a lot in common: Most were adventurous and entrepreneurial people with roots in Great Britain who viewed land ownership as a path to wealth. They also believed growing their economies couldn't happen without slave labor.

In South Carolina and in Georgia, Wright never hid his Englishness or the fact that he had the power of the British monarchy at his disposal, but he didn't always use it as a weapon. His skill as a diplomat was never more apparent than when he tried to quell the unrest over the Stamp Act of 1765, which taxed all paper products, such as wills, deeds, contracts, newspapers, pamphlets, writing paper and playing cards. Parliament enacted the law because the Seven Years War, which pitted England against France, left England with crushing debt, and British leaders reasoned that Americans benefited from England's victory so they should help relieve that debt.

Some Georgians supported the Stamp Act, and in fact, Georgia was the only colony in America that enforced the tax,[2] but the law was widely unpopular there. Even the pro-British *Georgia Gazette* publisher James Johnston, who "refused to admit to his Paper any of the Seditious (pro-independence) publications then circulating through the different Provinces,"[3] published 76 articles against the law and only 13 for it.[4] Johnston reported in the October 31, 1765, edition that an "...effigy of a stamp officer was carried through the streets (of Savannah), and afterwards hanged and burnt, amidst the acclimations of a great concourse of people of all ranks and denominations...."[5]

Gov. Wright was well aware that most Georgians hated the law. In one of his many panicky letters to the British Board of Trade in early 1766, he wrote that "the Liberty Boys, as they call themselves, had assembled together to the Number of about 200 & were gathering fast and that Some of them had declared they were determined to go to the Fort & break open the Store & take out & destroy the Stamp't Papers &c."[6] The numerous threats by the Liberty Boys, a branch of the national Sons of Liberty resistance movement, concerned Wright, who viewed the Stamp Act backlash as a serious threat to his authority. Widespread rebellion against the law could overwhelm his military forces, which numbered only about 150 colony-wide,[7] so he reached out to well-respected Georgians and urged them to spread the word that a violent rebellion against the law would benefit no one. His diplomacy paid off.

"... my Lords on my Sending Expresses with Letters to Many of the Most Sensible & Dispassionate People, I had the Satisfaction to find that my Weight & Credit was Sufficient to Check & Prevent all Commotions & disturbances in the Country," Wright wrote in early 1766, "& every thing is at Present Easy & quiet, & I hope Peace & Confidence will be Restored in general."[8]

Fortunately for Wright and royal governors in other colonies, Parliament repealed the Stamp Act on March 18, 1766, to avert mass rebellion, which seemed inevitable in many of the colonies. But the fact that Wright publicly supported the act harmed his reputation,[9] and exposed a fissure in his relationship with Georgians that increasingly grew wider.

The residents of rural St. John Parish, with their New England backgrounds, exacerbated the worsening relationship between Wright and the colonists. With an emotional tie to Massachusetts and Connecticut, they felt a strong bond with northern colonists and did not like what they were hearing about how the British were treating them. St. John was one of the more prosperous parts of Georgia in the early and mid-1770s, and that wealth empowered its residents. Many of them felt they were outgrowing the need for what the British had to offer, not unlike an older child who resents the presence of a babysitter, especially a strict one. St. John residents dubbed their parish Georgia's "cradle of liberty," and they would become a thorn in Wright's side.

His many years in Georgia gave him insight into the mood of the people, and by 1774 he realized that his relationship with Georgians had badly deteriorated. However, Wright, who professed "a real and affectionate regard for the people," held out hope that they would not embrace the independence movement.

As it turned out, 1774 was the year when revolution in America became inevitable. The tipping point came two weeks before that year began, when Bostonians, protesting a tax on tea, dumped 46 tons of British tea into Boston Harbor. To punish the colony for the Boston Tea Party, Parliament enacted the Coercive Acts, which closed the port of Boston, ended Massachusetts' right to govern itself, and barred colonial courts from prosecuting British citizens for everything, including murder. Massachusetts essentially became a police state. If there were another Boston Massacre, no one would have been prosecuted for it. Parliament thought all of this pain would force Massachusetts residents to acquiesce to British rule and serve as a deterrent to independence-minded people in its 12 other North American colonies.

Parliament miscalculated. Broad swaths of Americans despised these laws, and colonists had their own name for them — the Intolerable Acts.

Before 1774, the colonies didn't have a lot to do with each other, and that's how they wanted it. But after the Intolerable Acts were enacted, leaders from all of the colonies sought each other out, wanting to know how the British were treating people in other parts of America. They created correspondence committees to share information about how British occupation impacted from colonists from New Hampshire to Georgia. The Intolerable Acts also prompted the colonies to support Massachusetts residents. Virginia lawmakers urged residents to pray and fast for Bostonians, who bore the brunt of the laws. Georgians and South Carolinians donated rice for "the suffering poor of Boston."[10] Pennsylvanians sent flour, Marylanders and Virginians grain and cattle, and Connecticuters and Rhode Islanders food and money.[11] In all of the colonies, leaders formed militias, stockpiled weapons and gunpowder, and published newsletters that demonized Parliament.

To formalize their unity against the Intolerable Acts, Massachusetts cousins Samuel and John Adams and others led the creation of the First Continental Congress, which met on September 5, 1774, in Philadelphia, the largest city in North America at the time. Its mission was merely protest, not revolution. Looking back on it many years later, John Adams wrote that the First Continental Congress "resembled in Some respects, tho' I hope not in many, the Counsell of Nice in Ecclesiastical History."[12] Its main piece of business was to petition King George III to revoke the Intolerable Acts. He never considered it.

Georgia, with the highest percentage of British loyalists of any colony, wasn't ready to send a delegation to the First Continental Congress, but dissent was brewing there even before Congress met. Dissatisfaction with British rule revealed itself in Georgia on July 14, 1774, when this meeting notice appeared in the *Georgia Gazette*:[13]

"The critical situation to which the British colonies in America, are likely to be reduced, from the alarming and arbitrary impositions of the late acts of the British parliament, respecting the town of Boston, as well as the acts that at present extend to the raising of a perpetual revenue, without the consent of the people or their representatives, is considered as an object extremely important at this critical juncture; and particularly calculated to deprive the American subjects of their constitutional rights and liberties, as a part of the British empire. It is therefore requested, that all persons, within the limits of this province do attend at the liberty pole, at Tondee's Tavern in Savannah, on Wednesday the 27th instant, in order that the said matters may be taken under consideration; and such other constitutional measures pursued as may then appear to be most eligible."

It was signed by Noble Wimberly Jones, Archibald Bulloch, John Houstoun and George Walton, who were part of an established faction of the independence movement. Their names attached to the notice gave it weight and reflected the seriousness with which Georgia's leaders viewed the Intolerable Acts. The meeting was well attended — not just by more established Savannahians but also by "the radicals" who lived in St. John and other rural parishes. Letters complaining about the British from those in Boston, Philadelphia, Annapolis, Md., Williamsburg, Va., Charleston, S.C., and other cities were read aloud. The colony's leaders wanted to let people in those places know what was happening in Savannah, Sunbury, Augusta and the Georgia countryside, so they formed a committee of 31 men who would write dispatches on behalf of Georgians. Among those were Houstoun, Jones, Bulloch, Walton, Hall and George McIntosh, the youngest sibling of Lachlan McIntosh, the justice of the peace and rice planter who partnered with South Carolina slave trader Henry Laurens.

Button Gwinnett didn't attend the meeting and wasn't nominated to serve on the correspondence committee. He was consumed with his struggling plantation. Earlier that month, he borrowed an enormous amount of money from a wealthy merchant in South Carolina to keep it afloat.[14]

At the meeting, Georgia's leaders also discussed if and when — and how — the colony would participate in what became known as the Association, a proposed trade boycott of British products that was to include all 13 colonies. The purpose of the Association was to pressure Parliament to address the colonies' grievances, which focused on the Intolerable Acts.

When word of these discussions reached Gov. Wright, he quickly called a meeting of his closest aides, then on August 5 released this proclamation:[15]

> *"Whereas, I have received information, that on Wednesday the 27th day of July last past, a number of persons… did unlawfully assemble together at the Watch-house in the town of Savannah, under colour or pretence (sic) of consulting together for the redress of public grievances, or imaginary grievances; and that the persons so assembled for the purposes aforesaid, or some of them, are from and by their own authority, by a certain other hand bill issued and dispersed throughout the province, … (these) summonses and meetings must tend to raise fears and jealousies in the minds of his majesty's good subjects.*

> *"…in order therefore that his majesty's liege subjects may not be misled and imposed upon by artful and designing men; … all such summonses and calls by private persons, and*

all assembling and meetings of the people,
which may tend to raise fears and jealousies
in the minds of his majesty's subjects, under
pretence (sic) of consulting together for redress of
public grievances, or imaginary grievances; are
unconstitutional, illegal and punishable by law.

"And I do hereby require all his majesty's liege
subjects within this province to pay due regard
to this my proclamation, as they will answer the
contrary at their peril....

"JA. WRIGHT.
"God save the King."

On November 30, 1774, George III weighed in with an address to both houses of Parliament, declaring that his North American colonies were rebelling against his laws. He promised to respond.[16]

"It gives me much concern, that ...a most daring spirit of resistance, and disobedience to the law still unhappily prevails in the Province of the Massachusetts Bay, and has in divers parts of it broke forth in violences of a very criminal nature. These proceedings have been countenanced and encouraged in other of My Colonies and unwarrantable attempts have been made to obstruct the commerce of this kingdom by unlawful combinations. I have taken such measures, and given such orders, ...and for the restoring and preserving order and good government, in the

Province of the Massachusetts-Bay; and you may depend upon my firm and stedfast (sic) resolution to withstand every attempt to weaken or impair the supreme authority of this Legislature over all the dominions of my Crown; The maintenance of which consider as essential to the dignity, the safety, and the welfare of the British empire."

When the king's speech was distributed in America, it had no noticeable effect. By this time, many of the colonies were in a state of what amounted to pre-war mobilization. Militias were drilling and hoarding gunpowder and rifles. In Massachusetts, Thomas Gage, the royal governor, had lost control of the countryside. John Adams, a resident of Massachusetts, wrote, "The Revolution was in the Minds of the People."[17] Armed conflict was right around the corner.

Six weeks after George III's speech, on January 12, 1775, the leaders of Georgia's independence movement met at Tondee's Tavern in Savannah to discuss petitioning him to repeal the Intolerable Acts. "The mild and humble tenor of this instrument invited the signatures and influence of the most respectable men in the province," wrote McCall, Georgia's first historian.

Button Gwinnett wasn't one of them. He didn't attend the meeting.

Six days later, an even larger group gathered in Savannah for the inaugural session of the Georgia

Provincial Congress. Like the First Continental Congress, the creation of this body was a reaction to the Intolerable Acts. Georgia's first congress discussed the trade boycott and elected representatives to the Second Continental Congress' spring 1775 session. At the meeting, Archibald Bulloch, who by this time had become the leader of the independence movement in Georgia, said, "We are not Acquainted with an Individual in Georgia, who looks upon the Claims of Parliament as just, and all Men Speak with abhorrence of the measures made use of to enforce them..."[18] This was an exaggeration because about one out of three Georgians considered themselves British loyalists in 1775. But when Bulloch's words were read to Parliament a year later, it realized that Georgia, despite its reliance on England, would join the independence movement.

Gov. Wright, who attended the Provincial Congress meeting in January, told Georgia's leaders that he loved the colony and would hate to see it join the independence movement.[19] They responded diplomatically, disavowing violence and pledging an allegiance to the king, but demanding to be treated with the same rights and privileges enjoyed by British subjects. Those rights, they said, must be clearly defined and established. Wright saw through the carefully worded response, and a few weeks later, on Feb. 13, 1775, wrote a letter to Lord Dartmouth, England's Secretary of State for the Colonies, expressing his concern:

"Really, my Lord, a great many People have worked themselves up to such a pitch of political enthusiasm with respect to their ideas of Liberty and the powers of the British Parliament, and of their right to resist what they call unconstitutional laws, that I do not expect they will yet give up their pretensions."

At the same Georgia Provincial Congress meeting, Archibald Bulloch, Noble Wimberly Jones, Lyman Hall and John Houstoun were elected to the Second Continental Congress, which would meet in Philadelphia. Unlike the First Continental Congress, this congress wouldn't be focused on mere protest. It was intent on revolution.

Because delegates from only five of Georgia's parishes attended the Provincial Congress meeting, Bulloch, Jones and Houstoun didn't feel as if they had the authority to speak for all of Georgia, so they decided not to go to Philadelphia.[20] This abundance of caution infuriated the residents of St. John Parish who wanted Georgia to join forces with the other colonies, so they, sent Hall, one of their own, to Congress. Without asking for anyone's permission, he traveled to Philadelphia by sea with 160 barrels of rice and £50 of silver,[21] gifts to Bostonians, who were at the epicenter of America's opposition to England.

When Wright learned of Hall's plans to go to Philadelphia, he wrote another letter to Lord Dartmouth, dated April 24, 1775, expressing his frustration with the political climate in Georgia and the role that Hall and other former New Englanders in Georgia were playing in the colony:[22]

"The committees in the parishes were a parcel of the lowest people, chiefly carpenters, shoemakers and blacksmiths. It is really terrible that such people should be suffered to overthrow the civil government and most arbitrarily sport with other men's lives, liberties and property. I must mention that a few inhabitants of the Parish of St. John, chiefly descendants of New England people, …still retain a strong tincture of Republican or Oliverian principles, have entered into an agreement amongst themselves to adopt both the resolutions and Associations of the Continental Congress. …and I am told they have appointed a man, Lyman Hall, of New England extract to go from there to meet in Philadelphia next month, where, I expect (he) will be treated (poorly).

"And these poor insignificant fanatics no sooner entered into Association than they broke through it in many instances, and still do, although they pretend great sanctity, and to be strict adherents of religion and liberty, as they term it…."

Wright, as usual, had his finger on the political pulse in Georgia, but he was wrong about one thing: Lyman Hall wasn't shooed away when he arrived in Philadelphia. He was unanimously accepted into

Congress, which was dominated by like-minded people who were fed up with British rule.[23] However, Hall didn't have voting rights because he represented only one parish in Georgia, so he wasn't invited to sign Congress' petition to King George III. Hall told his fellow delegates that Georgia's leaders were fed up with British rule, and he assured them that the colony would send a full slate of representatives to Congress in the fall.

Meanwhile, news of the first battles of the Revolutionary War in the Massachusetts towns of Lexington and Concord reached Georgia on May 10, 1775. The next day, about 10 men met at Noble Wimberly Jones' house and made plans to break into a brick bunker at the eastern edge of Savannah where the British stored gunpowder. The structure, which was 12 feet underground, was secured by a thick wooden door and an iron lock that Gov. Wright was confident didn't need to be guarded. The men breached it late on the night of May 11 and stole about 600 pounds of powder, giving some of it to independence-minded men in nearby Beaufort, S.C.,[24] and stashing the rest in their basements and attics.

This marked the first aggressive action against the British by Georgians, and it triggered another proclamation from Wright and a reward of £150 sterling for the apprehension of the thieves. The reward would have funded about five years of living expenses for an average family, but no one turned in the gunpowder bandits. That powder was used by Georgians and South Carolinians against the British during the war.

About three weeks later, on June 5, a liberty pole — a centuries-old symbol of freedom, resistance and independence — was erected in Savannah. After the pole was secured in the ground, "the first regular toast drank on this occasion was to the King, but the second was to American liberty."[25] With relations frayed between the British and their Georgia subjects, British customs officers later that month seized a merchant ship in Sunbury's port, claiming there was illegal cargo aboard. More likely than not, trade duties weren't paid, but locals intimidated the officers, who eventually allowed the ship to leave port.

These three incidents — stealing the gun powder, erecting a liberty pole and challenging British customs officers — resulted in no punishments or consequences and helped to embolden Georgians who no longer wanted the British in charge of their colony.

Jones, Bulloch, Houstoun and Walton organized a meeting at the liberty pole on the morning of June 22 to choose a group to lead efforts to enforce the British trade boycott that Georgians had not yet formally endorsed. The 15-member group, called the Council of Safety, authorized itself to correspond with the Second Continental Congress as well as to the leaders of safety councils in other colonies and to parish leaders throughout Georgia. Again, Button Gwinnett wasn't there, wasn't chosen to be a member of the council and wasn't identified as a leader in his home parish of St. John. After the meeting, the men went to Tondee's Tavern to eat and drink, toasting 13 times and firing a cannon after each toast.

The "lowest people," as Gov. Wright referred to them in a letter two months earlier, were grabbing power in Georgia, and Wright appeared helpless to do anything about it. By the end of the year, the Council of Safety would almost entirely suppress Wright's authority.

The next act of British resistance in Georgia came soon afterward when a British ship called *Philippa,* en route to Florida with a cargo of gunpowder, guns and musket balls, decided to take refuge in the Savannah River to avoid a storm in the Atlantic Ocean.[26] Unaware of the growing anti-British mood in Georgia, *Phillipa* approached Tybee Island, where it was confronted by *Liberty*, a merchant ship fitted with 10 cannons. *Liberty*'s captain informed *Philippa*'s crew that his cargo "belonged to Savannah,"[27] and it escorted *Phillipa* to Cockspur Island at the mouth of the river, where it was boarded. *Liberty*'s crew discovered six and a half tons of gunpowder and 700 pounds of lead bullets as well as firearms.[28] *Liberty* wasn't large enough to take all of the cargo to Savannah, so *Philippa* was escorted to Savannah, where it was unloaded.[29] British forces never arrived to put up a fight, and Wright didn't bother to issue a proclamation condemning the act.[30]

On July 4, 1775, — around the time *Liberty* confronted *Phillipa* — 102 members of the Georgia Provincial Congress met at Tondee's Tavern in Savannah and unanimously elected Archibald Bulloch its president and George Walton its secretary. The next day, Georgia's congress allowed Gov. Wright's friend John Mulryne to read a resolution that Georgia, among other things, should not separate from "the mother country."[31] Right afterward, a motion was made that Georgia's leaders should "put the province upon the same footing with our sister Colonies."[32]

"This was Georgia's first secession convention," wrote 19th-century historian Charles Jones, Jr. "It placed the province in active sympathy and confederated alliance with the other twelve American colonies,...."

On July 6, Georgia's congress agreed that the colony would stop all trading with England, including buying "any slave, imported from Africa, or elsewhere, after this day."[33]

Georgia was the last colony to join the trade boycott against England because it depended on Great Britain for trade more than the other North American colonies, and that included the slave trade. The colony's economic survival depended on importing enslaved people to power its agricultural engine, and the ships that brought enslaved people to Georgia then were almost exclusively registered in Great Britain. Most of the leaders of the independence movement in Georgia — Bulloch, Walton, John Houstoun, Lyman Hall, Joseph Habersham and many others — owned slaves and needed them to operate their plantations, so they had a lot to lose financially from boycotting trade with England.

In fact, the importation of slaves into Georgia plummeted after the boycott. In 1774, at least 12 British-based ships brought enslaved people to Savannah, the port where Georgia-bound slaves disembarked.[34] After the colony joined the trade boycott, only one ship in 1775 and one in 1776 transported enslaved people to Savannah.[35] A British ship wouldn't bring enslaved people to Georgia again until 1784, the year the treaty that ended the Revolutionary War was ratified.[36]

Georgia's "secession convention" in the summer of 1775 didn't interest Button Gwinnett. He wasn't one of the 11 men from St. John Parish who served as a member of the Georgia Provincial Congress, and there is no record that he attended. At this time, Gwinnett and some others from St. John had very different priorities. They were on a mission to try to convince rural Georgians to join the radical political movement with the goal of weakening the more established and conservative leaders in Georgia,[37] such as Bulloch, Houstoun and Noble Wimberly Jones. These men were leading the independence movement in Georgia, but Gwinnett didn't care about that. He wanted to reduce their political power during a time when the colony needed its most effective leaders joining forces with leaders of the other colonies. A critical assessment of Gwinnett's efforts during the summer and fall of 1775 was included in an unrelated document published two years later. An excerpt stated: "While Gwinnett and his friends referred to themselves as 'The Liberty Society', the old conservatives of Savannah saw Gwinnett's group as a 'Nocturnal Junto' whose 'tyrannical proceedings' existed to 'keep themselves a while in power to be a scourge and a curse to the honest part of the community.'"[38]

During the Georgia Provincial Congress session, its members elected Lyman Hall, Bulloch, Houstoun, Jones and the Rev. John Joachim Zubly to serve in the Second Continental Congress in the fall.[39]

Bulloch could not wait to inform John Hancock, president of the Continental Congress, that Georgians were excited to join efforts with the other colonies:[40]

"Sr. As we appear so late in the American Cause, We must introduce ourselves with Expressions of Regret, that our Province has been so long divided,…. It gives us therefore pleasure to inform You, That a

Provincial Congress being appointed to be held at Savannah, was accordingly opened on Tuesday the 4th Instant,…. We flatter ourselves for the future You may look upon Us as a United People.

"…We have also proceeded to the Choice of Delegates to represent Us in Continental Congress,…. One of these Gentleman (Hall) is with you, and three others (Bulloch, Houstoun and Zubly) have agreed to attend the Congress with all convenient Speed, And we doubt not will be received as their great Zeal for the Common Cause deserves. …We have already Resolved strictly to adhere to the Association (boycott of British goods), and are heartily disposed Zealously to Enter into every measure that your Congress may deem necessary for the Saving of America…"

Zubly, born Hans Joachim Züblin in Switzerland, led Independent Presbyterian Church of Savannah and was considered the most influential pastor in Georgia at the time.[41] But he was an odd choice to join the Second Continental Congress. He never held public office, though he was known to Georgia's political leaders because he frequently opened colonial legislative sessions with a prayer and sometimes a sermon, as he did at the Provincial Congress meeting on July 4, 1775. What made him an odd choice is he wanted England to continue governing Georgia.

His view of the independence movement had taken a 180-degree turn, going from a supporter of colonists' rights in the mid-1760s to a staunch British loyalist in the mid-1770s.

Nothing makes this clearer than showing how his position on taxation changed during those 10 years. Most Georgians opposed The Stamp Act of 1765 because it required that "every newspaper, pamphlet, broadside, ship's clearance, college diploma, lease, license, insurance policy, bond, bill of sale, and every legal document be written or printed on stamped paper sold by public (British) officials."[42] In a sermon called "The Stamp Act Repealed," Zubly supported repealing the law but said colonists should obey it as long as it exists. Nine years later, in 1774, he published a lengthy essay titled, "Great Britain's Right to Tax Her Colonies, Placed in the Clearest Light, By a Swiss." Georgia's political leaders apparently didn't read it — or remember it — and they must not have listened to his sermon, called "Law of Liberty,"[43] at the July 4 Provincial Congress meeting, where he made it clear that Georgians should not separate from England.[44] Had Georgia's leaders paid attention, they never would have selected him to represent the colony in Congress.

Even *Zubly* couldn't believe he was selected. "Dr. Zubly expressed his surprise at being chosen, and said that he thought himself for many reasons a very improper person; but the choice was insisted upon," wrote George Walton, secretary of the Georgia Provincial Congress.[45]

Zubly has been described as "weak-kneed," but he was just the opposite. At a time when a growing number of Americans objected to British rule, he refused to compromise his beliefs. "In a day when many were willing and able to alter their thinking once the revolution came," his biographer wrote, "Zubly remained firm to his political and theological principles even though it cost him his land, his liberty and his reputation."[46]

Soon enough, Bulloch and Houstoun, who served in Congress with him, would hear more of Zubly's views.

In the summer of 1775, between the time when the delegates were chosen and when they served, the colonies became a dangerous place to praise King George III, criticize the independence movement or challenge Americans who spoke out against British rule. Reports of British loyalists being tarred and feathered, beaten or both occurred throughout America, in big cities and small towns. Two men in Georgia — one in Savannah and the other in Augusta — were tarred and feathered and paraded around those cities.[47] The victim in Savannah was threatened with death unless he drank to the "damnation of all

Tories (loyalists) and success to American liberty."[48] He did what he had to do to spare his life.

Gov. Wright witnessed the abuse: "…and soon after they brought him in a cart down by my house, and such a horrid spectacle I really never saw. They made this man stand up in a cart with a candle in his hand, and a great many candles were carried round the cart, and thus they went through most of the streets in town for upwards of three hours. And on inquiring what he had done I was informed that he had behaved disrespectfully towards the Sons of Liberty…."[49]

By the fall of 1775, Wright's duties were limited to little more than probating wills and writing administrative letters.[50] The man who for 15 years ruled Georgia as if he were the king himself was no longer able to see a role for himself there.

"It is really a wretched state to be left in," he wrote to Lord Dartmouth, England's Secretary of State for the Colonies, "and what it's impossible to submit to much longer — Government totally annihilated and assumed by Congresses, Councils, and Committees, and the greatest acts of tyranny, oppression, gross insults, etc., etc., etc., committed, and not the least means of protection, support, or even personal safety and these almost daily occurrences are too muck (sic), my Lord."[51]

When Bulloch, Houstoun and Zubly arrived in Philadelphia to serve in the Second Continental Congress, most of their fellow delegates were in no mood to hear anything resembling pro-England views. There were respected delegates in this Congress who thought 1775 — and even 1776 — was too early for America to split from England. But this Congress wanted revolution, and an opinion to the contrary could be seen as treasonous, depending on how forcefully it was delivered.

As Bulloch, Houstoun and Zubly arrived, Lyman Hall, who had been there since May, was leaving Philadelphia. Zubly wasted no time making it known that he opposed the trade boycott with England.

The debates on trade began on October 3, and Zubly spoke briefly on October 4 and 5.[52] On October 12, he elaborated, saying, "The measure, we are now to consider, is extremely interesting. I shall offer my thoughts. If we decide properly, I hope we shall establish our cause—if improperly, we shall overthrow it, altogether. Trade is important. We must have a reconciliation with Great Britain or the means of carrying on the war. An unhappy day when we shall. A Republican government (democracy) is little better than government of devils. I have been acquainted with it from 6 years old. We must regulate our trade so as that a reconciliation be obtained or we enable[d] to carry on the war. Can't say, but I do hope for a reconciliation, and that this winter may bring it. I may enjoy my hopes for reconciliation, others may enjoy theirs that none will take place."[53]

Six other delegates spoke before Zubly again chimed in, saying, "Georgia is settled along the Savannah River, 200 miles in extent, and 100 mile the other way. I look upon it (the trade boycott) altogether will be the ruin of the cause."[54]

Maryland delegate Samuel Chase, who was becoming increasingly angry, couldn't hold his tongue any longer: "I will undertake to prove that if the Revd. gentleman's positions are true and his advice followed, we shall all be made slaves. If he speaks the opinion of Georgia I sincerely lament that they (Georgians) ever appeared in Congress. They cannot, they will not comply!—Why did they come here? Sir we are deceived. Sir we are abused! Why do they come here? I want to know why their provinc[ial] Congress came to such resolutions. Did they come here to ruin America? That gentleman's advice will bring destruction upon all North America."[55]

On October 20, Zubly rejoined the debate. "We can't do without trade (with England)," he said. "To be, or not to be is too tariffing a question for many gentlemen. All that wise men can do among many difficulties, is to choose the least."[56]

Chase, revealing his anger again, accused Zubly of attending Congress to speak for and spy for Georgia Gov. James Wright. After Chase vowed to gather evidence to charge Zubly with treason, Zubly informed Bulloch and Houstoun that he was leaving Philadelphia.[57]

"I am setting off for Georgia greatly indisposed. ...in case of my first arrival I think not to make my Report to our Council of Safety till we are all present. I have left my Case with Spirits at my Lodging's which I advise you to take with you well filled... Should I arrive before you I will not fail to acquaint your friends but I can only travel slow — I wish you a pleasant journey."

Bulloch and Houstoun weren't convinced that Zubly planned to wait for them to return to Georgia before briefing the Council of Safety members, so Bulloch left for Savannah in time to attend a "special meeting" of the council on December 19, 1775.[58] But before Bulloch left Philadelphia, he and Houstoun became the 44th and 45th delegates to sign Congress' "Agreement of Secrecy" document, which reads:[59]

"Resolved, That every member of this Congress considers himself under the ties of virtue, honor and love of his country, not to divulge, directly or indirectly, any matter or thing agitated or debated in Congress in committee or Congress, before the same shall have been determined, without the leave of Congress; nor any matter or thing determined in Congress, which the majority of the Congress shall order to be kept secret."

Zubly had no intention of signing it.

By the time he and Bulloch appeared at the Council of Safety meeting, the tide had completely turned in Georgia. "... taking sides against the liberty people, he (Zubly) became so obnoxious that he was banished from Savannah with the loss of half his estate."[60] Looking back on his brief time in Congress, Zubly, who had relocated to South Carolina, was unapologetic. "I made it a point in every company," he wrote in his diary, "to contradict and oppose every hint of desire of independence or of breaking our connection with Great Britain."[61]

Bulloch wanted to attend that meeting not just to report on the trade debate — and Zubly's role in it — but because he had some good news to share: Congress gave Georgia an early Christmas present, agreeing to help the colony defend itself by funding a battalion of 728 men, led by a colonel who would be paid $50 a month.[62]

It's unclear exactly how Button Gwinnett learned of this development, but he didn't consider it good news. He considered it *great* news. He was going to Savannah.

8

A Reluctant Public Servant

Archibald Bulloch and John Houstoun didn't enjoy being in the room when Maryland delegate Samuel Chase confronted the British loyalist John Zubly during the trade debates at the Second Continental Congress. And they felt especially uncomfortable when Chase questioned whether they also aligned themselves with England.

"I think the gentleman ought not to take offense at his brother delegate," Houstoun told Chase.[1] Zubly-gate, as it might be called today, didn't just make Bulloch and Houstoun look bad. It also reinforced some congressional delegates' opinion that Georgia remained closely linked with England in 1775 and didn't share the other colonies' zeal for independence.

The leaders of the Second Continental Congress wanted the colonies to be unified so they could take the next step and declare their independence from England in 1776. That didn't mean *all* the delegates had to vote for independence, but Adams, who was counting the votes on this matter, wanted to make sure a majority of the men from each colony did so.

Georgia's leaders inexplicably chose a British loyalist to serve in Congress, so they wanted their colony's delegates to be 100-percent united when they met in 1776 in Philadelphia to vote for independence. As 1775 became 1776, it wouldn't be difficult to find a Georgian other than Bulloch, Houstoun and Lyman Hall who wanted to break free of England's grasp.

That said, Button Gwinnett wouldn't have been the first person to come to mind. In fact, Gwinnett might not have come to mind at all. He didn't organize or attend any of the pro-independence meetings in Georgia. He never gathered at the liberty pole in Savannah, nor did he participate in the raid on the British gunpowder magazine. He wasn't a member of the Georgia Provincial Council or the Council of Safety, nor was he a member of the colony's correspondence committee, and he wasn't identified as a leader in rural St. John Parish, where he lived. He didn't voice his opposition to British authority in Georgia, at least not publicly. Simply put, he had showed no interest in the independence movement.

For five years, he had mostly stayed on his planta-tion, dealing with his creditors and their lawyers, and sometimes going to nearby Sunbury to do busi-ness or socialize. So it must have come as a surprise to Georgia's leaders to see Gwinnett at the Council of Safety meetings in Savannah on January 7 and 8, 1776.[2] This was his first reported appearance at a government meeting in Georgia since February of 1771, when he was brought under warrant to the Commons House of Assembly session, where he was supposed to have represented St. John Parish. The minutes from that two-day meeting in January 1776 reported nothing that he said — if he said anything at all — and there is no explanation for why Gwinnett attended.

"While Gwinnett was out of the public eye, we can assume that he and Lyman Hall were correspond-ing," said Solomon K. Smith, associate professor of history at Georgia Southern University, "and Hall was filling Gwinnett in about what was happening in Savannah and in Philadelphia (with the Second Continental Congress)."[3]

Gwinnett very well may have heard about the Continental Congress' decision to fund a battalion in Georgia from Hall, and it is likely that that news brought him to the Council of Safety meetings. In January of 1776, Gwinnett was a former mer-chant, a former store owner and a deeply indebted planter. Without a trade or a college education, his money-making options were limited, and a career in the military represented a promising opportunity to earn a steady income. If he were forced to confront the British, whose navy was cruising the Georgia coastline and intimidating residents, he might as well get paid for it. And as always, he set his expectations high. He wanted to be the leader of Georgia's new battalion, the colonel.

Never mind that he had never served in the military and had never publicly expressed an interest to do so. In 18th-century America, a man didn't necessarily need military experience to become an officer. Experience was a good thing, but inexperienced men who possessed intelligence and leadership skills were sometimes given opportunities to lead soldiers. Gwinnett, who was confident and persuasive, would have made the case to the members of the Council of Safety — before or after the meetings — that Gov. Wright would not have appointed him a waterways commissioner and a justice of the peace if he didn't have what it takes to lead a battalion.

Gwinnett's desires aside, the money for the battalion could not have come at a better time for Georgia's leaders. On January 18, less than two weeks after the Council of Safety meetings, a group of men, led by 23-year-old Joseph Habersham, barged into the governor's residence, where Wright was conducting a meeting.[4] Habersham walked up to Wright, put his hand on his shoulder, and said, "Sir James, you are my prisoner."

Wright had reason to assume this was some sort of prank. After all, Habersham's recently deceased father James considered Wright a trusted ally, and the elder Habersham assumed Wright's gubernatorial duties when Wright was in England from the summer of 1771 to the winter of 1773. And now his friend's son was arresting him? In the governor's residence in front of his friends and allies? In the colony he had governed for 15 years?[5] But this was no prank. Wright was placed under house arrest, with a guard assigned to his front door to keep him from communicating with his aides and allies. The Council of Safety, which requested the arrest warrant, put the Scottish-born rice planter Lachlan McIntosh, a militia officer who was a justice of the peace in St. Mary Parish, in charge of overseeing the protection of Savannah.

During his five years away from Savannah, Gwinnett lost his land to creditors and although his plantation was earning money, a significant amount of it was being used to repay debts. So there is every reason to believe that he decided to abandon his dream of becoming a wealthy planter and pursue a stable career in whatever way he could.

He wanted the newly funded colonel job, but he had competition. Savannah merchant Samuel Elbert, a member of the Council of Safety who did have military experience, also applied. Elbert was aligned with the more conservative faction of Georgians who wanted independence while Gwinnett was aligned with the radical faction. Not surprisingly, a political power struggle ensued between the factions, leading to a compromise: Gwinnett wouldn't get the job, but neither would Elbert.[6] Instead, it would go to McIntosh. Elbert would serve under McIntosh as a lieutenant colonel, and Gwinnett would represent Georgia in the Second Continental Congress. There is nothing in the historical record that explains why Gwinnett wasn't offered the lieutenant colonel job. However, he and McIntosh had worked together in the justice of the peace court in St. Mary Parish, and the men who were deciding who would get these appointments may have had reason to believe that a McIntosh-Gwinnett pairing would be a bad idea.

Regardless of how exactly it was decided that Gwinnett would represent Georgia in the Second Continental Congress, this point should not be lost: Before Gwinnett expressed interest in the colonel job, he knew — because of his relationship with Lyman Hall —that Congress planned to declare independence from England in the summer of 1776, but he didn't care enough to be want to be there and cast a vote. He had to be, figuratively speaking, shoved with two hands to the back in the direction of Philadelphia, where Congress met. Although he could have refused to serve in Congress, not doing so meant returning to St. Catherines Island, where for 10 years he had been unable to turn his plantation into a successful business venture. The place must have been a constant reminder to him of a missed opportunity — his latest chance to fulfill his dream of becoming wealthy.

Gwinnett's selection to Congress became official on February 2, 1776, at the Georgia Provincial Congress meeting. Lyman Hall, Bulloch, Houstoun and George Walton were also selected, with the understanding that three of the five would go to Philadelphia to represent Georgia. (Georgia's relatively small population — the least populous of the 13 colonies in 1776 — and its late entry into the independence movement meant only three of its delegates could attend as voting members. Virginia, the most populous colony, sent seven delegates.)

With the exception of the compromise that led to Gwinnett's selection, there is no explanation in the historical record for why the other men were chosen, and none is needed. Houstoun and especially Bulloch had become important leaders in Georgia, and they were urgently needed in the colony, so they decided to stay there while Hall, Walton and Gwinnett served in Congress.[7] Hall, who had been active in the independence movement for as long as just about anyone in Georgia, was an obvious choice, as was Walton, a lawyer and military officer who served on the Council of Safety and the Georgia Provincial Congress and had the respect of many of the colony's most important civilian and military leaders.

But why Gwinnett? He had a few things going for him: He lived in St. John Parish, which was at the forefront of Georgia's independence movement. He was close friends with Hall, who had the respect of the colony's leaders and had influence on Gwinnett. A third explanation for Gwinnett's selection was less obvious:

"In colonial and revolutionary America, absenteeism was not rare when it came to serving in the legislature at the colonial and the federal levels," said Smith, the Georgia Southern University historian. "John Adams complained about it all the time. Congress never had a full body. So Gwinnett could have been an attractive selection because he had the time to serve in Congress."

In other words, because he didn't have a role in government and because his plantation was puttering along and didn't require his constant attention, nothing was keeping him from serving in Congress and staying at least long enough to vote for independence.

The irony should not be lost on anyone: If Bulloch or Houstoun had served in that session of Congress instead of Gwinnett, very few people today, including Georgians, would have any reason to know anything about Button Gwinnett, who is now viewed as a Founding Father on the national stage. And Houstoun or Bulloch would be much better known than they are today. By virtue of voting for independence and signing the Declaration of Independence, Bulloch or Houstoun — and not Gwinnett — would be viewed as a Founding Father and not solely as an influential figure in colonial and revolutionary Georgia.

Bulloch wrote John Adams, explaining why he would not serve in Congress and informing him that George Walton would brief Adams on what was happening in Georgia:[8]

"As a Multiplicity of public Business prevents my revisiting Philadelphia, I have embraced an Opportunity by Major Walton of enquiring after your Welfare; and as he is capable of giving you the amplest Account of the State of this Province, I wou'd take the Liberty of introducing him to your Notice and Acquaintance. I make no Doubt but it will afford you the highest Pleasure to see one irresistible Spirit of Freedom."

Bulloch's time in Congress in the fall of 1775 had clearly impressed Adams, who replied: "I was greatly disappointed, Sir, in the Information you gave me, that you Should be prevented from revisiting Philadelphia. I had flattered myself with Hopes of your joining Us soon, and not only affording Us the additional Strength of your Abilities and Fortitude, but enjoying the Satisfaction of Seeing a Temper and Conduct here."[9]

Gwinnett's selection led to this question: Who was Button Gwinnett? Outside of Georgia, no one could answer that question. Proof of that can be found in the Second Continental Congress meeting records, where during his brief stint, his name was sometimes spelled *Gwinn* or *Guinet* as well as Gwinnett. Those who knew Gwinnett had another, very different question in the weeks before he was to serve in Congress: Would he actually show up? When it came to fulfilling his legislative duties, he had been unreliable, to put it kindly. Practically speaking, he had no legislative experience because he hadn't attended the Commons House of Assembly sessions to which he was elected in 1770 and 1771 without being brought to Savannah under warrant by the Assembly's messenger, an 18th-century sergeant at arms. Hall, who would have known about Gwinnett's dismal attendance record as a colonial legislator, decided to accompany him every step of the way — from the Georgia coast to the Pennsylvania State House, later named Independence Hall.

Before the two men left for Philadelphia, it seemed that all hell was breaking loose in and around Savannah.

On February 11, three weeks after being placed under house arrest, Gov. Wright escaped out the back door of the governor's residence in Savannah with the help of his friend and British loyalist John Mulryne. Mulryne took Wright to his house on the banks of the Wilmington River before Wright hopped on a boat to the Savannah River, where *Scarborough*, a British warship, was anchored, waiting for him. Two days later, from a cabin in the ship, Wright wrote a letter, which was forwarded to the Georgia Commons House of Assembly. The first part of the letter asks that England's navy ships be allowed to dock in Savannah's port and receive fresh supplies, with the guarantee that its naval forces "will not commit any hostilities against the province." The remainder of the letter is a desperate, last-gasp attempt to persuade Georgia's leaders to disassociate themselves from the independence movement:[10]

"...His majesty has been graciously pleased to grant me leave to return to England, and (whatever may be thought) my regard for the province and people is such that I cannot avoid, (and possibly for the last time) exhorting the people to save themselves and their posterity from that total ruin and destruction, which although they may not, yet I most clearly see at the threshold of their doors; and I cannot leave them without again warning" them, in the most earnest and friendly manner, to desist from their present plans and resolutions: it is still in their power, and if they will enable me to do it, I will (as far as I can) engage to give, and endeavour to obtain for them, full pardon and forgiveness for all passed crimes and offences; and this I conjure you to consider well, and most seriously of, before it's too late: but, let things happen as they may, be it remembered, that I this day, in the king's name, offer the people of Georgia the olive branch, that most desirable object, and in estimable blessing, the return of peace and happiness, to them and their posterity.

"... I am also to mention, that the same armed sloop will be sent up tomorrow, to Four-mile point, in order to get fresh water, and for no other purpose. This letter, which I consider as of the utmost con-sequence and importance to the whole people of Georgia, I must desire you will be pleased to commu-nicate to the assembly, if sitting, and if not, to those who are called the council of safety, and especially to the inhabitants of the town and province in general, and acquaint them, that I shall expect their full and clear answer to every part of it, in a reasonable time.

"I am, with perfect esteem, gentlemen,

"Your most obedient and faithful servant,

"JAMES WRIGHT."

Unlike his other public letters and proclamations, this one does not end with "God Save the King."

The Assembly recognized receiving the letter but adjourned without addressing it — a clear sign that Georgia's leaders wholeheartedly had committed to the independence movement and viewed Wright as irrelevant and unworthy of their time and attention.

After Wright's missive was ignored, he realized there was not even the most remote chance of reconciliation between himself and Georgia's leaders. And on March 2, four British ships, including *Scarborough* with Wright and 20 guns aboard, *Tamer* with 16 guns, *Cherokee* with 10 guns, and *Hinchinbrook* with eight guns, sailed into the mouth of the Savannah River toward 11 merchant ships loaded with rice and prepared to depart Savannah.[11] The British wanted the rice for their soldiers in Boston and elsewhere who needed food.

Two of the ships cruised into the port, but one of them, *Hinchinbrook*, a schooner, ran aground and was fired upon by soldiers led by Maj. Joseph Habersham, the 23-year-old who placed Gov. Wright under house arrest.[12] During the next high tide, the ship freed itself from the muddy river bottom and escaped, and in the early morning hours of March 3, about 250 British soldiers and marines boarded several of the merchant ships to take as much rice as they could steal.[13]

When they were spotted, more than 300 Georgia militia and about 100 South Carolinians, led by Col.

Lachlan McIntosh, fired upon the British for "several hours" from Yamacraw Bluff.[14] McIntosh reported that British troops abandoned the ships and were "running in the marsh in a laughable manner for fear of our rifles."[15] However, the British would have the last laugh. They burned three merchant vessels, dismantled six others and stole another two before their fleet passed through the mouth of the Savannah River and escaped out to sea.[16] In a letter on March 10 to Lord Dartmouth, England's Secretary of State for the Colonies, Wright exaggerated the success of the British raid, claiming they made off with "14 or 15 merchant ships."[17] McIntosh conceded that the British took 1,600 barrels of rice "without paying a farthing for it."[18]

The two-day fight, called the Battle of the Rice Boats, ended with both sides claiming victory. The British got rice for their troops in the northern colonies, and Georgians and South Carolinians chased the British warships out of the port and back out to sea. For Georgians, this military battle and Wright's departure marked yet another opportunity to choose sides. The loyalists who remained either had to pledge allegiance to the independence movement or suffer the abuse that came with staying and continuing to align themselves with England.

Although the Battle of the Rice Boats emboldened many Georgians, the colony had become dysfunctional. It was losing population, particularly loyalists, many of whom were political appointees with government jobs. With many of them gone, the courts weren't working well, and road maintenance, harbor improvements and mail delivery stopped. And, of course, British troops weren't around to protect colonists from attacks from hostile Native Americans.

For the first time in the 43-year-old history of the colony, Georgians needed to figure out how to run things without British oversight. Members of the Georgia Provincial Congress decided to get out of Savannah and meet in Augusta, where they began work on a broad outline for how a new, independent government would operate. It drafted the generic-sounding "Rules and Regulations," a 13-paragraph document, which expressed Georgia's desire to govern itself and served as a temporary state constitution.[19] Like the first official Georgia constitution that would be adopted a year later, Rules and Regulations called for executive, legislative and judicial branches, with a strong legislature.

The colony's congress also elected Archibald Bulloch president of Georgia and commander-in-chief of its militia. He was an obvious choice. He was a trusted, credible and willing leader, and more than anyone else in Georgia at that time, Bulloch understood the colony's problems and had given a lot of thought to the solutions.

Born in Charleston, S.C., in 1730, Bulloch, whose parents had emigrated from Scotland, became a lawyer and a lieutenant in the South Carolina militia. He arrived with his family in Georgia in 1758 and moved to Savannah in 1764. Four years later, he was elected to the Commons House of Assembly. Unlike Gwinnett, he became a leader in the legislature, led the independence movement in Georgia and served as a militia officer, fighting under Lachlan McIntosh at the Battle of the Rice Boats.

On April 5, 1776, just before Gwinnett and Hall left for Philadelphia — George Walton went later — Bulloch wrote to Georgia's congressional delegates, instructing them to request money from Congress for the colony's defense against "the Indians, upon our backs" and "the fortified town of St. Augustine," where many British nationalists and loyalists now lived and planned attacks against Georgians.[20]

"Our remote situation from both the seat of power and arms, keeps us so very ignorant of the counsels and ultimate designs of the Congress, and of the transactions in the field, that we shall decline giving any particular instructions, other than strongly to recommend it to you that you never lose sight of the peculiar situation of the province you are appointed to represent: The Indians, both south and northwesterly, upon our backs; the fortified town of St. Augustine made a continual rendezvous for soldiers in our very neighborhood; together with our blacks and Tories with us; let these weighty truths be the powerful arguments for support. At the time we also recommend it to you, always to keep in view the general utility, remembering that the great and righteous cause in which we are engaged is not provincial, but continental. We, therefore, gentlemen, shall rely upon your patriotism, abilities, firmness, and integrity, to propose, join and concur, in all such measures as you shall think calculated for the common good, and to oppose such as shall appear destructive."

While Georgia's leaders were working urgently to decide how to operate the colony and protect it from its enemies, Gwinnett, who was making plans to leave for Philadelphia, was concerned about his personal safety and his property. He decided he needed some protection during his trip to Philadelphia, so he borrowed a pistol from Sunbury resident Patrick Mackay,[21] an acquaintance who once asked Gwinnett to sign as a witness on a deed of gift. At this time, the powerful British navy, facing no opposition from the tiny, fledgling Continental Navy, continued to sail along the Georgia coast, unnerving Gwinnett and other coastal residents whose slaves, cattle and hogs were at risk. Gwinnett asked to be kept informed about what the British navy was doing while he was away.

In a May 1 letter to Gwinnett from Lt. Col. Samuel Elbert, he wrote, "D(ea)r Guinette, I suppose nothing extraordinary has happened, or (other)wise I should be informed. Our Enemys (sic) ha(ve) attempted nothing worth notice, save some (of their) Vessels Attempting to pilfer in the Southern Fr(ontier) and makeing (sic) some captures in them, ..."[22]

Under the circumstances, that was good news for Gwinnett. Philadelphia awaited him. The fewer distractions, the better.

On May 20, Gwinnett and Hall, traveling by horseback, reached Philadelphia,[23] where Hall introduced Gwinnett to John Adams, who recorded seemingly everything that happened during the session. Adams noted that, "The Delegates from Georgia Made their appearance this day in Congress with unlimited powers, and the gentlemen are very firm."[24] *Very firm* related to their resolve to vote for independence, and that pleased Adams. In a letter to Archibald Bulloch, he sounded confident. "...the colonies will have republics for their government let us lawyers and your divine (Rev. John Zubly) say what they will."

For Hall, it was mission accomplished: Not only did he and Gwinnett make it to Philadelphia, a 750-mile trek from coastal Georgia, but Gwinnett was on board. He would vote for independence. Hall has been given much of the credit for whatever zeal for independence Gwinnett possessed at that time. "... there is every indication that it was Hall's influence that germinated the intensity of spirit in Patriot Gwinnett,"[25] according to Hall's biographer. Whether or not Gwinnett considered himself a patriot and possessed an "intensity of spirit" at that time, there is no question what he would do when it was time to vote for independence.

On their day of arrival, Hall and Gwinnett signed the "Agreement of Secrecy," the same document that Bulloch and Houstoun signed during their time in Congress in the fall of 1775. The message behind the decision to sign this document was clear and obvious, as former Pennsylvania Gov. Richard Penn said, "If you do not (hang together), gentlemen, I can tell you that you will be very apt to hang separately."[26]

The Second Continental Congress, which met behind locked doors and shuttered windows, had very ambitious goals, and that became clear to everyone on June 7, when Richard Henry Lee, a delegate from Virginia, introduced a brief but impactful resolution "that these united colonies are and of right ought to be free and independent states."[27] This is Lee's resolution, as it was read aloud to Gwinnett and the other delegates:

"Resolved, That these United Colonies are, and of right ought to be, free and independent States, that they are absolved from all allegiance to the British Crown, and that all political connection between them and the State of Great Britain is, and ought to be, totally dissolved.

That it is expedient forthwith to take the most effectual measures for forming foreign Alliances.

That a plan of confederation be prepared and transmitted to the respective Colonies for their consideration and approbation."

The resolution, seconded by John Adams, was nothing short of groundbreaking, and it met with resistance from a minority of delegates who wanted independence eventually but weren't convinced that this was the right time to declare it. Congress tabled the resolution to allow the hesitant delegates — from New Jersey, Pennsylvania, Delaware and South Carolina — to discuss it and perhaps get more comfortable with it.[28]

While those discussions continued, Congress on June 11 appointed a five-person committee to flesh out Lee's resolution.[29] Thomas Jefferson, who had recently turned 33, was viewed by his fellow delegates as an impactful writer, and he holed himself up in a nearby townhouse and began the first draft of what would become the Declaration of Independence.[30]

The other members of the committee — John Adams, Benjamin Franklin, Roger Sherman and Robert Livingston — served as Jefferson's first editors. Jefferson borrowed heavily from his own preamble to the Virginia Constitution and George Mason's Virginia's Declaration of Rights, a precursor to the U.S. Bill of Rights.[31] Led by Franklin, the editors created another version. Then the entire Congress weighed in, deleting Jefferson's assertion that George III perpetuated the slave trade in order to appease slave-owning delegates in the southern colonies and elsewhere.[32]

In total, Congress made 86 changes to trim Jefferson's draft to 1,337 words,[33] a fact that must have irked the man who was so confident in his beliefs and in his writing skills that years later he rewrote sections of the bible with which he disagreed.[34] Because Jefferson wrote the first draft, he has been given most of the credit for creating its guiding principles, but he later said it included no new ideas. The ideas, he said, came from English philosopher John Locke, known as the "Father of Liberalism;" French philosopher Baron de Montesquieu, who devised an account to explain how governments might avoid corruption; and the Scottish Enlightenment, a period in the 18th century known for its plethora of intellectual and scientific accomplishments.[35]

During the summer of 1776, Gen. George Washington, who sent frequent letters to Congress ever since he was appointed commander in chief of the Continental Army in 1775, popped in and out of the Pennsylvania State House to meet with members of a congressional military committee. Gwinnett confidante Lyman Hall served on that committee. It is unknown if Gwinnett met Washington, but during the 10 weeks Gwinnett spent in Philadelphia, he attended committee meetings with many of the nation's most influential Founding Fathers, such as Benjamin Franklin, Samuel Adams and Robert Morris. Gwinnett almost certainly made little or no impression on these men during his brief time in Congress. He doesn't appear in any of their memoirs or biographies, save for a one-sentence mention of him and Lyman Hall in John Adams' autobiography.

While in Congress, he volunteered for the so-called "Secret Committee," a fact that irked his fellow Georgian George Walton, who didn't trust Gwinnett's judgment and viewed him as an ill fit for that committee. Gwinnett was assigned to four other committees: marine, Indian affairs, one that focused on "establishing expresses between the several continental posts," and one that began brainstorming what would become the Articles of Confederation, which laid out how the federal government would work after America gained its independence.[36] He served on the latter committee with Samuel Adams, Roger

Sherman, Robert Livingston and others, giving him a front-row seat to the initial discussions and debates in what became a six-year process to have the articles ratified by all 13 states. Assuming he attended the committee meetings, he would have heard delegates discuss the role that government should play in people's lives. This insight would have benefited him if he decided then that he wanted to help write Georgia's first formal constitution. By then, John Adams had urged the delegates in colonies with no constitutions to draft one, a crucial step to transition from a British colony to an American state.

Gwinnett possessed the gift of persuasion, according to Hugh McCall, Georgia's first historian, but for whatever reason, he was very quiet — at least in public settings — in Philadelphia. John Adams, who took voluminous notes of committee meeting discussions and floor debates, mentioned Gwinnett only once in his thousands of pages of notes.[37] It had to do with a matter called Article XIV, which gave Congress the power to regulate the trade of and manage the affairs of Native Americans. Article XIV was the subject of heated debates, largely pitting South Carolina delegates, who opposed it, against delegates from other states. South Carolina worried that regulation would hamper trade with Native Americans, making it less profitable. Other delegates, such as George Walton of Georgia, said hostile tribes posed a security threat, and Walton used Article XIV to make the case that

Congress needed to give money to Georgia to protect and defend itself from them.

Adams used 122 words to summarize Walton's comments, which echoed what Archibald Bulloch had instructed Georgia's delegates to say.[38] Adams reported that Gwinnett agreed with Walton: "Gwinnett is in favor of Congress having such power."[39] Nine words. Gwinnett served in the Second Continental Congress for 10 weeks — six days a week — and his recorded contribution merited nine words from John Adams.

Solomon Smith, the Georgia Southern University historian who teaches colonial and revolutionary history, pointed out that "Adams is known for only mentioning the people who he thinks were important to the cause."[40] So giving practically no notice of Gwinnett reflects Adams' opinion of Gwinnett and his role in Congress.

As the vote on independence approached, Adams wrote to Archibald Bulloch, assuring him, "Your Colleagues Hall and Gwinn(ett), are here in good Health, and Spirits, and as firm as you your self could wish them."[41]

Adams added, "This morning is assigned for the greatest Debate of all,"[42] referring to Richard Henry Lee's independence resolution. John Dickinson of Pennsylvania assumed the lead role in arguing against it. In his autobiography, Adams wrote, "No Member rose to answer him: and after waiting some time, in hopes that some one less obnoxious than myself, who had been all along for a Year before, and still was represented and believed to be the Author of all the Mischief, I determined to speak."[43]

On July 1, nine colonies were prepared to vote in favor of the resolution. The New York delegation was instructed at the time to pursue reconciliation with England — a lost cause by 1776 — and were not authorized by its colonial government to vote on such a weighty resolution. That left South Carolina, Pennsylvania and Delaware as the holdouts. A majority of the delegates from Pennsylvania were opposed to the resolution, as were all of the South Carolina delegates. The two Delaware delegates who were in Philadelphia, George Read and Thomas McKean, were split. Congress' desire to show George III and Parliament that the colonies were unified appeared doomed. But then it granted a request by 26-year-old South Carolinian Edward Rutledge, the youngest delegate, to postpone the vote one day.[44]

Things changed overnight. McKean, who supported independence, had summoned fellow Delaware delegate Caesar Rodney, who was leading an investigation into loyalist activity, to nearby Philadelphia, where Rodney on July 2 cast a tie-breaking vote for Delaware in favor of independence. The South

Carolina delegates, who thought it was too soon to declare independence, changed their minds, and the two Pennsylvania delegates who opposed independence at the time chose not to vote on July 2 so that their delegation could unanimously vote in favor of independence. With a majority of delegates from Delaware, South Carolina and Pennsylvania on board, Lee's resolution passed 12 to 0, with the New York delegation abstaining.

In a letter to his wife, Abigail, John Adams predicted that Americans would forever commemorate their independence with a festival every second of July.[45] "The Second Day of July 1776," he wrote, "will be the most memorable Epocha, in the History of America."

With the vote for independence settled, adopting the Declaration of Independence on July 4 became a formality. (On July 9, the New York Provincial Congress voted for independence, a decision that allowed New York delegates to sign the Declaration.) The document was sent to the printer, and on July 19 Congress had it enlarged and printed on thick paper.

August 2 just as easily could have been the date that Americans celebrate their independence. On that date, 49 delegates signed the Declaration of Independence. John Hancock, president of the Second Continental Congress, signed it first, in the center and directly below the text, with his oversized and flowing signature. The others signed with their delegations, starting with the northernmost state, New Hampshire, and ending with Georgia, the southernmost state. Rather than starting on the left side of the page, New Hampshire delegates signed just below the last sentence of the document on the right side of the page, followed by Massachusetts delegates, and so on and so forth.[46]

When the time came for the Georgia delegates to sign, the signatures took up four full columns. A fifth column allowed for plenty of room for the three Georgians to sign toward the bottom of that column. Georgia's delegates decided to sign in alphabetical order, with Gwinnett going first and Walton last. For reasons that have never been recorded, Gwinnett started a sixth column, and he signed at the top. Lyman Hall, one of four doctors to sign the Declaration, signed next, below Gwinnett's signature, and George Walton signed below Hall's signature. Knowing that he was the final delegate to sign the Declaration that day, Walton placed a period after his name, the only delegate to do so.

Seven delegates, most notably Richard Henry Lee, signed after August 2, as did George Wythe, Elbridge Gerry, Oliver Wolcott, Lewis Morris, Thomas McKean and Matthew Thornton, who joined Congress in November of 1776 but was permitted to sign the Declaration. There was no room for Thornton to sign with his fellow New Hampshire delegates, so he signed at the bottom of the right-hand column, furthest from where Gwinnett signed.

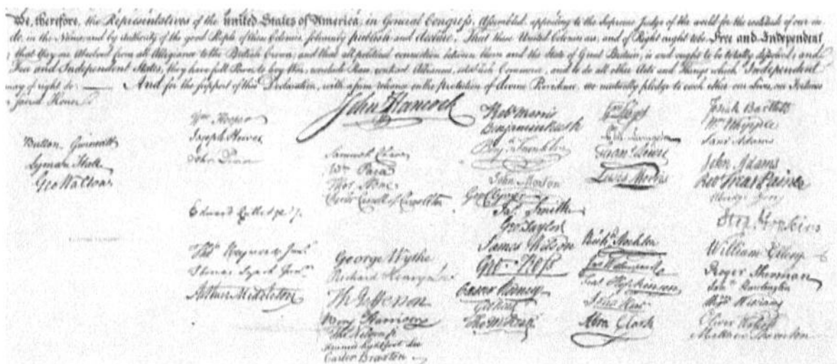

Gwinnett chose to sign at the top of the left column.

In the western world, the first place the eye goes when reading anything is the top left, so, with the exception of Hancock's large, showy signature, the signature of Button Gwinnett — an Englishman who failed at every business he ever tried, who didn't voluntarily show up for the colonial legislature to which he was elected, who would have rather become a colonel in the Georgia militia than serve in the Second Continental Congress — is the first signature many people see on arguably the most significant and well-known document in American history.

9

An Unworthy Founding Father

Americans love their Founding Fathers. Even with all their faults, they are viewed as intelligent and courageous visionaries who put their country before themselves. There is no getting around the fact that many of them owned slaves and considered women and non-white men inferior to them in every way, but they created the first modern nation-state based on the overriding principle that regular folks, not kings and queens, should be in charge. And they gave a new name to the people who would live in this nation-state. They would forever be called citizens, not subjects.

To get to that point, these relatively few men accomplished three remarkable feats: They organized and executed the overthrow of the most powerful military and economic power in the world. They created the first large-scale republic in the modern era. And they separated church and state, the first nation in the world to do so. More than 25,000 Americans died during the Revolutionary War, but the Founding Fathers managed to do those things without the widespread massacres that accompanied revolutions in other countries, most notably France, Russia and China. Taken as a whole, America's Founding Fathers introduced modern democracy to the world, one of the most significant achievements in human history. And their movement reshaped the global economy and accelerated debates in America and elsewhere about slavery and human rights.

For these reasons, these men are generally respected, if not admired. John Adams, Thomas Jefferson and Benjamin Franklin are the best known signers of the Declaration of Independence. However, nearly all of the lesser-known signers deserve to be called Founding Fathers because of their accomplishments, their sacrifices and their courage.

Button Gwinnett is the exception. Of the 56 signers, he is the least worthy to hold the Founding Father title.

To quantify what must sound like a subjective claim, consider three areas that the vast majority of the signers have in common: successful careers, involvement in colonial government and an early and burning passion for the independence movement. These three distinctions contributed to their status as leaders in their communities and in their colonies. And their commitment to public service and their desire for independence highlighted their altruism and selflessness. The fact that Gwinnett failed in his chosen professions, had no desire to govern and didn't speak out against British rule until well after many others did not make him inferior to his fellow Americans, many of whom remained neutral or aligned with the British in 1776. Nor did it make him stupid, unambitious or lazy. He was none of those things. But his life's work, his lack of public service and his disinterest in the independence movement up to that point question his worthiness to sign his name on arguably the most important document in our nation's history. Career success and government involvement aside, when it came to leading the colonies away from British rule, Gwinnett was not a leader. Nor was he a follower. He was apathetic, which set him apart from the vast majority of the Declaration signers and other leaders of the independence movement.

To be fair, not every one of the other signers enjoyed successful careers, governed at the local and colonial level and burned with an early passion for ridding the colonies of British control, but everyone except for Gwinnett could check at least two of those three boxes by 1776. He eventually could check one, but not until soon before he served in the Second Continental Congress. A review of the credentials of the other 55 signers makes it clear that Gwinnett was out of his league in Philadelphia, where Congress voted for independence on July 2, 1776, adopted the Declaration of Independence two days later, and signed it on August 2.

To prove that point, consider all the signers as a member of one of three groups: the writers and editors of the Declaration; other leaders who historians widely view as exceptional; and the lesser-known signers, who make up the largest of the three groups.

First, the four men who wrote, edited and signed the Declaration of Independence: chief writer Thomas Jefferson, and editors Benjamin Franklin, John Adams and Roger Sherman. (Robert Livingston also served on the committee that created the document, but he wasn't in Philadelphia when most of the delegates signed it, and he didn't sign it at a later date.)[1] Leading up to the summer of 1776 and afterward, Jefferson, Franklin, Adams and Sherman did much more than create the Declaration, but even if they had done nothing else, their impact far exceeded Gwinnett's. They created arguably the most bold and impactful document in the nation's history in addition to their many accomplishments before and after 1776.

Next are six signers who historians widely view as unquestioned leaders and influencers of the independence movement and more than worthy to sign the Declaration:

- John Hancock, who graduated from Harvard at 17, excelled as a merchant and spent much of his own money financing the revolutionary cause and the war effort, including building the U.S. Navy. His peers voted him president of the Second Continental Congress,[2] making him the first national leader of the independence movement, and he later served more than a dozen years as governor of Massachusetts.

- Elbridge Gerry graduated from Harvard at 18, became an early patriot, the governor of Massachusetts and then a diplomat. As a recognized expert in finance and military matters, he advocated for better pay and better equipment for soldiers during the war. He also advocated for the Constitution to include a Bill of Rights, and he served as John Adams' second vice president.[3] (Forgive him for now for creating an oddly shaped congressional district that some say looked like a salamander, thus the term gerrymandering.)

- Richard Henry Lee, an early voice against British rule and a member of the Virginia House of Burgesses, introduced a resolution to seek independence from England that inspired the

Declaration of Independence.[4] In 1785, he served as president of the Continental Congress.

- James Wilson, a lawyer and judge who attended the universities of St. Andrews, Glasgow and Edinburgh, later served as a delegate to the Constitutional Convention of 1787, where he made several critical contributions to the new constitution, including ideas that served as the basis for the presidency.[5] The Pennsylvanian is the only person who signed both the Declaration and the Constitution and served as a U.S. Supreme Court justice.

- George Clymer, a successful Pennsylvania merchant, helped supply the army and in 1775 was appointed joint treasurer of the nation.[6] He was one of only six men to sign both the Declaration of Independence and the Constitution, and he was elected to the first U.S. Congress in 1789. His work to establish the Bank of North America in 1781 helped stabilize the nation's finances.

- George Wythe, an intellectual giant, became America's first law professor (at the College of William and Mary) and pioneered the use of moot courts and mock trials. He mentored many of the younger Founders, including Thomas Jefferson, Supreme Court Chief Justice John Marshall, Speaker of the House Henry Clay and President James Monroe.[7]

No one, including Gwinnett's most fervent admirers, can make a sound argument that he was on equal footing with those men as a professional, a public servant or a patriot.

The 46 remaining signers, with one exception, are not household names, except possibly among history buffs in their home states. Of those, 40 check all three boxes: colonial government involvement, a successful career and a well-chronicled zeal for independence prior to 1776.

That leaves these six men who could check only two of the three boxes in 1776:

- Often mistaken for John Adams' brother — they were cousins — Samuel Adams received a Harvard education and served multiple terms in the Massachusetts House of Representatives, advocating for colonial rights and against British rule. He was arguably the most vocal opponent of the British in New England. He organized the Boston Tea Party and wrote numerous articles — under various pseudonyms — calling for the colonies to expel the British from America. He was a master of propaganda who shaped the opinion of New Englanders, and Thomas Jefferson credited him with steering Congress toward independence.[8] However, like Gwinnett, he lacked a head for business. He failed as a brewer and was a lenient and arguably incompetent tax collector. For that reason and that reason alone, he makes this list.

- James Smith, a real estate attorney in Pennsylvania, became active in the independence movement in the early 1770s, when he began serving on safety and correspondence committees. As part of his resistance work, he gained status in Pennsylvania by raising and training a militia company in that colony. After he served in Congress, he stayed active in the state legislature and helped oversee Pennsylvania's military and logistical support during the Revolutionary War. But he didn't begin serving in the Pennsylvania Provincial Assembly until 1776, giving him virtually no little colonial government experience compared with the vast majority of his fellow signers.

- Arthur Middleton studied law at Cambridge University and served multiple terms in the South Carolina House of Assembly starting in 1765. Unlike most of the aristocratic gentlemen of his time in South Carolina, he spoke out boldly and early that the colonies should free themselves from British rule. His attitude toward loyalists was ruthless.[9] After he signed the Declaration, he fought in defense of Charleston and was captured by the British. Upon his release, he became involved in politics and lived a life of public service. He lived many years on his family's plantation and is referred to as a planter or a gentleman farmer, but he was largely uninvolved in the family business and can't claim to have contributed to its success.

- George Read became a lawyer at 19 and served as the crown-appointed attorney general in Delaware for 11 years. During much of that time, he was a state lawmaker and then served in the First Continental Congress. As a member of Congress, Read signed the 1774 Petition to the King, a plea to George III to repeal the Intolerable Acts, a series of laws passed by the British Parliament to punish Massachusetts for the Boston Tea Party. Read generally opposed British policies and supported colonial rights, but he voted against independence on July 2, 1776.[10] However, he ended up signing the Declaration of Independence, supported the war effort and later signed the U.S. Constitution and became a U.S. senator and Delaware's chief justice.

- Like Gwinnett, Robert Morris was born in England, attended a small school and became a merchant, but that's where the similarities end. Morris was a member of the Pennsylvania Provincial Assembly, where he argued for colonial rights and against taxation without representation. He was such a successful merchant that he was thought to be one of the wealthiest men in America in the 1770s. As a member of the Second Continental Congress, he was a leader and a key member of the marine committee and was described as the "de facto commander" of the continental navy. He also helped draft the Model Treaty, which was designed to serve as a template for relations with foreign countries and advocated for free trade. And he served as chairman of the Secret Committee of Trade, which established a network of agents charged with procuring supplies for the Revolutionary War. He didn't favor declaring independence on July 2, 1776,[11] but he signed the Declaration one month later. In October of that year, he explained his decision: "I am not one of those politicians that run testy when my own plans are not adopted. I think it is the duty of a good citizen to follow when he cannot lead. ...I do not wish to see my countrymen die on the field of battle nor do I wish to see them live in tyranny."[12] He oversaw the financing of the war and levied his personal fortune to help finance the war effort. He lost nearly all of it.

- Edward Rutledge, the youngest signer by three months, was born in Charleston and studied law in London before he served in the South Carolina Commons House of Assembly. That led to his selection to the Second Continental Congress, where John Adams later described him as a "peacock."[13] He was in no hurry to break ties with England, where his mother was born, and he opposed independence as late as July 1, but he voted for it the next day.[14] He did so, he said, because he understood the importance of the colonies appearing unified. He later served in South Carolina's legislature and in the militia, fought in the Siege of Charleston in 1780 and was a prisoner of war in Florida before he was released in a prisoner exchange. He became governor of South Carolina.

Gwinnett has been described as "a reluctant revolutionary,"[15] but what to make of Read, Morris and Rutledge? Read and Morris didn't even vote for independence on July 2, 1776, as Gwinnett did, and Rutledge was even more reluctant than Gwinnett. It's true that the trio thought 1776 was too early to break from England, but they understood the importance of unity and compromise during a crucial time in our nation's history, unlike Gwinnett, as the final nine months of his life make clear. What's more, these three men's pre- and post-1776 careers, accomplishments and sacrifices far exceeded Gwinnett's.

As for Gwinnett, it's telling that the historical record includes compliments from only two of his contemporaries. On May 20, 1776, the day he and Lyman Hall and Gwinnett showed up to serve in Congress, John Adams wrote they are "both intelligent and spirited men, who made a powerful addition to our Phalanx."[16] Adams knew Hall, but he had just met Gwinnett that day, and his words only reflected Gwinnett's commitment to vote for independence. The second compliment came almost exactly a year later, when Gwinnett was on his death bed, and Hall, his close friend, described him as a patriot, "a whig to excess."[17]

A more recent positive comment about Gwinnett came from Harvey H. Jackson III, a historian who has written extensively about colonial and revolutionary Georgia. Jackson, eminent scholar in history at Jacksonville State University in Alabama, wrote that Gwinnett's political skills have been underappreciated. In the second half of 1775, Gwinnett rallied support for the radical political faction in Georgia's rural southern and western parishes with the goal of displacing established Savannah-based leaders, many of whom led the independence movement in the colony.[18] Jackson opined that Gwinnett's revolution was about empowering radicals in Georgia as much as it was about the colonies gaining their independence from England.[19]

In fact, Gwinnett's actions make it clear that he wanted to empower *himself*. He realized that Congress planned to vote for independence in the summer of 1776, but rather than serve as a delegate, he wanted the colonel job in the Georgia militia. Unfortunately for him, the faction he worked to enlarge wasn't powerful enough to secure the job for him. He didn't get it because Georgia's leaders couldn't stomach seeing this debt-ridden rabble-rouser get what he wanted. Whatever politicking Gwinnett did in rural Georgia in 1775 doesn't change the fact that he provided no meaningful public service prior to his selection to the Second Continental Congress, and while in that body, was never more than a quiet follower.

But doesn't Gwinnett deserve respect and admiration for associating himself with the independence movement during a time when the British hunted American leaders and threatened them with imprisonment and even death? Shortly after the Declaration was signed, about 32,000 British troops and 8,600 German soldiers arrived in New York to try to crush the rebellion. "Upon the whole there can be no doubt but that Philadelphia is their object, and that they will pass the Delaware as soon as possible," George Washington wrote to John Hancock. "Happy should I be, if I could see the means of preventing them. At present I confess I do not."[20]

Later that year, New York Declaration signer Francis Lewis, a wealthy merchant, had his house and possessions destroyed or taken and his wife imprisoned.[21] As the troops moved inland, New Jersey signer Richard Stockton was targeted. He was "dragged from his bed by night, stripped and plundered of his property" by loyalists before being jailed in a notoriously brutal prison.[22]

On December 20, 1776, a few weeks after the Stockton's abduction, Congress began meeting in Baltimore after British troops forced the delegates to leave Philadelphia, just as Washington predicted. Gwinnett, who was again selected to serve in Congress, chose not to attend that session. He remained in Georgia, a safe place for leaders of the independence movement from 1776 to 1778 because the British had been expelled and their troops were focusing their efforts on the northern colonies. During the first half of the 1770s, with the British in Georgia and many Georgians publicly objecting to British rule, Gwinnett attended no independence-related meetings, served on no security or correspondence committees or in the Georgia Provincial Congress, sat out the Battle of the Rice Boats in Savannah, and made no known public comments critical of British authorities and their occupation of the colony.

After the British recolonized Georgia on December 29, 1778, they and their loyalists made life miserable for Georgians who had led the independence movement. Long-time Assembly Speaker Noble Wimberly Jones was captured and imprisoned while the British chased current or future governors John Adam Treutlen, Richard Howly, John Houstoun and Edward Telfair all over Georgia in 1779, 1780 and 1781. Lyman Hall fled to South Carolina and then to his home state of Connecticut. George Walton and

Lachlan McIntosh, both military officers, fought the British army and became prisoners of war. After the war ended, Hall returned to Georgia in 1782 to find his Liberty County plantation burned to the ground. McIntosh's plantation near Darien met the same fate, as did Walton's, near Augusta.

Gwinnett wasn't around for that, so he never suffered England's wrath for voting for independence and signing the Declaration of Independence.

10

A Hometown Hero

A "special messenger" in what amounted to an 18th-century Pony Express arrived in Savannah on August 8, 1776, with an unsigned copy of the Declaration of Independence and a cover letter from John Hancock, president of the Second Continental Congress.[1] Archibald Bulloch gathered Georgia's leaders and read it to them, and two days later, he read it publicly, kicking off a huge party. Led by Col. Lachlan McIntosh, Savannahians marched to the liberty pole and celebrated with another reading and the firing of 13 guns, symbolizing the 13 colonies.[2] After that, they ate together "under the cedar trees and cordially drank to the prosperity and perpetuity of the United, Free, and Independent States of America."[3] The dinner included 13 toasts, followed by a funeral procession — the largest gathering in Savannah up to that time — which ended in front of the courthouse, where an effigy of King George III was buried.

An unidentified person closed the festivities with what could be described as a political statement or a prayer, or both.[4]

> *"For as much as George the Third of Great Britain, hath most flagrantly violated his coronation Oath and trampled upon the Constitution of our country and the sacred rights of mankind: we, therefore, commit his political existence to the ground — corruption to corruption — tyranny to the grave — and oppression to eternal infamy; in sure and certain hope that he will never obtain a resurrection to rule again over these United States of America. But, my friends and fellow citizens, let us not be sorry, as men without hope, for TYRANTS that thus depart — rather let us remember America is free and independent; that she is and will be, with the blessing of the Almighty, GREAT among the nations of the earth,*
>
> *"...May God give us his blessing, and let all the people say, AMEN."*

Smaller but similar celebrations occurred elsewhere in Georgia, including in St. John Parish, the home of

Lyman Hall and Button Gwinnett, who by this time were hometown heroes.

After Gwinnett signed the Declaration of Independence, he couldn't wait to leave Philadelphia. He left that very day, August 2 — about 10 weeks into his nine-month term — missed a committee meeting and didn't show up in the congressional record after that. He was replaced on that committee by fellow Georgian George Walton,[5] who arrived in Philadelphia after Gwinnett and Hall. Gwinnett left Philadelphia with Virginia delegate Carter Braxton, who served on a committee with him. The two parted ways after Braxton, a planter with 18 children, reached his home along the Mattaponi River near Chesapeake Bay, leaving Gwinnett to travel the rest of the way alone.

Like so much about his life, there is no existing explanation for Gwinnett's decision to leave Philadelphia on the day he signed the Declaration, but there are four plausible reasons why he left when he did:

First, he might have wanted to check on his home on St. Catherines Island, which, along with the rest of the Georgia coast, was threatened by the British navy. That's understandable, but if true, it reveals that he prioritized his possessions over his congressional duties, unlike many other Founding Fathers who made great financial sacrifices for the cause. Second, he might have missed his wife and daughter and wanted to see them. Also understandable, but that was unlikely to be his main motivation, given that he had been away from them for years at a time during much of the 1760s and part of the 1770s. Other delegates no doubt missed their families, but many of them stayed in Philadelphia to continue their work. Like the first explanation, this one makes him look more concerned with his needs than the needs of his adopted country. Third, he might have wanted to be the one to share the news of — and take credit for — Congress' decision to give Georgia money for its defense. He knew how important the money was to the colony, and he couldn't wait to tell its leaders of his role — whatever it might have been — in securing the appropriation. The fourth reason is related to the third: Gwinnett wanted to waste no time lobbying for a high-ranking military position funded by the money from Congress.[6] Of the four possible explanations for his departure from Philadelphia, the third and fourth most closely align with someone as ambitious and job hungry as Gwinnett.

A lot had changed in Georgia since he had left four months earlier. The British were gone, and the colonists got a taste of what life was like with this new-found freedom. It wasn't all good. In fact, living in Georgia in 1776 was difficult.

The *Georgia Gazette*'s pro-British publisher left, so the newspaper wasn't publishing, causing an information deficit for Georgians. But that was the least of their problems. Many British loyalists also left and took with them the know-how to run the government and the courts, and Georgia's remaining leaders struggled to fill the void. The colony's economy was a mess in 1776. Slaves owned by loyalists dispersed or were moved out of state, causing rice production to plummet.[7] Georgians endured the effects of inflation because its currency, which was always weak, further depreciated and wasn't accepted in other states.[8] Even if someone had plenty of money to spend, the usual trade channels were closed because of the trade boycott against England, making imported goods scarce.[9]

If all that weren't bad enough, the British and their American loyalists in Florida supported the efforts of mercenaries who occasionally crossed the border into Georgia and wreaked havoc. And then there were the Native Americans. The British, who made great efforts to keep the peace with them during the colonial period, turned them against Georgians during the revolutionary period. Emboldened by the British, they worked as scouts and often ambushed militia soldiers and others in the swamps and woods of south Georgia. By the time Gwinnett returned to Savannah in late August of 1776, it was obvious that Georgia, the least populated and most remote of the 13 colonies, was struggling to defend itself from its enemies.

So he must have relished the opportunity to share his good news: Congress gave Georgia $60,000 — about $2.2 million in purchasing power in 1776 — for a regiment of rangers, two battalions, two artillery companies and the construction of four ships.[10] Two weeks earlier, Congress allocated $300,000 to South Carolina for its defense,[11] a clear sign that Georgia mattered less to the independence movement in the minds of John Hancock, John Adams, Robert Morris and America's other leaders.

Declaring a desire to become independent was one thing, but achieving independence would cost a lot of time, a lot of effort and potentially a lot of lives. Georgia would have liked more than $60,000, but this money provided something concrete that would help Georgia immediately. (When Gwinnett was only two days from arriving in Savannah, Congress gave the colony an additional $5,000 to buy "riffles (sic) for the troops ordered to be raised for the defence (sic) of that state."[12])

On August 30, 1776, the day Gwinnett made it to Savannah, he attended a Council of Safety meeting, where he presented a letter from John Hancock about Congress' allocation."[13] A summary of the Council of Safety meeting discussion only mentions "Mr. Gwinnett," not the other two Georgians who served in Congress with him. And it states, "In compassing the passage of these resolutions and in carrying them into practical effect he (Gwinnett) was largely instrumental."[14]

Despite what Gwinnett may have said to lead the meeting attendees to that conclusion, he almost certainly played little or no role in helping Georgia secure the money from Congress. When Gwinnett arrived in Philadelphia in the late spring of 1776, he knew no one in Congress, except for Lyman Hall. While there, Gwinnett said virtually nothing when Georgia's delegation was given an opportunity to make a case for the money. George Walton made a lengthy argument for it, as John Adams made clear in his reporting of the discussion. It made sense that George Walton, a major in the colony's militia, was "largely instrumental." Georgia's senior militia officers communicated their needs to him before he traveled to Philadelphia.[15] And Archibald Bulloch told John Adams that Walton would brief him on what was happening in Georgia. Lyman Hall, who served in Congress in 1775 and was a member of the congressional military committee in 1776, was better known — and would have had more influence — than Gwinnett. What's more, Congress received Bulloch's letter requesting money for Georgia's defense. For that reason alone, the colony may have received money even if Walton failed to make a solid argument for it.

Although there's no reason to think that Gwinnett had anything to do with convincing Congress to allocate the money, he was ambitious and clever enough to know that taking credit for this could increase his status among Georgia's leaders.

"At some point while he was serving in Congress, we can assume he saw that political opportunities could lead to other opportunities," said Solomon Smith, the Georgia Southern University historian.[16]

When Gwinnett left the Council of Safety meeting in Savannah on August 30, he was a former merchant and an unsuccessful planter who had lost his land and his house, and he owed money to numerous creditors. He had no role in colonial government. He needed money — and he needed purpose and direction. Then Archibald Bulloch made a decision that benefited him. Bulloch realized that Congress' decision to end ties with England was a monumental event that warranted an election to allow Georgians to establish a new government and create a state constitution, so he called for elections to the Commons House of Assembly to occur during the first 10 days of September 1776.[17] Now Gwinnett wanted to play a role in the legislature, and because signing the Declaration of Independence made him into something of a hero in Georgia, his election to the Assembly was assured.

Meanwhile, Bulloch had cemented his position as the unquestioned leader of Georgia. He was the right leader at the right time, and according to Hugh

McCall, Georgia's first historian, his call for elections was the right thing to do. Bulloch believed "America must stand or fall by the virtue of her inhabitants," McCall wrote. "...consequently, the utmost caution must necessarily be used by the people of this state, in choosing men of unsuspected characters, men whose actions had proved their friendship to the cause of freedom, and men whose depth of political judgment qualified them to frame a constitution for the future government of the country."

Bulloch may have been the most politically power-ful man in Georgia, but some who knew Gwinnett believed that his brief time in Congress made him hungry for some of that power, and his ambition was the subject of gossip among influential Georgians.

In a letter in September of 1776, Samuel Elbert, who competed with Gwinnett for the colonel position that Lachlan McIntosh received, wrote, "I am glad to find the alarm from your quarter is nothing — - pray has the President (Bulloch) or me most to fear from Gwinnett. I tell him G (Gwinnett) will be president (of Georgia). He tells me G will be colonel. Mr. (John) Wereat (Georgia's liaison to Congress) has wrote word that he (Gwinnett) rally (sic) come home to get the Second Regiment. Can this be possible (?)"[18]

A colonel position no longer interested Gwinnett. Congress had authorized money for a brigade in

Georgia to be led by a brigadier general. He wanted *that* job, and he might have felt confident that it was his for the asking because his former colleagues in Congress would make the decision. Gwinnett had voted for independence with them, so he had reason to believe he had earned their support. The problem for him was fellow Georgian George Walton had the respect of many influential delegates,[19] and he wasn't going to recommend Gwinnett for the job.[20] A military officer, Walton viewed Gwinnett as undisciplined, unqualified and unworthy to lead a brigade. What's more, influential South Carolina delegate Henry Laurens, who was in line to become the next president of the Second Continental Congress, preferred another man for the job.

On September 16, the day Congress announced that Georgia would receive an additional $50,000 to defend itself, it also revealed that *Colonel* Lachlan McIntosh would become *General* Lachlan McIntosh, Laurens' friend and business partner.[21] For the second time in seven months, the tall, handsome Scottish-born planter received a job that Gwinnett badly wanted.

Gwinnett's feelings aside, a full brigade couldn't have come at a better time for Georgians, who worried about attacks from the British in Florida as much as James Oglethorpe had worried about the Spaniards who lived there 40 years earlier. The Council of Safety ordered that all livestock on St. Catherines and the other sea islands be moved inland or destroyed by November 1 to remove temptation for the British navy, whose warships patrolled the Georgia coast in search of whatever they could steal.

In a four-page letter dated September 20, Gen. Robert Howe of the Southern Command wrote to Bulloch:[22] "The idea of defending the islands ...is too absurd for anybody but a madman to entertain. ...The knowledge I have of these islands, particularly Sappelo, St. Simons, St. Catherines, Ossabaw and Skidaway, make me certain how valuable they would be to the Enemy..."

Despite Howe's pessimism, Georgia's leaders felt compelled to mount a defense. They instructed McIntosh to station soldiers at various places along the coast, including 50 in Darien and another 50 in Sunbury,[23] across St. Catherines Sound from where Gwinnett lived. McIntosh also assigned his older brother William, a lieutenant colonel, to oversee the construction of a tiny wooden fort — really nothing more than a 100-square-foot stockade — on the Satilla River, about 120 miles south of the Savannah River. It was to be called Fort McIntosh. It is impossible to believe Gwinnett was pleased that the man who beat him out of two high-ranking officer positions would now have a military post named after his family, regardless of its size.

Gwinnett lacked the support in Congress he needed to get the brigadier general position, but his political ascension in Georgia was nothing short of astonishing. The radical faction, which wanted to lessen the power of the more established and conservative leaders in Georgia, was always closely aligned with the independence movement. And after the Declaration of Independence was signed, radicals gained political power. No Georgian benefited more than Gwinnett. He was elected to the Commons House of Assembly in September, and at the Georgia Provincial Congress session in October, he became speaker of the Assembly as well as a member of the prestigious Council of Safety, though his contributions were never recorded in meeting minutes that continued into 1777.[24]

His job as speaker made him the most powerful lawmaker and the second most powerful politician in Georgia — second only to Bulloch, the colony's president and commander-in-chief. In less than a year, Gwinnett went from a debt-ridden planter who played no role in government to a heartbeat from leading the affairs of a state. The conservatives in Georgia were shaking their heads at this meteoric rise, but with the radicals in the majority, Gwinnett had no reason to worry about his political adversaries.

He wasted little time using his political power, targeting Lachlan McIntosh and his brothers, William and George. He set out to make them miserable. Or as 19th-century Georgia historian Charles C. Jones, Jr., put it: "He gladly availed himself of the opportunity thus afforded to mortify General Lachlan McIntosh and vent his wrath against him upon his brother(s)."[25]

His first step was to order an investigation of William, the eldest brother, who commanded the calvary forces that patrolled the Georgia-Florida border. That was a thankless job if there ever was one: Georgia's militia was shorthanded and underfunded, and the British, with a garrison in Florida, had no shortage of instigators willing to cross the border into Georgia and wreak havoc. William was accused of failing to protect some plantations during fights between the Georgia militia and British forces and their allies. The Council of Safety eventually exonerated him,[26] but he obtained a leave of absence because he was "quite worn out with yr. hardships & fatigue of the service & obtained leave to retire for a while."[27]

Thanks to Gwinnett, Georgia lost an experienced military officer at a time when it needed all it could get.

A week after he became speaker of the Assembly, Gwinnett was selected to serve as a delegate in the next Second Continental Congress session, along with John Houstoun, Lyman Hall, George Walton and Nathan Brownson, a future governor who, like Hall and Gwinnett, lived in St. John Parish. As he had done in the spring of 1776, Houstoun turned down an opportunity to serve. So did Gwinnett, leaving Hall, Walton and Brownson to attend.

Gwinnett could be forgiven for not wanting to serve again in the body that had denied him the brigadier general position, but unlike during the early months of 1776, when he didn't have a lot on his plate, he was swamped. Besides the duties he had as speaker, he put himself in charge of a committee that oversaw the creation of Georgia's first official constitution. Although one distinguished, 20th-century historian wrote it is impossible to know for sure who wrote that constitution because records have been lost,[28] others have concluded that Gwinnett led that effort. The committee members, whomever they were, referred to themselves as "...representatives of the people, from whom all power originates."

As many state constitutions from that period did, Georgia's reflected the mood of the time, opening with these words:[29]

"...the conduct of the legislature of Great Britain for many years past has been so oppressive on the people of America that of late years they have plainly declared and asserted a right to raise taxes upon the people of America, and to make laws to bind them in all cases whatsoever, without their consent; which conduct, being repugnant to the common rights of mankind, hath obliged the Americans, as freemen, to oppose such oppressive measures, and to assert the rights and privileges they are entitled to by the laws of nature and reason..."

There is no evidence that Gwinnett left the Second Continental Congress with a detailed draft of a constitution written by John Adams, as some have alleged, but Adams gave specific instructions to future state constitution writers to include broad, overriding principles, such as separation of powers; protection of basic rights, such as freedom of speech and religion; and the proposition that all men are created equal. Although these principles made their way into state constitutions, they often were not put into practice, at least not by modern standards. The declaration that individuals are created equal, for example, did not include enslaved and Native American men, or women of any race. As for religion, anyone could worship however they chose, but in many states, including Georgia, Protestants controlled the government and received all of the important civic and military positions.

Assuming Gwinnett led the effort to write Georgia's constitution, he would have benefited from the insight he had gained while listening to independence-related discussions in Congress in Philadelphia and from serving as a member of the committee that began drafting the Articles of Confederation, America's first framework of government.

The 10-page, 1777 Georgia constitution is relatively succinct, easy to understand and inarguably Gwinnett's most significant accomplishment.

"It is believed that he had more to do than any one else with framing that important document," wrote Charles Jones, the 19th-century Georgia historian.[30]

Like Thomas Jefferson's Declaration of Independence, Georgia's 1777 constitution included no new ideas. It incorporated many of John Adams' recommendations and elaborated on the Georgia Provincial Congress' Rules and Regulations document, which had served as the first unofficial state constitution.

Georgia's new constitution allowed for freedom of press and freedom of religion, "provided it not be repugnant to the peace and safety of the State."[31] It called for legislative, executive and judicial branches, with lawmakers receiving the most power. This echoed Georgia's Rules and Regulations document, and it was a complete reversal from the days when royal Gov. James Wright ruled the colony as if he were King George III, vetoing legislation he didn't like. That top-down style of governing had been the rule in all the British colonies, but this constitution made it clear that those days were over.

It dictated that lawmakers would elect a governor to a term of only one year to keep him from accumulating too much power. The governor would also serve as commander-in-chief, but legislative leaders would advise him. He would have the power to grant pardons and appoint people to important government positions, as Wright did.

The constitution replaced Georgia's eight original parishes with the state's first eight counties, all of which would have public schools, courts and jails.[32] The counties of Burke, Camden, Chatham, Effingham, Glynn, Richmond and Wilkes were named in honor of members of the British Parliament who sympathized with the colonies. ("If I were an American, …while a foreign troop was landed in my country, I never would lay down my arms. Never, never, never!" said William Pitt, 1st Earl of Chatham. "I rejoice that America has resisted. Three millions of people so dead to all the feelings of liberty as voluntarily to submit to be slaves, would have been fit instruments to make slaves of us all.")[33] St. John's Parish, which viewed itself as the state's "cradle of liberty," was named Liberty County.

"The legislature of this state shall be composed of the people," stated Paragraph II of the new constitution,[34] but Gwinnett and his fellow radicals took advantage of their new political power. The constitution spelled out that the Commons House of Assembly would be made up of 14 residents from rural Liberty County, 10 each from Burke, Chatham, Effingham, Richmond and Wilkes counties, and one each from the sparsely populated Camden and Glynn counties. In addition, Georgia's largest city, Savannah, which was — and still is — part of Chatham County, was given four additional delegates, and Sunbury, in Liberty County, two more. So the radicals made sure that Liberty — a hotbed of radicalism — would have two more legislators than Chatham, the state's largest county and the place where Georgia's conservative leaders lived. Only Protestants could be elected.

Georgia's constitution allowed more people to vote. The British had required a man to own at least 50 acres of land to be eligible to vote. Under the new constitution, a man who was at least 21 years and six months old with £10 of taxable property, or who worked in "a mechanics trade" could vote.[35] In other words, most employed white men could vote, except for those who claimed a nobility title. Eligible voters who did not could be fined as much as five British pounds unless they had an acceptable excuse,[36] but this was rarely, if ever, enforced.

Although the constitution writers expanded voting rights, they limited how much power they were willing to share with the masses. The British allowed men with at least 500 acres to be eligible for elected office. This constitution reduced that to 250 acres or property worth at least £250. So holding public office was still reserved for people who were doing well, as long as they weren't clergymen. This bias was likely due to

British loyalist Rev. John Zubly, who, as a congressional delegate in the fall of 1775, advocated for trade with England and caused delegates in other colonies to question Georgia's commitment to the independence movement.

The constitution also mandated trial by jury "to remain inviolate forever," with civic and criminal matters adjudicated within the county where they originated, assuming the county had enough people to assemble a jury.[37]

"Mr. Gwinnett, from the committee appointed to revise and consider the draught (sic) of the Constitution for the government of this State, brought in their report, which was received and read for the first time," according to the minutes of the Assembly's January 29, 1777, meeting. It was adopted on February 5, after which 500 copies were made. By this time, New York and Massachusetts were the only states that did not have constitutions. (New York's constitution was co-written by Robert R. Livingston, who helped edit the Declaration of Independence, and by John Jay, the state's second governor and the first U.S. Supreme Court chief justice. John Adams, not surprisingly, wrote Massachusetts' constitution, which served as a model for the U.S. Constitution.)

As for Georgia's constitution, Connecticut congressional delegate Roger Sherman, the only person to sign four of the key documents related to the founding of the United States — the Continental Association, Declaration of Independence, Articles of Confederation and U.S. Constitution — reviewed it at Lyman Hall's request and approved of it "in the main."[38] In other words, he liked most of it.

Overseeing the creation of Georgia's first official constitution may have been Gwinnett's crowning achievement, but that didn't mean everyone liked it.

Although it was inclusive by 18th-century standards, not all Georgians valued that level of inclusiveness. To some, it went way overboard. Savannah merchant and politician Joseph Clay wrote that it "is so very Democratical & has thrown power into such Hands as must ruin the Country if not timely prevented by some alteration in it."[39] Clay, sounding a lot like former Gov. James Wright, added that the government was run by individuals "whose ability or situation in Life does not intitle (sic) them to it."[40] He added that the authors of the constitution was harming Georgia as much as King George III.

John Wereat, a future governor of Georgia and the state's liaison to the Continental Congress at the time, said Georgia's constitution was the work of a few men "at a nightly meeting in a Tavern," and it deserved whatever criticism it received.[41] Lachlan McIntosh commented that those who volunteered to write the constitution saw it as an opportunity to cement their positions as career politicians, and "some I fear lust after the old flesh pott,"[42] a literal reference to a pot used to cook meat and a metaphorical reference to steady income.

Just before the constitution was released, Georgia was faced with a bombshell request: Merge with South Carolina.

South Carolina planter, lawyer and congressional delegate William H. Drayton, Sr., made the case that a merger would benefit Georgia in five ways: Reduce expenses, avoid "dangerous disputes about boundaries," place Georgia's weak currency on equal footing with South Carolina's, enhance Savannah's port, and lessen competition, which can "lead to jealousy and defeat of each other's plans."[43] Drayton, who announced his proposal in Charleston on January 23, spoke for about an hour and when he was finished, passed out copies of his speech,[44] which were rushed off to Georgia.

Soon afterward, the state's leaders convened a public meeting in Savannah to respond to the proposed merger. Drayton, who attended, was not permitted to speak, but he took a lot of notes.[45]

One of the speakers was Gwinnett. Drayton later recalled, "And so Mr. Button Gwinnett appeared as the champion against me, when he had taken care to deprive me of an opportunity of exposing the fallacy of his arguments. However, I had taken notes of the principal answers to what I had said; and in an hour after, of presence of an Officer of high military rank, and in three or four members of the Convention, I produced those notes, and asked if they were just; and they agreed with me that what he had said was either a gross misrepresentation of what I had said, or no answer to my arguments. In the afternoon, the Convention delivered to me a paper containing their objection of the proffered union; founded as, I apprehend, upon a reason that does not exist in nature."[46]

Whether or not Gwinnett misrepresented Drayton's arguments, the last thing Georgia's leaders wanted at this time was to merge with a state that it considered more of a rival than an ally. If the merger occurred, many Georgians feared they would be bullied by their neighbor to the north, which was more established, more populous and more prosperous than Georgia. And the merger proposal included no assurances from South Carolina to help protect Georgians from the British and their hostile allies.

On this matter, Gwinnett spoke for the majority of Georgia's leaders, but Drayton continued to work behind the scenes to interest influential Georgians in the merger, leading to a proclamation months later that included an offer of a 100-pound reward to anyone who apprehended Drayton.[47] He described the proclamation as full of "nonsense and false-hoods."[29] That was the end of the merger discussion, but it was not the end of disputes between Georgia and South Carolina, which quarreled over their border until a solution was agreed upon in 1788.

Regardless of the merits of the merger proposal, its timing could not have been worse. Georgia's leaders had more pressing matters, particularly how it would defend itself against its enemies. Archibald Bulloch had recently received a letter from Continental Army Gen. Robert Howe, who was convinced that the state did not have ample resources to do that.[48]

"... It gives me Sir, great anxiety to find your State so destitute of almost Every Military requisite, and deficient in every necessary provision for the Soldiery. No Barracks built for the Men, nor any that I have heard of preparing to be built, no Publick stores furnished with Goods where the Soldiers may lay out their Money in Necessaries.... No Arsenal furnished with Military Stores, no arms purchased, or Commissions appointed to purchase them, very little Powder or Lead and no effectual measures taken to encrease (sic) The quantity..."

Gwinnett and Georgia's other leaders knew Howe accurately summarized the state's predicament. They counted on Bulloch to figure out what to do about it.

◆❖◆

When Bulloch signed the state constitution on February 20, 1777, his title changed from president to governor, the first American-born person to lead Georgia. His fellow Georgians, excluding the significant number who remained loyal to the British, considered Bulloch as wise and as able as any leader in any of the other states. During those difficult times, they took comfort in that.

Just two days later, he, Gwinnett and five others, attended a Council of Safety meeting.[49] With the security of the state at great risk, the council members were experiencing a great deal of stress, as the meeting summary made clear: "Whereas the present alarming situation of this State makes it absolutely necessary, that every friend of American liberty should stand forth and support the same; and whereas a great part of the militia of this State, are now ordered out in service, and the remainder ready to turn out, at a moment's warning...."[50]

And then, at seemingly the worst possible time, Georgia lost its most indispensable leader. Bulloch died later that day, suddenly and mysteriously. He was 47. (A white male in the South in the latter part of the 18th century who made it to 20 typically lived an additional 40 years,[51] so Bulloch died relatively young. He would have expected to live another 12 to 15 years.) Speculation that he was poisoned was never proven,[52] and the historical record includes the names of no one accused of any wrongdoing. Autopsies rarely occurred in 18th-century America, and one was not recommended to try to determine his cause of death. He was buried in Colonial Park Cemetery in Savannah.

His death was a great loss to Georgia, as Hugh McCall, Georgia's first historian, made clear:

"He had filled the most important offices that the state could confer upon him; and by his mild, firm, and dignified deportment, commanded the respect and esteem of his fellow-citizens. He was one of the four gentlemen who invited the republicans of Georgia, to rally round the standard of freedom, at the liberty pole in Savannah. The remainder of his useful life, was ardently and zealously devoted to the union of Georgia with the other states in the common cause."

Charles Jones, Jr., who wrote his history of Georgia seven decades after McCall's, also heaped praise on Bulloch:

"Of all the patriots who encountered peril and made strenuous exertion to deliver Georgia from kingly domination and pave the way for her admission into the sisterhood of the confederated American colonies, no one was more earnest, self-sacrificing, valiant or influential than the honorable Archibald Bulloch. Of irreproachable character, firm in his convictions, brave of heart, bold in action, wise in counsel, jealous of individual and political rights, and thoroughly identified with the best moments of Savannah ...at an early stage of the revolutionary proceedings he became an acknowledged leader of the rebels, and was by them was rapidly advanced to the highest post of danger and of honor."

Gwinnett, who was inarguably ambitious and arguably power hungry, benefited from Bulloch's death, becoming president of the Council of Safety. A more important decision involved picking the interim governor. Whoever replaced Bulloch would have huge shoes to fill, and on March 4, the Assembly's Executive Council decided Gwinnett could handle the responsibilities.

As the interim governor and commander-in-chief of the militia, Gwinnett was now the most powerful politician in Georgia as well as its top military civilian. In a mere six months, he went from playing no role in Georgia's government to leading it.

The Executive Council, in its commission of Gwinnett, wrote:

"...we do by these presents give and grant unto you, the said Button Gwinnett, with the advice and consent of the Council, by yourself, or by your Captain and Commander by you to be authorized, full power and authority to levy, arm, muster, command and employ all persons whatsoever residing within the said State of Georgia under your Government...."

That same day, Gwinnett, hoping to remove the interim title sooner rather than later, called for elections on May 8 to select a governor and an executive council.[53] And the next day he exercised his authority by issuing his only known proclamation: To "prevent any Intelligence or Supplies being carried to our Enemies," he forbade any ship or boat from leaving any port or harbor in Georgia "until further orders."[54]

Around this time, he found a letter that John Hancock, president of the Second Continental Congress, had written to Archibald Bulloch two months earlier. The letter, written while Bulloch was alive, claimed that George McIntosh, Gen. Lachlan McIntosh's youngest brother, "seems is a Member of the Congress in Georgia, and under that Character, is secretly supporting by every Act in his Power, the Designs of the British King & Parliament agt. (against) Us."[55] The accusation referred to a shipment of rice that was en route to the tiny South American nation of Dutch Guiana (now the Republic of Suriname) in the summer of 1776 but ended up at the British military post in St. Augustine, Florida. When George McIntosh found out the shipment had been diverted, he told Archibald Bulloch that a business partner of his had deceived him.[56] Bulloch believed McIntosh and told him to be prepared "to put (his story) in force" if he were ever accused of wrongdoing.[57]

Gwinnett, a waterways commissioner in coastal Georgia, learned about the shipment sometime after he returned from Philadelphia at the end of August 1776 and gave McIntosh even more information about it than he knew.[58] Gwinnett also believed McIntosh's story and told him he "would never see a farthing" from the sale.[59] McIntosh replied that he didn't care as long as the incident didn't harm his reputation.[60] McIntosh, a surveyor who had laid out the fledgling port city of Brunswick, had by then a long history as a leader in Georgia. He represented St. Andrew Parish in the Commons House of Assembly for most of the 1760s and served on the prestigious Council of Safety in 1776, and on the Assembly's Executive Council in 1777.

But John Hancock insisted in his letter to Bulloch that strong evidence incriminated McIntosh, and he wanted him arrested.

Bulloch apparently ignored Hancock's request because he had served with McIntosh in the Commons House of Assembly and in the Georgia Provincial Congress and viewed him as a man of integrity. Gwinnett, who presumably also knew what had happened with the shipment of rice, also didn't act on Hancock's request to arrest McIntosh after he initially read the letter.

On the day the Executive Council chose Gwinnett to be interim governor, George McIntosh's wife died, and he didn't attend the council meeting.[61] Shortly afterward, when the council met to officially sign off on Gwinnett's commission, McIntosh was present, but he refused to support Gwinnett, saying Gwinnett was unfit to serve as governor.[62] McIntosh reportedly said Gwinnett "would be the last person in the world he would choose" to lead Georgia, and Gwinnett replied, "By God, this will be the last day you and I will ever sit together in Council."[63]

That turned out to be true, and after the confrontation, Gwinnett decided to have McIntosh arrested. However, Gwinnett faced a conundrum: He didn't know what, if anything, Bulloch had written to Hancock in reply. McIntosh had not been arrested, so as far as Gwinnett knew, Bulloch either had not replied to Hancock, or he had replied to say he didn't believe the accusation. So Gwinnett chose his words carefully in a letter to Hancock, dated March 28, 1777, when he wrote, "On reconsidering your letter & the aggravating Circumstances of McIntosh's crime, I thought it advisable to apprehend him immediately."

Gwinnett ordered the "Body of the Delinquent," as he called McIntosh, to be taken into custody. McIntosh, not knowing at the time why he was arrested, was shackled and taken to jail in Savannah, where Gwinnett ordered the jailer to keep McIntosh in "iron handcufs" (sic) even while he was in his cell because his crime was treason.[64] The Council of Safety met soon afterward in Savannah — without Gwinnett, who was in Sunbury — and ordered the jailer to release McIntosh because he was ill,[65] and the poor jail conditions were worsening his condition. He was released on a bail of 20,000 in Georgia currency and was ordered to report to Congress under guard.[66]

Gwinnett, who claimed to have his finger on the pulse of the nation, wrote to Hancock that independence-minded Americans were upset that McIntosh was freed.[67] He added that McIntosh was one of many Georgians helping supply the British in Florida, and those loyalists needed to suffer the consequences.

McIntosh's alleged act of treason "has given great Offence (sic) to all the friends of America in this Country," Gwinnett wrote to Hancock, "& notwithstanding all the artifices of the McIntoshes & their numerous connections will kindle a blaze among the people not easy to be extinguished."[68]

Gwinnett accurately predicted the consequences of McIntosh's arrest. It not only infuriated the McIntoshes, but it created an enormous distraction in Georgia at a time when the state needed to focus on governing and protecting itself. Bulloch understood the consequences of arresting McIntosh and chose not to act on Hancock's accusation. Gwinnett's decision to poke at the McIntosh bear again divided Georgia's leaders when unity would have better served the fledgling state.

Having a prominent Georgia political leader arrested was a significant event, and it may have damaged Gwinnett politically, but the George McIntosh saga was a sideshow for him. Bulloch had been instructed to devise a plan to secure Georgia's southern border. Now that task became Gwinnett's top priority.

Like other Georgians before him, Gwinnett proposed an attack on St. Augustine, where many British nationalists and loyalists had relocated after they fled Georgia in 1776.[69] The Assembly approved his plan, but executing it would be extremely difficult. For one thing, there wasn't much of an inland supply line between Savannah and St. Augustine. It didn't exist in 1740 and 1743, when Georgia's founder James Oglethorpe unsuccessfully attacked St. Augustine. It wasn't much better by 1776, when Gen. Charles Lee, commander of the Southern Department, ordered an attack. And a year later, it hadn't improved. Roads and bridges were few and far between, and with the exception of the town of Darien, which was a military and trading outpost, there wasn't much of anything or anyone between Savannah and St. Augustine except old-growth forests and fresh-water swamps. (Brunswick, which became a busy commercial port city starting in the mid-19th century, was still in its infancy in 1777, with only about 100 residents.)

Even if there were a good inland route to Florida, Georgia didn't have enough soldiers to carry out the mission, as Gwinnett would discover. The British didn't have that problem. Their side included loyalists who fled Georgia as well as Native Americans, who joined them in the fight. And then there were the 18th-century mercenaries who reveled at creating chaos. Hugh McCall, Georgia's first historian, explained their impact and motive:

"Florida royal Gov. Patrick Tonyn had previously commissioned privateers, to cruise on the coast of the southern provinces, to plunder the property of the inhabitants, and the adventures of merchants lying in the harbours. ...The southern settlers in Georgia, had been frequently disturbed by the predatory incursions of these banditti. The more effectually to excite terror in the inhabitants, they had constantly small parties of Indians in their train. Property which was moveable, conflagration and murder, were the principal objects of their enterprise. They had no attachment for king, country, or anything at variance with pillage and interest."

Not only were the Georgia militia outmanned, but it and the U.S. Continental army lacked coordination. Gwinnett, as the militia's interim commander-in-chief, played a key role in that dysfunction. Having run William McIntosh out of the army[70] and arrested George McIntosh, Gwinnett moved on to their brother, Gen. Lachlan McIntosh, the highest-ranking Continental Army officer based in

Georgia. In the days and weeks before a military mission of this magnitude, Gwinnett should have wanted as many experienced officers as he could get — and he would have been wise to seek their input — but he was intent on getting rid of the man who had twice received military positions that he sought.

As the start of the mission drew near, Gwinnett undermined McIntosh by ignoring him and communicating only with the colonels who reported to him and with McIntosh's superior officer, Gen. Robert Howe, the commander of the Continental Army in Georgia and South Carolina. Gwinnett went so far as to ask Howe to transfer McIntosh out of Georgia,[71] but he admitted he had no legitimate charge against him, so Howe refused.[72] Howe, who thought Gwinnett's plan to attack St. Augustine couldn't succeed, also turned down his repeated requests for troops under Howe's command. He "came, he saw, and left us in our low Estate," Gwinnett wrote to John Hancock about Howe's lack of support.[73]

Hancock was aware of the pressure on South Carolina and Georgia to protect their citizens from attacks. He had written as early as March of 1776, "The Situation of the Middle and Southern Colonies hath engaged the Attention of Congress. …there is Reason to think the Force of our Enemies will be directed against the Colonies in the Southern Department."[74] And later that year he wrote a letter to Georgia's leaders, exhorting them to do everything in their power to stop the British from re-colonizing Georgia.[75]

Knowing of Hancock's interest in Georgia's security, Gwinnett complained to him about Howe's lack of cooperation,[76] not seeming to care that Howe's chronically understaffed command couldn't spare troops for his mission. As Gwinnett made clear, Howe and his soldiers left Georgia for South Carolina just weeks before he planned to attack St. Augustine.

Gwinnett's decision to ignore McIntosh caused some officers and soldiers in McIntosh's command to question McIntosh's authority. In a letter written a couple of months later, McIntosh opined that Gwinnett was disappointed that Congress didn't make him a brigadier general and when he became the interim governor and commander-in-chief, he made it his mission to undermine McIntosh's authority. Gwinnett, McIntosh wrote, lost "sight of everything else, than (sic) to render the army obnoxious, & Create the utmost Confusion & disorder in it."[77]

Gwinnett knew the McIntoshes didn't like or respect him, and his vendetta against them at the very least created a distraction in Georgia at a time when its civilian and military leaders were struggling to protect the colony against British-planned attacks from Florida. Leaders in other states often humbled themselves, showed grace and compromised in the interest of advancing the American independence movement. Gwinnett observed that first hand when he served in Congress in the spring and summer of 1776. Founding Fathers, such as Robert Morris of Pennsylvania and Edward Rutledge of South Carolina, said as much when they signed the Declaration of Independence even though they thought the Continental Army and state militias were unprepared in 1776 to take on the powerful British army.

Not Gwinnett.

"When he (Gwinnett) assumed the reins of government, he permitted not his anger to slumber," according to McCall, the Georgia historian. What's more, Gwinnett, as interim commander-in-chief, meddled in military matters, such as court martialing, that were tradition-ally left for McIntosh and other military leaders.[78]

> "...*The exercise of the powers assumed by Gwinnett, over the army, produced the contempt and disrespect of some of the inferior officers toward the general, and destroyed the basis of military discipline. When any of the officers were charged with offences, civil or military, Gwinnett claimed the right of trying the offenders before the executive council. If an officer was ordered on command or detachment, he was selected by, and received his orders from the president and council. ...he intervened in Army matters to such*

an extent that he seriously impaired the discipline of the troops, and incited among the officers a spirit of insubordination toward the commanding general (McIntosh). Gwinnett ...being of imperious will and implacable in his hate, was firmly resolved to supplant Gen. McIntosh and subject him, if possible, to humiliation and further disgrace."

As Gwinnett's power increased, George Walton, who had served with him in the Second Continental Congress, warned others about him.[79]

"This great Hero that has set our Country in a flame cannot last long & no gentleman could have suffered long under accusations trumped up for time serving purposes," he wrote to Lachlan McIntosh. "I find that the Laws are taken out of the Judges (sic) hands and exercised by your dictator who I presume has suspended the Habeas Corpus Act as I find no writ was brought upon a certain occasion. I am treading upon delicate ground in my present situation. If I was at home I would speak my mind in the market place against this Lord of the earth."

In a follow-up letter to McIntosh, Walton continued to rail against Gwinnett:[80]

"I cannot readily dismiss him; not from any partiality to his virtues, but from an abhorrence of his vices. Mark him at the first moment of his arrival in that

Country & trace him (if it be possible to follow him thro the great variety of his shiftings & turnings) down to the present crisis; and you will find no criterion by which you might fix any character. A mere Proteus in principle, he makes virtue subservient to his vices; to cover the multitude of the latter he affects to be possessed of the former. With the loudest clamorings for Liberty he would ruin the Country whose cause he pretends to advocate; and with the warmest declaration of Friendship he would stab the most virtuous of Characters. Counteract one machination and he will have recourse to another.

"Disgrace him for discovered crimes, he will seek a palliation and founds a reestablishment in the delusions of Patriotism. Has he not deserted all parties with which he was ever known to be engaged? Has he ever professed a friendship (save one perhaps [Lyman Hall]) but to betray? ...This self elected Demaacque (demagogue) is dispised (sic) more or less every where. His election by his own vote is detested beyond measure. If he has not fascinated the senses of the whole people and has not the power of preserving the infatuation, he must, sooner or later atone for these things."

Walton's comment that the "flame cannot last long" — written to McIntosh, of all people — turned out to be prophetic.

* ◇ *

In 1777, after British nationalists and loyalists left Georgia, only about 33,000 people lived in the state,[81] but when Gwinnett planned the attack on St. Augustine, he didn't anticipate that it would be so difficult to recruit soldiers. McCall, the early Georgia historian, put it simply: "The province contained but few actual inhabitants."[82] Nearly half of those 33,000 were enslaved, and in 1777 the Georgia militia didn't arm enslaved men for fear of revolt. What's more, about half of the white people were women and children. That left a pool of 8,000 or so potential soldiers.

The fact that a mission to attack St. Augustine failed just one year earlier also must have made it more difficult to find Georgians willing to fight that same fight. But that didn't stop Gwinnett, whose effort matched his confidence. He recruited in his home parish of St. John, which had just been renamed Liberty County, and he enlisted others to help him. In March of 1777, he paid an army captain named Clement Nash a fee to round up soldiers,[83] but it's safe to say that Nash wasn't very successful. In the end, Gwinnett managed to assemble an army of only about 200 men, many of whom lived in Liberty and were willing to help out a hometown hero.

With no support from Gen. Howe, he found himself in the incredibly awkward position of having to ask Lachlan McIntosh for help.[84] This turn of events had to have given McIntosh great satisfaction, and he might have been tempted to turn down Gwinnett's request. But in a letter dated March 28 to Gwinnett, McIntosh, after noting that Gwinnett's initial plan included no input from "any Military Gentlemen," agreed to cooperate.

"I have the pleasure to inform you that the Continental Troops under my Command are always ready to march at the Shortest notice, & Asst & Co-operate with y[ou] in any measure that appears to hav[e a] probability of Success, or tends to prom[ote the] Interest of this or the United States."[85]

McIntosh's Continental Army troops and Gwinnett's Georgia militia soldiers gathered in Sunbury on April 14, 1777.[86] Gwinnett then called for a meeting to strategize, but McIntosh and his officers refused to attend.[87] McIntosh wrote that the meeting request "was out of his Line, quite improper for the (governor) of the State, & interfering with the particular province of the Officers of the Military, & more especially as there was few or no Militia to join them...."[88] The general said he would lead his troops and recommended that the militia's officers and soldiers join his men. Gwinnett, who had no military experience, countered that *he* should command all troops, continental and militia.[89] As governor, he had no authority over continental troops, but that didn't prevent him from asking for it. On April 17, McIntosh's contingent began marching to Florida[90] while Gwinnett and the Georgia militia remained in Sunbury. Gwinnett's critics could claim that he stayed put because he didn't want to risk his life on a mission that he should have known couldn't succeed.

The Georgia Council of Safety lost patience with Gwinnett and McIntosh and ordered them to report to Savannah. On April 22, McIntosh wrote that he was suspended, and Samuel Elbert, who had been promoted to colonel in the Continental Army, was ordered to lead the mission.[91] The mission predictably failed, and the Assembly began an investigation to learn why it went so wrong. Elbert, who later would become a general and governor of Georgia, was able to lead many soldiers back to Savannah, where Georgia's political leaders would decide who was more at fault for the failure — Gwinnett or McIntosh.

Before the inquisition occurred, the Assembly met on May 8, 1777, to elect a governor and an executive council. With the radical faction in the majority, Gwinnett had to like his chances to remove *interim* from his title. However, most of the lawmakers, including many radicals, apparently were not impressed with his two months on the job, and "by a large majority," they chose John Adam Treutlen from the radical political faction to be Georgia's third governor.[92]

Born Hans Adam Treutlen, he and his family arrived in Georgia from southern Germany in 1746 as indentured servants.[93] Treutlen was 12 at the time, and his family was beholden to a man who lived 10 miles south of Savannah. A minister who met Treutlen was impressed with him and enrolled him in school, where he did very well. After his schooling ended, he began acquiring land and became a planter and a merchant.[94] Like Gwinnett, Treutlen's accumulation of land led to his appointment to justice of the peace, and that led to his election to the Commons House of Assembly. He also served as commissioner and surveyor of roads.[95] Unlike Gwinnett, Treutlen became a successful businessman and earned the respect of his fellow lawmakers during his time as a legislator. Most Germans who settled in Georgia, Treutlen included, trusted American leaders more than British authorities, and they tended to align themselves with the radical political faction, which was more vocal in opposing British occupation.

Henry Muhlenberg, an 18th-century German-born clergyman who is considered the patriarch of the Lutheran church in the United States, knew of Treutlen, a lay leader in the church. He called Treutlen a man of "native intelligence" who replied "coolly and laconically" under pressure from his political opponents.[96] Treutlen was well suited, Muhlenberg said, for the difficult task of leading the new state during a time of stark political divisions and frequent attacks from the British, their sympathizers and Native Americans.

According to McCall, Treutlen won the gubernatorial election by "a handsome margin," and Gwinnett's disappointment was "grievous."[97] The newly elected Executive Council was split between conservatives and radicals, with radicals holding a slim majority.

The Assembly met again on May 15 to hear from Gwinnett and McIntosh about why the Florida mission that it had approved failed so miserably. By this point, the two had become "inveterate enemies."[98] In the days before the hearing, McIntosh submitted a letter that contained what he considered "a plain candid" account of what happened.[99] "Since I was concerned or had any knowledge of an Expedition first formed to gratify the dangerous Ambitions of this Man (Gwinnett), & which distressed this Country so much & so amazing an Expence, & tho' not well equipt for want of knowledge for him at last."[100] McIntosh also bristled at what he considered Gwinnett's interference in military matters. This was not the first time McIntosh complained about this. He once asked the like-minded George Washington "how far we are under the control of the Provincial Congress, & c., of this or any other Province where we are upon duty."[101]

At the hearing, Gwinnett blamed McIntosh, arguing that the Continental troops underperformed and McIntosh did not properly support him. McIntosh countered that Gwinnett interfered with military operations and only communicated with him until after he realized he needed more soldiers and could not persuade Gen. Howe to provide them. Civilian leaders in America in the 18th century, including those in Georgia, generally supported civilian oversight of the military. In the end, the Assembly frowned on McIntosh's refusal to discuss strategy with Gwinnett in Sunbury and sided with Gwinnett.

The decision momentarily unhinged the usually composed McIntosh — and with Gwinnett now a *former* governor — he felt emboldened to call Gwinnett "a scoundrel and a lying rascal" in the presence of many members of the Assembly. Lyman Hall later wrote that he did not hear the insult,[102] but others did.

The Assembly's leaders could have suggested that McIntosh apologize,[103] and that might have prevented what happened next. But there is no record that anyone did that, leading to speculation that Gwinnett lost the respect and support of Georgia's leaders during his two-month stint as interim governor and commander-in-chief. Perhaps they thought Gwinnett's poorly executed plan to attack St. Augustine disqualified him from serving as governor. Perhaps George Walton wasn't the only one who thought Gwinnett was power hungry and needed to be put in his place. Perhaps some of them even agreed that Gwinnett really was a scoundrel and a lying rascal.

Whatever their opinions were, McIntosh did not feel the need to apologize, or if he did, he decided to wait.

Gwinnett, meanwhile, stewed over the insult. *A scoundrel? A lying rascal?* He made his own decision that day about how to resolve the situation. It started with a letter.

11
A Duel to the Death

Benjamin Franklin scoffed at duels and duelists, as he made clear to a friend:[1]

"It is astonishing that the murderous practice of Duelling should continue so long in vogue. Formerly when Duels were used to determine Lawsuits from an opinion that Providence would in every Instance favour Truth and Right with Victory, they were more excusable. At present they decide nothing. A man says something which another tells him is a Lie. They fight, but whichever is killed, the point in question remains unsettled.

"To this purpose they have a pleasant little Story here: A Gentleman in a Coffee house desired another to sit farther from him.—Why so?—Because, Sir, you stink.— That is an Affront and you must fight me.— I will fight you if you insist upon it: But I do not see how that will mend the Matter. For if you kill me I shall stink too. And if I kill you, you will stink, if possible, worse than you do at present. How can such miserable Sinners as we are, entertain so much pride as to conceit that every Offence against our imagined Honor merits Death! These petty princes in their own opinion would call that Sovereign a Tyrant, who should put one of them to death for a little uncivil Language, tho' pointed at his sacred Person. Yet every one of them makes himself Judge in his own Cause, condemns the Offender without a Jury, and undertakes himself to be the Executioner."

Petty or not, nothing else made sense to Button Gwinnett. If Lachlan McIntosh wouldn't publicly apologize for calling him "a scoundrel and a lying rascal" in the presence of Georgia's leaders, then McIntosh should face the barrel of a dueling pistol. It was as simple as that.

Gwinnett said as much in a letter that George Wells, his political ally, delivered to McIntosh at his house on St. James Square in Savannah "late on the evening of May 15, 1777."[2] Wells waited while McIntosh read Gwinnett's request to meet just before sunrise the next day in a pasture at one of the plantations owned by former Gov. James Wright,[3] about a mile east of McIntosh's house.

After McIntosh read it, he joked to Wells that he would prefer to meet at a more reasonable hour, but if that's what Gwinnett wanted, he would be there. And he would bring the pistols.[4]

The morning of May 16 was hot,[5] and McIntosh arrived before Gwinnett, who was not known for his punctuality. Each man was accompanied by a "second," an ally who would make sure rules were clearly communicated, agreed upon and followed. Gwinnett's second was Wells, who not even three years later would serve for a mere 11 days as Georgia's governor, his term cut short after dueling against James Jackson, a fiery British-born politician who became governor from 1798 to 1801, then quit to serve in the U.S. Senate. McIntosh's second was Joseph Habersham, the same man who had arrested Gov. Wright a year earlier in the governor's residence and rose to the rank of lieutenant colonel in the Georgia militia. Based largely on his arrest of Gov, Wright, President George Washington named Habersham the third-ever postmaster general of the United States in 1795, a job he kept until Thomas Jefferson became president in 1801.

Lyman Hall also attended the duel[6], not in the capacity of a doctor but to support his friend, Gwinnett. A handful of others, presumably those who got word of the duel, watched from a distance. McIntosh and Gwinnett agreed to move to block their view. Even with only five men present, the duel was documented as thoroughly as any event in Gwinnett's life. There wasn't a lot of chit-chat. After all, Gwinnett and McIntosh had no desire to be in each other's presence and avoided any conversation "but the business on hand."[7]

During the first half of the 18th century, men often fought duels with swords, but by 1777, dueling pistols, which came in pairs and fired lead balls, were the weapon of choice. "After politely saluting each other," McIntosh and Gwinnett inspected the pistols and confirmed that each was loaded with "a single Ball."[8]

Georgia was something of a hotbed for dueling during the latter third of the 18th century, but in 1777 there was no established distance for duelists to stand apart from each other, as there was by 1838, when 10 to 20 paces was the recommended distance.[9] The seconds asked the duelists how far apart they would like to stand while shooting, and Gwinnett said, "Whatever distance the general pleases."[10] McIntosh suggested a mere eight to 10 feet. Without waiting for Gwinnett to answer, Habersham suggested four paces, the equivalent of 10 to 12 feet, and Gwinnett and Wells agreed.[11]

Then there was the matter of what *type* of duel Gwinnett and McIntosh preferred. The two most common were the British and the French.[12] The French duel — the kind often recreated in movies — required the duelists to stand back-to-back and walk the agreed-upon number of paces before spinning around and firing. In a British duel, the men stood at the agreed-upon distance and waited to fire their pistols when they received a signal. (In *War and Peace*, Leo Tolstoy added to the drama by having his duelists walk toward each other as they fired their pistols.)

When it was suggested that Gwinnett and McIntosh stand back-to-back and walk the four paces before firing, McIntosh said he preferred standing face to face.

"By all means, let us see what we are all about," he said.[13] Like most men of his day, Gwinnett owned rifles and presumably knew how to fire them, but McIntosh, a military officer, had been firing guns since he was a boy, and now he suggested that the two men stare each other down before firing. Despite any reservations Gwinnett might have had, he and Wells again agreed to the request.[14]

When the signal was given, the men fired at the same time. A bullet struck Gwinnett just above the left knee, causing him to fall and announce, "My thigh is broken."[15] (It wasn't.) McIntosh, who was shot "through the thick of the thigh," remained standing and almost immediately afterward asked Gwinnett if he wanted to fire another shot. Gwinnett said he would if someone would help him to his feet,[16] but Wells and Habersham thought enough damage had been done, and they objected, putting an end to the duel.

McIntosh then limped over to Gwinnett, and they shook hands and went their separate ways in search of medical treatment. The seconds reported that McIntosh and Gwinnett "behav'd like Gentlemen & men of honor" before, during and after the duel.[17]

The work of their doctors was not documented. Doctors in 18th-century America would have offered their patients several swallows of hard cider or rum to try to distract them from the pain. Then the doctors would try to locate the lead ball, first by poking their index fingers into the wound.[18] If the bullet was lodged deeper than finger length, they would use a metal probe to poke around for something hard that wasn't a bone.[19] After locating the bullet, they would jam a forceps, like tweezers with a long handle, into the wound to try to remove the lead ball. If that didn't work, they would use a bullet extractor, an 18th-century surgical instrument with a screw at one end. Lead is a relatively soft metal, so the doctors would try to pierce the lead ball with the screw end of the extractor and then twist it, like a corkscrew, into the ball.[20]

With the screw deep inside the lead ball, it could be pulled out, like a cork yanked from the neck of a wine bottle. All of this would occur without anesthesia. To dress the wound, the doctors would either suture it closed with linen thread, or pack it with wool or lint, and as it healed, replace the bloody cloth with clean cloth.[21]

McIntosh recovered from his wound. As for Gwinnett, Lyman Hall wrote, "Mr. Gwinnett was bro't in, the weather, Extrem (sic) Hot — a Mortification came on — he languished from that (Friday) Morning till Monday Morning following, & expired."[22]

He died on May 19, 1777, from the "mortification," a gangrene infection. At 42, he was the second of the 56 signers of the Declaration of Independence to die (after John Morton of Pennsylvania), and the second youngest (after Thomas Lynch Jr. of South Carolina).

In 1777, the state's only newspaper, the *Georgia Gazette*, was not publishing, but newspapers in South Carolina, Pennsylvania, Connecticut and Massachusetts each published two- or three-sentence stories about the duel during the next two months. On May 26, 1777, the *South Carolina Gazette*, the first newspaper to report on the duel, stated that it was the result of "an unhappy dispute," and inaccurately reported, "The General, we hear, lay dangerously ill."[23]

In Georgia, there was no need for a newspaper to report what occurred. Word of the duel and Gwinnett's death spread quickly, and there was no shortage of finger-pointing. Everyone who played a role — McIntosh, Habersham, Wells and James Houstoun, the doctor who treated Gwinnett — were blamed for contributing to Gwinnett's death.

McIntosh eventually realized that killing a former governor, even if he was just a former *interim* governor, could have unwelcome repercussions for him, so he took affidavits from Habersham and Wells to document the event.

Days later, he sent the affidavits and a letter that provided his side of the story to the Army's Judge Advocate General Col. John Lawrence, who prosecuted many of the most important military trials during the Revolutionary War. By this point, McIntosh had two weeks to think about the duel and its immediate aftermath.[24]

In the rambling letter, which he began writing on May 30, McIntosh explained that his relationship with Gwinnett fell apart after Gwinnett didn't get the brigadier general position. He described Gwinnett as "unfortunate" and blamed his death on Gwinnett's doctor, James Houstoun. McIntosh wrote that he was the duel's second victim. He claimed his enemies took advantage of his "declar'd aversion from principle to private Dueling," and he explained that he was in a no-win situation: If he accepted the duel and injured or killed Gwinnett, he would be seen as taking advantage of Gwinnett, and if he declined the duel, he would be viewed as "unworthy ...to hold his (military) Commission." He wanted Lawrence to know that Gwinnett's widow, Ann, often asked him how he was feeling and didn't blame him for her husband's death. He added in a P.S., dated June 3, that she wanted Dr. Houstoun, "who seems to be generally blam'd for the death of her husband," prosecuted.

McIntosh's self-serving letter raises a lot of questions: Why does a man with a self-proclaimed aversion to dueling own dueling pistols? Why would someone who insulted his adversary in front of the state's political leaders claim to be an innocent victim of "personal abuse?" During a time when doctors often struggled to treat wounds that would be considered non-life threatening in later centuries, why would McIntosh be so quick to shift the blame to the doctor for not effectively treating a wound that he caused? Why would he think Lawrence would believe that? And what to make of his statements about Ann Gwinnett?

If McIntosh accurately reported what she told him, her opinion of him changed drastically soon afterward. On August 1, she wrote to Second Continental Congress President John Hancock, asking him to "take proper notice" of McIntosh and Habersham and strip them of their military commissions.[25] At a time when America needed all of the military officers it could get, that wasn't going to happen. She also described the duel's seconds, Habersham and Wells, as "cruel and bloodthirsty" for allowing her husband and McIntosh to shoot at each other at such a short distance.[26] She neglected to share with Hancock — if she was aware — that Habersham and Wells ended the duel by refusing to allow McIntosh and her husband to fire a second shot at each other, though they were both ready and willing.

It's reasonable to assume that McIntosh never intended to kill Gwinnett. McIntosh, who grew up in a Scottish clan that came to America to protect Georgians from Florida-based Spaniards, was a military cadet as a teenager and had a lifetime of experience with guns. At a distance of only about 12 feet, he could have shot Gwinnett in the torso or the head if he wanted to kill him, but the lead ball entered Gwinnett's thigh. In their affidavits, the seconds, Wells and Habersham, didn't say there was an agreement that Gwinnett and McIntosh would aim below the belt to reduce the likelihood of someone dying. And in McIntosh's lengthy letter to Col. Lawrence, he could have claimed that he shot Gwinnett in the leg because he never intended to kill him, but he didn't make that claim — and never did afterward.

Intentional or not, Gwinnett's death devastated Lyman Hall, whose grief turned to anger when the authorities initially declined to charge McIntosh with murder. Hall and Wells accused the local judges of neglect of duty, and only then did an investigation begin. It led to an arrest and a trial, but few people, including Ann Gwinnett,[27] thought McIntosh would be convicted. Not only did her husband request the duel, but there was the widespread belief in the 18th century that duels, while viewed as unsavory, were a legitimate and lawful way for consensual males to settle their disputes. In short, that was how gentlemen sometimes handled their disagreements back then, and whatever consequences they suffered should be confined to the damage done by the lead balls. This duel was different because it occurred during a time of extreme partisanship in Georgia, but the rule of law ignored it, and McIntosh was acquitted.

Hall, meanwhile, began trying to shape Gwinnett's legacy, describing him as a hero and a patriot. In a letter he started writing on the day of the duel to fellow Congressman Roger Sherman of Connecticut, he heaped praise on his friend. "Gwinnett is, if possible, a whig to excess." (Not to be confused with the 19th-century Whig Party, *whig* was used interchangeably with patriot, originating from the British Whigs, who opposed total sovereignty.[28])

Hall, who finished the letter after Gwinnett's death, wrote, "O, Liberty! Why do you suffer so many of your faithful sons, your warmest votaries, to fall at your shrine! Alas my friend! My friend!!"[29]

Three decades later, Hugh McCall, Georgia's first historian, portrayed Gwinnett as power hungry, emotional and undisciplined:

"Gwinnett appears to have been a man of considerable literary talents, but hasty in his decisions, overbearing in his temper, and wild and excentric (sic) in his plans. "...he was ambitious, grasping of power, strong in his prejudices, intolerant of opposition, and violent in his hate. Rising like a meteor, he shot athwart, the zenith of the young commonwealth, concentrating the gaze of all, and in a short moment was seen no more."

Except for Gwinnett's role in overseeing the creation of Georgia's first constitution, 19th-century Georgia historian Charles Jones also struggled to compliment him. He wrote, "we have no monument of his literary or public effort. He wrote and spoke but seldom."

The historical record makes this much clear: During the final 10 months of Gwinnett's life, he proved himself to be selfish, ambitious and unwilling to compromise. Serving in Congress was only a consolation prize for the man who wanted a job with a salary: the colonel's position in the Georgia militia. He abandoned his congressional duties as soon as he could to return to Georgia and wrongly take credit for convincing Congress to appropriate money for Georgia's defense. His brief time as a congressional delegate in Philadelphia led to political power in Georgia, and he used it to ruin — or try to ruin — the careers of the three McIntosh brothers, who were leaders in Georgia during a time when the state needed all the leaders it could get. As interim governor, his plan to attack the British in Florida was ill-conceived and doomed from the start. Not only that, but Gwinnett's actions as governor widened the political division between radicals and conservatives, contributing to instability when unity and compromise would have better served the fledgling, embattled and isolated state. Archibald Bulloch realized that partisanship wouldn't benefit Georgia as it transitioned from a colony to a state, and he strayed from it as much as possible.

As it turned out, Gwinnett's death also further divided Georgia's leaders.

In the summer after Gwinnett died, John Wereat, a member of the conservative faction in Georgia, said Gwinnett and his allies in the so-called "Liberty Society" labelled conservatives and others with whom they disagreed politically "with the hateful name of Torey [sic], . . ."[30]

"The business of this Cabal as far as I am capable of Judgeing (sic) seems to be principally intended to poison the minds of the people throughout the State, & to set them at enmity, with every Man who is not of their party," Wereat wrote. "They or the leaders of them seem to be void of every sentiment of honour, & truth is a stranger to their proceedings, they bellow Liberty, but take every method in their power, to deprive the best part of the community of even the Shadow of it. Those wretches appear to me to have a manifest intention to destroy the reputation of their neighbors; in order to raise themselves fortunes, & political fame upon the ruins of the real Friends of their Country, and the American Cause."

Around the time Wereat wrote that, Lachlan McIntosh's allies tried to shield him from backlash as radicals sought to tarnish his reputation and even banish him from the state. It didn't help that he was linked with his youngest brother, George, who was charged with treason for allegedly being part of a group that sold rice to the British army in Florida. John Hancock said a letter intercepted from Patrick Tonyn, Florida's royal governor, incriminated McIntosh.[31] In it, Tonyn described George McIntosh as "a loyal attachment to the King and Constitution. He would, my Lord, be in a dangerous situation was this known."

George McIntosh was so well connected in Georgia that the state's leaders, including its new governor, Adam Treutlen, questioned whether the state's judges could objectively rule in the case. Treutlen asked John Hancock if Congress would decide McIntosh's guilt or innocence.[32] McIntosh didn't help his cause by disobeying an order to report under guard to Congress. He went missing, and rumors spread that he was on the run, hiding somewhere in coastal Georgia. To make matters worse for Lachlan McIntosh, Treutlen suspected that he was helping George avoid capture.

While accusations against Lachlan and George McIntosh circulated throughout the state, Lachlan complained to his political ally George Walton about his family's enemies. His brother George, Lachlan wrote, "is now hunted through the woods and swamps like a partridge in Liberty County and the most respectable characters in the State who have spirit to asert (sic) his innocence is looked upon almost as bad."[33]

Treutlen dispatched a military party to search for George McIntosh, who was found in North Carolina, making his way on the long journey north to Philadelphia to face Congress' judgment. A guard escorted him the rest of the way, carrying with him a thick stack of correspondence that Treutlen believed incriminated McIntosh and showed that the most patriotic Georgians viewed him as a trai-tor. Congress spent much of October 4, 1777, dis-cussing what to do with him.[34] Fortunately for him, the McIntoshes had allies in Congress, most notably George Walton and South Carolina delegate Henry Laurens, Lachlan's longtime mentor and business partner. Congress assigned a committee of three delegates — John Adams and two others — to make a recommendation, and it concluded there was not enough evidence to convict George McIntosh, so he was released. However, in the Georgia court of public opinion, he was guilty of treason, and Georgians who thought otherwise were deemed disloyal to America.

Even Laurens had his doubts, saying that at the least George had exercised poor judgment.[35]

This good news for George McIntosh didn't release Lachlan McIntosh from the miserable limbo in which he found himself in his home state. Lachlan may have been acquitted of Gwinnett's murder, but the judge's ruling didn't sway the opinions of many influential Georgians, including the new governor and members of the Assembly's Executive Council. This was not a position in which anyone — let alone a high-ranking military officer — would like to find himself.

Lyman Hall was one of those who believed the worst of Lachlan McIntosh, and Hall was not done with him. He and Joseph Wood, a Pennsylvanian who recently moved to Liberty County and became a planter and a politician, led an effort to have McIntosh's military commission stripped. They organized a petition that 574 like-minded Georgians signed. Banishing him from the state would be "a more deadly stroke to Toryism in this State than any other can be," according to the language on the petition from rural Wilkes County.

McIntosh was beside himself, and he dashed off another letter to George Walton. "Wood & Co, surely must think if they could remove me out of there (sic) way they could carry on everything at pleasure. I never spoke twenty times in my life to that man

(Wood). Yet he & his party are indefatigable in their research for slander against me."[36]

The petitions organized by Hall and Wood — and a separate one from the Commons House of Assembly — were presented to Congress, which again was tasked with cleaning up one of Georgia's messes. But before Congress could do anything, Walton intervened, asking George Washington if transferring McIntosh under his command would "derange the Army. ... He is a man of sense and judgment, with a great experience of the world; and, in point of bravery, he is fit to fight under the banners of General Washington." Washington replied that he was "very agreeable" to the transfer, so Lachlan McIntosh — now a man without a state — joined him at Valley Forge, in Pennsylvania.[37] Congress could move on to more pressing matters.

For Lyman Hall, 1777 was shaping up to be a terrible year. His long-time friend lost his bid for governor and was killed in a duel. The man who had shot him had gotten away with murder, as far as Hall was concerned, and was allowed to remain in the military, under George Washington's command, no less. And now Hall had to focus on the nearly impossible job of settling Button Gwinnett's debt-ridden estate.

1778 wouldn't be much better for Hall. Neither would 1779, 1780 or 1781.

12

A Tangled Mess, Part 2

Button Gwinnett wrote his first and only will on March 15, 1777, two months and a few days before he died. Archibald Bulloch, Georgia's first American-born governor, had very recently dropped dead, and Gwinnett may have wanted to make his wishes known in case his end-time was also closer than he hoped. He also may have prepared his will when he did because he was directed to deal with British threats to Georgia's southern border, and as interim commander-in-chief, he may have envisioned a potentially dangerous role for himself on the battlefield. Or his wife, Ann, who had written her first will seven years earlier, may have convinced him that he should finally get around to writing his.

Whatever the reason, he decided this was the right time to prepare his will, which he kept relatively succinct:

Savannah, March 15, 1777

I'm sound in Body and Mind for which I am
under the highest obligations to the Supreme being;
How long I shall remain so God only knoweth;
I therefore dispose of my property both real and
personal in the following manner:

First let all my just debts be discharged then one half
of my real and personal estates remaining be divided
between my wife and daughter in equal shares.
The other half of my estates both real and personal
shall belong to and apertain (sic) unto the Rev. Mr.
Thomas Bosomworth his heirs and assigns for ever,
the said Thos Bosomworth first giving
as rec(eip)t in full of all other demands.

This is my last Will and Testament and I hereby revoke
all other wills and Codicils.
The above is only intended to convey my estate in America.
I hereby Appoint Thos Savage and Lyman Hall Esquires
as executors to this my last will and Testament.

Button Gwinnett

There is no reason to believe he had assets anywhere but in America, but he clearly wanted to leave that impression. The will, which was admitted to probate on May 30, 1777,[1] included this key phrase: "First let all my just debts be discharged." This would prove much easier said than done. Gwinnett's friend Thomas Savage III, a wealthy, Bermuda-born merchant who lived most of his life in Charleston, S.C., realized that and decided he wanted no part of the job. He waived his right to serve as co-executor, leaving Lyman Hall to do the work himself.[2]

As his friend, mentor and confidante, Hall would have known a lot about Gwinnett's financial problems and his many creditors. Satisfying all of Gwinnett's creditors would be akin to trying to feed 5,000 people with five small loaves and two small fish. Hall wasn't a miracle worker, just a hard worker. He knew he would need to sell all of Gwinnett's assets to repay Gwinnett's creditors, and then hope something would be left over for Ann and Elizabeth, his friend's widow and teenage daughter.

He got right to it. His work began shortly after Gwinnett died on May 19, 1777. An estate document, filed in Chatham County court, listed debts of £4,928, five shillings and five and a quarter pence[3] — about $1.35 million today. This was all the debt Hall knew about at the time. Unfortunately for him, there would be much more to discover.

Hall needed to begin selling Gwinnett's possessions, so he ordered an inventory of his belongings. Gwinnett no longer owned the land where his plantation was located, nor did he own the house and barns on the land. He owned the items in the house and the barns, but the inventory made it clear that Gwinnett's most valuable assets were enslaved people.

Of his 61 enslaved people, 19 were men, 12 were women, and 30 were children. The inventory listed their names — seven children were unnamed by Gwinnett — their race, and their appraised values (in British pounds):[4]

A Mulatto Wench named Moll	120	A Negro Boy named Stafford	80
A Negro Girl named Charlotte	60	Negro Fellow Cato	90
Negro Fellow Will	80	Boy, by name, Scipio	55
Negro Fellow John	85	Boy, by name, Friday	45
Negro Fellow Quako	90	Boy, by name, Jack	55
Negro Fellow Frank	80	Boy, by name, Frank	50
Negro Fellow Sam	45	Boy, by name, Lazarus	45
Negro Fellow Fyon	50	Boy, by name, Mingo	50
Negro Fellow Ceasar	85	Boy, by name, Bijou	40
Negro Fellow Joe	85	Boy, by name, Wednesday	50
Negro Fellow Jemmy	75	Boy, by name, Paul	50
Negro Fellow Start	80	Boy, by name, Dick	50
Negro Fellow Ned	50	Boy, by name, Tom	70

Negro Fellow Jack	40	Boy, by name, Prince	50
Negro Fellow Zingo	80	Boy, by name, Monday	50
Negro Fellow Bob	50	Mulatto, by name, Jack	30
Negro Fellow George	55	Mulatto, by name, Bacon	30
Negro Fellow Congo	55	Wench, Sylvia & 2 Children	100
Boy, by name, Captain	60	Wench, Bettey & Son	80
Boy, by name, Tuesday	55	Wench, Lora & Son	75
Boy, by name, Daniel	55	Wench, Fortymore & Child	80
Boy, by name, Job	50	Wench, Celia	65
Boy, by name, Cupit	50	Wench, Phillis	50
Boy, by name, Pansau	50	Wench, Molley & Child	75
Wench, Joanna & Child	65	Wench, Bella	55
Wench, Bela	60	Girl, Fanny	50
Wench, Cumb	55	Girl, Caroline	35

A review of the entire inventory makes it clear how much enslaved people were valued financially in 18th-century Georgia. The appraisers valued 50 sheep at £62 — about half as much as the bi-racial woman named Moll, who clearly was a valued contributor to the plantation.[5]

Ann Gwinnett, who by this time had lived on St. Catherines for several years, almost certainly provided information to help the appraisers value the enslaved people and her husband's other belongings. She would have known the age and abilities and skills of the enslaved people and the quality of each possession. Much of the rest of the non-human assets in the inventory included furniture and other household items, many of which the appraisers described as old.[6] There was one mahogany table, two tea tables, two old desks, five old chairs, two old chests, 16 old pictures, 120 quart bottles, eight pairs of sheets, three new "super fine" table cloths, five "half worn Damask" napkins, one old feather bed, 10 old blankets, 14 old knives and forks, four silver teaspoons, two mustard pots, two glass candlesticks, and much more.[7]

The inventory included weapons: one small sword, one pair of pistols and holsters, and one brass rifle. As expected on a plantation, there was no shortage of tools: six whipsaws, a chest of carpenter's tools, four wedges, three hoes and an ax, among many others. And many books: one Jacobs Law Dictionary, two "family" dictionaries, one "general" dictionary, one on horseshoeing and husbandry, one on "life, death and immortality," two on agriculture, two bibles, one spelling book, one grammar book, a book of poetry called *The Seasons* by the Scottish poet and playwright James Thomson, and a few others.[8]

All of these possessions and everything else in the inventory had a total value of £4,175 and four shillings, according to the appraisers[9] — about $1.15 million in 1777. His known debt at the time exceeded his assets by £753 (about $207,000), but could have ended up being more than that if his possessions sold for less than their appraised value. If there was anything else on the property, the appraisers deemed that it had no value and was left there for someone to gather and burn unless it had sentimental value to Ann Gwinnett.

The first sale of Gwinnett's non-human possessions occurred on August 14, 1777, in Sunbury, his home away from home in Georgia.[10] At least a couple of Gwinnett's creditors attended the sale. Thomas Bosomworth bought a flock of 50 sheep, and Levi Sheftall purchased Gwinnett's schooner called *Beggar's Benison,*[11] which Gwinnett had used to go to and from St. Catherines and Sunbury, sometimes with crops. Lyman Hall bought a few of his friend's books.[12] The sale raised about £4,175, making it clear that many buyers were willing to pay well over the appraised value. That was great news for Ann Gwinnett, who hoped she and her daughter would inherit something from her husband's estate. It looked at the time that she would get her wish.

Proceeds from the sale allowed Hall to pay a debt owed to the Second Continental Congress for £2,513, 19 shillings and three pence,[13] which was given to John Wereat, the state's liaison to Congress and a future governor of Georgia. As a member of its Secret Committee, Congress had entrusted Gwinnett with $20,000 in 1776 to buy arms and ammunition from the West Indies to protect Georgians from hostile Native Americans.[14] In the months after Congress allocated that money, George Walton, a fellow signer of the Declaration of Independence, said he wrote to then-Gov. Archibald Bulloch, questioning whether Gwinnett was actually using the money for its intended purpose.[15] Walton was under the impression that Bulloch forwarded his letter to the Assembly when Gwinnett was the speaker, but the letter never surfaced, infuriating Walton. "The iniquity of the proceeding," Walton wrote, "speaks so loudly that it calls for vengeance."[16]

In 1776 and 1777, Gwinnett owed a lot of money to a lot of people, and given his financial pressures, it would be reasonable to assume he used at least some of Congress' money to repay his debts. This money was almost certainly gossiped about. Ann Gwinnett, Button's wife, mentioned "the Matter about the Continental Money" in a letter she wrote in the summer of 1777 to Second Continental Congress President John Hancock, but she claimed to know nothing about it.[17] No records exist that show Gwinnett bought any firearms and ammunition with the funds, so no one will ever know what he did with it. Hall only knew what Gwinnett's bookkeeping records showed at the time of his death: Gwinnett hadn't used the equivalent of £2,513 of Congress' money, slightly more than half of what Congress allocated.

Gwinnett's records also showed that he had been repaying his £7,182 debt to John Neufville, the wealthy South Carolina merchant who lent him money in 1774. With some of the proceeds from the August 14, 1777, sale, Hall paid Neufville the balance of what Gwinnett still owed him: £1,960, 15 shillings and 11 and a quarter pence.[18]

Three months after the Sunbury sale, 18 of Gwinnett's 61 slaves were sold at a public auction in Savannah to repay additional creditors.[19] About six months later, in April of 1778, another sale of Gwinnett's things in Sunbury attracted Ann Gwinnett, who bought many household items that she would need for her new residence in Charleston, S.C., where her teenage daughter, Betsy, lived at the time. While at the auction, Ann almost certainly spoke with Hall about his progress in settling her husband's estate. She also would have told him about her needs as she planned her move to Charleston. In July, Hall bought her a horse and gave her £50, an amount that disappointed her.[20] Tom, the most highly appraised enslaved boy owned by her husband, accompanied her to Charleston. He was her most valuable possession.

Sometime around the time that the British returned to re-colonize Georgia on December 29, 1778, the remainder of Gwinnett's slaves were moved for safekeeping from St. Catherines Island, further inland, to Hall's plantation in Liberty County. They were moved again a few months later to Charleston before the British torched the buildings on Hall's plantation and his house in Sunbury in 1779. While in Charleston, Hall bought this advertisement in the *South Carolina Gazette*:

"The Sale of the THIRTY SLAVES belonging to the Estate of Button Gwinnett, Esq; is unavoidably postponed until Wednesday April 21, at which time they will be sold, as advertised, without reserve, at Mr. Strickland's."

The planters and others who bought these enslaved people paid a total of £1,050 and 11 shillings — or about £35 each — much less than their appraised value on Gwinnett's estate inventory. At that auction, Hall spent £66 on alcohol, which was served to the attendees, as was the custom. No doubt Ann Gwinnett, who lived in Charleston at the time and may have attended the auction, would have appreciated an additional £66 from her husband's estate, but it wasn't to be.[21]

Not long after that auction, Hall, hoping to stay ahead of British soldiers who wanted to jail him and other leaders of the independence movement, fled to his home state of Connecticut. He left South Carolina before the British won the Siege of Charleston in the spring of 1780. By then, Hall may have thought his work as Gwinnett's executor had ended, but these advertised estate sales and slave auctions led to more of Gwinnett's creditors coming forward to file claims against the estate.

One of the creditors was William Gibbons, a lawyer and one of the10 men who broke into the British powder magazine in 1775 in Savannah, the first recorded act of aggression against the British in Georgia. Another was Sarah Bosomworth — who, along with her husband Thomas, sold Gwinnett the lease to his plantation on St. Catherines Island. Thomas Bosomworth and his heirs were listed as heirs in Gwinnett's will, so the Bosomworths were in the same position as Ann Gwinnett, hoping the estate would end up with more assets than debts. But Sarah, who became a widow in 1782, likely assumed there would be nothing left after creditors recovered their money, so her lawsuit can be viewed as a last-ditch effort to get something for herself.

Hall learned of those and other lawsuits when he returned to Georgia later in 1782. That year he also reclaimed his land and restarted a life of public ser-vice. He served as governor for one year, in 1783. As governor, he advocated for the chartering of a state university, leading to the creation of the University of Georgia in 1785.[22] In January of 1784, as Hall's one-year term as governor was ending, he bought a public notice, which was published in the *Georgia Gazette* on January 22, 1784 — nearly seven years after Gwinnett died:

"Lyman Hall, executor of the estate of Button Gwinnett, Esq., deceased, gives the publick notice, that he is

desirous to settle the concerns of said estate as soon as may be, and requests all persons concerned to give in their demands without delay.

"He has a Waggon and Team for Sale."

After Hall's term as governor ended, he resumed his medical practice, but he was still dealing with Gwinnett's creditors. Hall heard from a merchant named Patrick Mackay, who had lent Gwinnett a pistol in the spring of 1776, when he was preparing to leave for his brief Second Continental Congress stint in Philadelphia. According to Mackay, Gwinnett owed him for a large cask of rum and six flasks of olive oil, as well as for the pistol that he claimed Gwinnett never returned. Mackay wanted three pounds for it.[23]

Hall, who had sold what was left of his 2,000-acre plantation in Liberty County, moved in 1790 to Burke County — just south of Augusta, near the South Carolina border — where he died on October 19 of that year.[24] He was 66, and he deserved the rest.

As hard as he tried, Hall never settled Gwinnett's estate. The *Georgia Gazette* published a series of notices that advertised tax collector sales on properties in Brunswick, McIntosh and Camden counties to satisfy taxes owed by Gwinnett's estate. Those notices, which reveal that Gwinnett owned more land than previously known, were published from May to August of 1802 — 25 years after Gwinnett died.

13

A Missing Button

Button Gwinnett has been described as mysterious because, unlike many other Founding Fathers, relatively little is known about him. He has no direct descendants who can shed light on him. If he wrote a diary, it has never surfaced, nor has any personal letter written to him from a friend or family member. He wrote only one personal letter that is known to exist, and it's only two sentences long. His signature is so rare that it was big news in 1956 when an archivist at Yale University Library found a receipt that Gwinnett wrote in 1762 to a sea captain who owed him money. When a receipt qualifies as "an exciting new find," as Yale described it back then, it's clear there isn't a lot on the record to chronicle a man's life.

This scarcity of information about Gwinnett has led to debates over everything from when he was born, when he arrived in America, what he looked like, and how he spent long periods of his life. However, no Gwinnett-related mystery has been more thoroughly investigated than where he was buried after his death on May 19, 1777.

Until 1848, no one seemed to have given it much thought. That year, a monument to the three Georgia signers of the Declaration of Independence — Gwinnett, Lyman Hall and George Walton — was dedicated in Augusta, a riverfront city at the border of South Carolina that today is best known for hosting the Masters golf tournament. Hall's and Walton's remains were re-interred under the monument, where they remain to this day. Gwinnett's could not be found, and during the next 110 years, there appeared to be no great urgency to find them. Once in a while, a newspaper would publish a story about it, including one in 1948 with the headline, "Where's Button Gwinnett's grave?"

Then in the 1950s, the Savannah-Chatham County Historic Site and Monument Commission oversaw what can only be described as an exhaustive investigation. It involved, among others, a Smithsonian Institution archaeologist, two dentists, a doctor, a Georgia Historical Commission archaeologist, a Georgia State Crime Laboratory senior toxicologist, an FBI evidence analyst, a ballistics expert and a local public school educator. The latter, Savannah native Arthur J. Funk, would have impressed Sherlock Holmes. Not only did Funk convince the commission to conduct the investigation, but he found and analyzed more evidence than anyone else involved in the effort.

The first question the commission attempted to answer was whether Gwinnett was buried in Savannah's Colonial Park Cemetery. If you lived in and around Savannah and you were white and a Protestant who died between 1750 and 1853, you very well may have ended up there. Gwinnett spent most of his time in Georgia living on the coast — about 40 miles east of Savannah — but it made sense that he would have been among the 9,000 or so Georgians put to rest in Colonial Park. During the final eight months of his life, he was a prominent member of the Georgia government, and many of his peers were buried there. If the commission could determine that Gwinnett was also buried in Colonial Park and if his gravesite was located, it would set in motion an effort to have a monument and a historical marker erected there.

The fact that no one seemed to know where he was buried encouraged the belief that his remains were on St. Catherines Island in Liberty County, where he lived for his final 11 years. Those who believed that also believed the gravesite would never be found.

Arthur Funk was not one of them. He believed that Gwinnett was buried in Colonial Park.

Answers came on Sept. 28, 1959, when the commission released its report to Savannah's mayor and aldermen.[1] The report, aptly titled *The Burial Place of Button Gwinnett*, opened with an admission that the commission's job was made more difficult because Gwinnett was not well known, even though he was once — briefly — the state's most powerful politician and one of 56 men who signed the Declaration of Independence. It added that he was known in the 20th century more for the value of his signatures. The scarcity of his signatures makes them very valuable — seven-figure valuable today.

"…some of the difficulty (we) have experienced in preparing this commentary," the commission's report stated, "is due to the fact that Button Gwinnett is a famous name rather than the name of a famous man."[2]

When those words were written in 1959, there was no internet — and fame *is* a subjective thing, after all — but google America's Founding Fathers today, and Button Gwinnett's name shows up on countless lists. That quote notwithstanding, the report was light on commentary and heavy on facts, and it revealed a trove of evidence, much of which came from Funk. In 1959, he was a 60-year-old retired public school educator, having worked 18 years as a high school teacher and 14 as a principal.

One of the most significant pieces of evidence Funk found was a one-page document entitled the "Estate of the Hon. Button Gwinnett." It was filed in 1777 in the Office of the Ordinary of Chatham County by the estate's executor Lyman Hall. The document's top line refers to "Cash paid the Sexton."[3] A sexton is a church employee who maintains its property, rings the church bell and digs graves if the church property includes a cemetery. Colonial Park Cemetery was vested in 1758 by Christ Church — known as the Mother Church of Georgia — and the only sexton in Savannah in 1777 was employed by Christ Church. That sexton must have dug Gwinnett's grave, Funk argued, and it had to be in what was then Christ Church Cemetery, now called Colonial Park Cemetery. That, more than anything else, convinced the commission that Gwinnett was buried in Colonial Park Cemetery.[4]

But where?

The gravesite couldn't be found in 1848, when an effort was made to locate Gwinnett's remains and re-inter them under the Signers Monument in Augusta. Sixteen years later, when Union Gen. William T. Sherman ended his well-known "March to the Sea" military campaign in Savannah, about 1,000 of his 60,000 soldiers pitched their tents in the cemetery, where some of the soldiers — young, bored and emboldened — reportedly vandalized headstones during the five or so weeks they were there. It is anyone's guess if the soldiers defaced Gwinnett's headstone. But about 90 years after they left Savannah, Arthur Funk was confident he had located Gwinnett's gravesite.

What was left of the headstone was a trip hazard more than anything else, a stone stump, two and a half inches thick and 25 inches wide and made from red sandstone.[4] In 18th-century America, most head-stones were made of sandstone, a soft rock, and that could explain how so much of this one could have deteriorated over the years. If it had crumbled to the ground little by little, the pieces probably would have been picked up and discarded, not saved and reas-sembled. Gwinnett had no direct descendants. Who would have cared that his gravestone was crumbling?

What was left of this headstone was excavated, revealing two markings that had been underground for nearly two centuries — a T and a 7.[5] When Funk saw those, he was certain he had found Gwinnett's headstone. He said the T and the 7 were examples of the stonecutter practicing his Ts and 7s. After all, there are four Ts in BUTTON GWINNETT and four 7s in 1735-1777, his birth and death years.[6] Funk the-orized that the stonecutter had no reason to believe that anyone would ever unearth the headstone and see those markings, so what was the harm in practicing his Ts and 7s on a part of the stone that would forever be underground?

This news was leaked in 1957 — two years before the historical commission released its report — to *The New York Times,* which cared enough about this discovery to let the world know: "Lost Grave of Button Gwinnett is Believed Found in Savannah." Believed by Funk, at least. Not everyone was convinced, so he vowed to build his case.

Funk pointed out that this gravesite was near the sites of other prominent people who died during the latter quarter of the 18th century, most notably Archibald Bulloch, Georgia's first American-born governor, who died three months before Gwinnett. In fact, Bulloch was buried a mere 10 paces north from Gwinnett's suspected gravesite. That fact lent additional credence to the possibility that the gravesite that Funk had identified was, in fact, Gwinnett's.[7]

To learn more, the gravesite's remains were exhumed and examined twice in 1957. Two dentists concluded that the mandible and teeth belonged to someone who had lived about 40 years.[8] Gwinnett lived 42 years. An FBI analyst said the individual's hair came from a male Caucasian.[9] A tiny amount of grease from the hair was even examined, but nothing could be learned from it in that time, before DNA helped identify human remains and solve forensic mysteries.

However, other evidence caused doubters to question whether these remains were, in fact, Gwinnett's. For example, the coffin was six feet long, several inches shorter than a coffin would have been made for a person who was six feet tall, Gwinnett's commonly reported height.[10] But Funk argued that the person who reported that — Hugh McCall, Georgia's first historian — wasn't always accurate with those sorts of details. Funk pointed out that Gwinnett's ancestors came from Wales, and the *Encyclopedia Britannica* at that time described Welshmen as short and slight[11] — as if a Brit with Welsh ancestors could not possibly grow to six feet tall. Based on the length of the femurs more than anything else, Funk and others believed the person buried there was about 5-foot-6, making it more likely that a 6-foot-long coffin would have been made for him.

The most contentious debate revolved around the examination of the left femur.[12] There is no dispute that Gwinnett was shot — in the duel that killed him — just above the left knee, so that bone received a lot of attention from the doctor, toxicologist and forensic archae-ologist who examined it. In fact, the bone just above the left knee was slightly damaged, but Antonio J. Waring, a local doctor who was present at the initial exhumation, said, "That looks like a woman's skeleton to me."[13]

The femur was sent to Marshall T. Newman, a renowned Smithsonian Institution archaeologist who specialized in human skeletal analysis. After examining the remains, Newman wrote "neither the surface appearance of this crushed area nor the x-rays… show any indication of trauma during life." He added, "In all probability, the femur belonged to an adult woman," who stood about 5-foot-4. Newman concluded that it is "highly unlikely, if not fully impossible for this bone to be that of Button Gwinnett."[14]

Those who agreed with Newman pointed out that Gwinnett, upon being shot, said the bullet broke his leg. How could anyone with a femur that looked like this, they say, think his leg was broken? Others say Gwinnett may have had a low threshold for pain, and he wasn't a doctor, so he wouldn't have known if the bullet actually caused a fracture, unless the bone poked through the skin. They argued that Gwinnett only knew for sure that he was in a great deal of pain.

Funk vehemently disagreed with Newman's "highly unlikely, if not impossible" conclusion. Funk took the femur to Charles Sullenger of the Georgia State Crime Laboratory, who had identified "a circular depression" just above the left knee, perhaps a sign of a wound from a lead ball.[15] This was exactly what Funk wanted to hear. He then spoke with a ballistics expert who said many 18th-century duels involved "light powder charges" because the intent of those duels was to injure, not to kill.[16]

McIntosh and Gwinnett despised each other, but it can be argued that they intended only to injure each other. If true, they also might have used light powder charges that slowed the acceleration of the lead balls. How else to explain the fact that the lead ball that hit Gwinnett's femur above the left knee at close range barely impacted the bone? The historical record, which includes affidavits from two witnesses at the duel, makes no mention of an intent to kill or an intent to injure, only that there was an intent to shoot, and that is exactly what happened.

In the end, the historical commission concluded that the evidence showed "beyond a reasonable doubt" that Gwinnett was buried in Colonial Park Cemetery, though it pointed out that the evidence was not irre-futable.[17] As for whether his remains were in the gravesite identified by Arthur Funk, the commission said they "probably" are Gwinnett's remains, but not beyond a reasonable doubt.[18]

These conclusions were definitive enough to trigger a tug-of-war over what were thought to be Gwinnett's remains. Augusta, where the Signers Monument is located, wanted to re-inter them next to the remains of the other Georgia Declaration of Independence signers as well as Gwinnett's friend Lyman Hall and his foe George Walton.

"Forget it," Savannah's mayor literally said. But Augusta officials didn't. They asked Georgia's secretary of state and attorney general to weigh in on this, but those officials said the state lacked the authority to decide where Gwinnett's remains should end up. Augusta's mayor eventually backed off, saying that if the remains might not be Gwinnett's, Augusta didn't want them.

This uncertainty led one doubter to write this frivolous unsigned poem, which made its way into a file folder at the Georgia Historical Society's library in Savannah:

The Ballad of the Missing Bones or He's a She, Suh:

Button Gwinnett and Zipper Funk.
One was dead. The other thunk.
Dig, dag, dug. Bones galore.
Maybe Buttons. Plenty more.
"Bingo," cried the Zipper. "Bunk,"
Said the Doctor. Think, thank, thunk.
Got his friend to say so, too.
Now what more can the Zipper do?
Think, thank, thunk. "Lee," he cried.
"Call commission to your side."
"Look and listen. Weigh. Compare."
"A wag, a bone, and a hank of hair."
"Sniff, snaff, snuff. To-wit, to who:
"This is what we think is who,
"Buttons missing though there be,

"That it's proba-bully he."
Six conniptions! Seven fits!
Tear the silly thing to bits.
Son of a Smith: And who are you,
To sniff, snaff, snuff, the way you do?
Think, thank, thunk. Commission head.
Klink, klank, klunked. And then he said:
"Now let's everyone relax.
"Quake no more and stick to facts.
"I'll agree you both are right.
"Button's a long lost transvestite."

The commission's conclusion that the remains *probably* are Gwinnett's was good enough for the Georgia legislature, which passed a bill to provide $5,000 for a monument made of veined Georgia marble. Speaking in support of the bill, state Sen. Spence Grayson of Savannah said he planned to vote for it because "I want to get those bones out of Arthur Funk's living room." Funk replied, "Grayson had better watch how he goes shooting his mouth off. Button Gwinnett did it once too often and look what happened to him."[19] The truth is the remains were in a copper-lined oak coffin in Funk's *guest bedroom* — for five and a half years. He wanted it known that no living human slept in the room while the remains were there.

"It was talked about as a hush-hush thing," Funk said. "People said, 'He's got the bones in his garage, and he won't let anybody see them.' That was ridiculous.

They were in the guest room, and nobody asked to see them."[20]

During the late 1950s and early 1960s, when reporters wrote stories about Gwinnett's remains, as they often did, they frequently contacted Antonio Waring, the local doctor who had concluded that the remains that Funk dug up belonged to someone several inches shorter than Gwinnett and "probably" a female. Funk was never swayed by conclusions that differed from his, even if they came from doctors and archaeologists.

In 1965, Funk told a magazine writer, "He (Waring) would simply lip off in the paper all the time. I didn't give a damn." Funk insisted there was nothing personal between him and Waring, who was deceased by the time the magazine article was published in 1966, but he admitted that he saw Waring on the street one day and gave him a "verbal dressing down and maybe a bit of a push."[21] Funk clearly wanted all of his hard work to lead to recognition for Gwinnett, and it did.

The monument, unveiled on October 17, 1964, includes a bronze marker, which reads:

"BUTTON GWINNETT ... SIGNER OF THE DECLARATION OF INDEPENDENCE ... WHOSE REMAINS, BURIED IN THIS CEMETERY, ARE BELIEVED TO LIE ENTOMBED HEREUNDER."

The tall, granite monument is within sight of a historical marker and a weathered headstone for Gen. Lachlan McIntosh, Gwinnett's dueling partner and foe. There can be no debate that neither one of them would have been pleased that their burial places are so near each other, but Gwinnett, who was a proud man, would be happy to have the grand, attention-grabbing monument.

He finally got the better of his archenemy.

14

A Final Look Back

Button Gwinnett

It's safe to say that Button Gwinnett would be shocked to know that someone paid $1.4 million for a piece of paper with his signature on it.[1] For more than a century, autograph collectors have competed for signatures of the signers of the Declaration of Independence, and Gwinnett's are prized because they are so rare. He also might be surprised to know how many people over the years have wanted to know what he looked like. No one who knew him ever provided a written description of his face. At least not one that has survived. Georgia's first historian, Hugh McCall, who published his first history of the state only 34 years after Gwinnett died, recorded Gwinnett's height (6 feet tall) and his stature ("lofty" and "commanding"), but he didn't describe his facial features, either because he didn't think it was important or he forgot to ask those who would have remembered.

A few images have surfaced that claim to depict Gwinnett. The most credible — and debatable — one is a portrait attributed to the Swiss-born American artist Jeremiah Theus, who worked in Charleston, S.C., where Gwinnett occasionally visited his friend Thomas Savage III. Theus, one of Charleston's "court painters," painted a portrait of Savage's sister, Elizabeth, so Gwinnett would have been familiar with his work.

The man in the painting that some have attributed to Theus — and some think is Gwinnett — has dark brown hair and eyes, which stare blankly. The man's receding hairline makes his forehead look large, and he has a slight double chin. His hand is tucked inside his jacket, a common pose for men painted by Theus and 18th-century portraitists in England and elsewhere.

So did Gwinnett sit for Theus?

No one disputes that Gwinnett valued artwork enough to own paintings. A detailed inventory of Gwinnett's assets conducted after his death in 1777 lists "16 old pictures,"[2] so could one of those be a Theus portrait? It's possible, but the portrait would not have been particularly old at that time, and it's difficult to believe that Gwinnett's wife, Ann, would have parted with something that would have had more value to her than it would have had to a stranger who saw it an estate sale. John Park, a Philadelphia art collector, owned the painting at one time, but it's unclear when he acquired it and who sold it to him. It surfaced in 1957, when an Atlanta savings and loan association bought it for $5,000 from a New York City gallery, which "unconditionally guaranteed the genuineness of the portrait."[3] The savings and loan association showed the portrait to two New York City "art experts," one of whom said it could have been painted by Theus and the other said there is "every reason to believe" Theus painted it.[4]

However, Margaret Simons Middleton, a Charleston historian who has written the only full-length biography of Theus, wrote in 1958 of the painting, "In my opinion, it is not by Theus."[5] Middleton was considered an expert on Theus' work, but her opinion didn't stop the savings and loan association from attributing the portrait to him when it was unveiled later that year. And it didn't stop someone from paying $115,700 for it at a Sotheby's "Important Americana" auction in January 2001, according to *The Atlanta Constitution*. It sold again as an unattributed "Georgia Colonial Portrait" to an anonymous collector for $18,000 at an auction in Asheville, N.C., in 2016. (Prices for Theus portraits tend to vary widely. At the same auction house in Asheville, a Theus painting sold in 2017 for $150,000 — a record for the artist — while a Theus portrait of James Habersham, Jr., a speaker of the Georgia House of Assembly, went for only $26,000 in 2023.)

Art historian Martha R. Severens, who has written a scholarly article about Theus' artistic style, agrees with Middleton. "The portrait was not done by Theus," said Severens, whose career has focused on Southern art and artists. "It does not have the quirky facial expression so typical of Theus."[6] The Gibbes Museum of Art in Charleston, which has 20 portraits by Theus or attributed to him, shared the contents of a folder marked Theus-Gwinnett, but it contains little more than letters and newspaper clippings from 1958 that cast doubt on whether Theus painted Gwinnett's portrait. Beyond that, an associate curator there said the museum is "not able to provide an opinion…."

The circumstantial evidence — that Gwinnett would have been familiar with Theus' work and occasionally visited Charleston when Theus was painting there — is too weak to overrule Severens' and Middleton's opinion that Theus did not paint the portrait. So the mystery of what Gwinnett looked like will not be solved here, unfortunately, and that explains the blurred face on the book's front cover.

The fact that no one can know what Gwinnett's face looked like hasn't kept his name and imagined likenesses from being plastered all over Georgia. There's the Button Gwinnett Statue at the Mall of Georgia in Buford, Georgia Gwinnett College in Lawrenceville, Button Gwinnett Drive in Atlanta, Gwinnett Elementary School in Hinesville, Gwinnett Street in Savannah, Button Gwinnett Place in Norcross, the Button Gwinnett Historical Marker in Liberty County, the Button Gwinnett gravesite monument in Savannah, Gwinnett Distribution Center in Atlanta, the Button Gwinnett chapter of the Georgia Society of the Sons of the Revolution in Lawrenceville, the Button Gwinnett House on St. Catherines Island, the University of Georgia's Gwinnett Campus in Lawrenceville, and, of course, Gwinnett County, just northeast of Atlanta. Gwinnett County boasts the Gwinnett School of Mathematics, Science and Technology, widely viewed as one of the best — if not *the* best — public high school in Georgia.

About 4,000 miles northeast of the Georgia coast is the Button Gwinnett Course at the Cottrell Park Golf Club outside Cardiff, Wales, the country where his ancestors lived. And at The Collegiate Church of St. Peter in Wolverhampton, England, is a plaque that notes his marriage there in 1757, his role as a signer of the Declaration of Independence in 1776 and his brief stint as governor of Georgia in 1777.

Gwinnett has also attracted the attention of 20th- and 21st-century writers and entertainers.

In his 1953 short story called *Button, Button*, the acclaimed science fiction writer Isaac Asimov tells the tale of an eccentric professor and inventor who is trying to raise money to create a flute that can be played by mental power alone. To do this, he enlists the help of a shady nephew to use another one of his inventions, which can reach into the past to retrieve objects. Their plan is to obtain a document signed by Button Gwinnett and sell it to finance the cost to design and manufacture the flute. They manage to retrieve an original document with Gwinnett's signature on it, but when they try to have it authenticated some 175 years after it was signed, they face an insurmountable problem: The 175-year-old document doesn't look 175 years old. It looks relatively new, and 20th-century appraisers won't authenticate it because it doesn't look nearly as old as it should. So the professor and his nephew are stuck with an incredibly valuable Gwinnett-signed document that they can't sell.

More recently, *Hamilton* creator and star Lin-Manuel Miranda also was drawn to Gwinnett. He wrote a rap song about Gwinnett, called *Button!*, and performed it with Steven Colbert on the latter's late-night talk show in 2015. The video is on YouTube, but here are Miranda's clever lyrics:

John Adams:

Barmaid, one ale if it's not too much bother

Pay attention! Did I mention I'm a Founding Father?

Don't try to front me, I won't play that, madam

I'm a founder of this country and my name's John Adams

Button Gwinnett:

I knew it was you, my boy Johnny Ace

Has it really been since Philly since I've seen your face?

Adams:

Thank you very much, always nice to meet a fan

Gwinnett:

Hold on a second, Adams, you know who I am

It's me, Button Gwinnett, I don't need a citation

Cause we met tête-à-tête when we signed the Declaration

Big-wig style, how could you forget?

I'm your brother founding father, Big B Gwinnett!

Adams:

Sorry, didn't hear, can you repeat that name?

Was it Bilbo Gimlet, what's your claim to fame?

I don't remember any hobbits on the signature roster

You say you're a Founder but you look like a Loster

Gwinnett:

What?! What!

You can call me Gwinnett, you can call me Button

All the shorties call me over when they see me struttin'

I'm a patriotic player, I don't need to cajole

I got the lady-folks unbuttoning their buttonhole

Yeah, ask Abigail, she knows

Adams:

I'm John frickin' Adams, come on, show respect

I ain't never heard of no buster named Button Gwinnett!

I'm the O.G. V.P. and I know every signer

From Hancock in Boston to Lynch in Carolina

Gwinnett:

It's a mystery why you're pissed at me

But Button Gwinnett will make history

I'm a glutton for attention so don't you forget

Tell him my name:

Button Gwinnett!

What's my name?

Button Gwinnett!

What's my name?

Button Gwinnett!

What's my name?

Button Gwinnett!

Ann Bourne Gwinnett

Very little is known about Button Gwinnett's wife, Ann, except that her father was a successful grocer in Wolverhampton, England, and she married Button in 1757, at the age of 22. During the first half of their 20-year marriage, she mostly lived in England while he was out to sea or in America. She outlived him and all three of their children.

Ann's paper trail consists of three wills and three other documents — a petition and two letters, which she sent to John Hancock, president of the Second Continental Congress. In the longer of the two letters, dated August 1, 1777, she referred to herself as an "exceedingly dejected widow," and stated that, "Mr. Gwinnett neglected his private Interests to serve this Publick (sic) Cause."[7] This was largely untrue, but perhaps she assumed that Hancock, who lived in Massachusetts and mostly worked in Philadelphia, wouldn't know any better. She asked Hancock if Congress would give her some money, but it never did. It did, however, recognize receiving "a letter and memorial from A. Gwinnett, of Georgia" on October 1 of that year.[8]

Ann Gwinnett's first will, dated August 24, 1770, listed her mother as her heir — not her husband, curiously enough — and named three creditors and the amounts they were to receive from her estate if they were not repaid by the time of her death. The second will, signed on October 20, 1780, three years after Gwinnett's death, named Elizabeth Ann "Betsy" Belin, her only living daughter, as her heir. By this time, she and Betsy, who was married, lived in Charleston, S.C., and Lyman Hall, the executor of her husband's estate, was still hard at work trying to satisfy her husband's creditors. The third will, dated May 4, 1785, referred to Betsy as deceased and named

Peter Belin, Betsy's widower, as Ann's heir. Ann, who had filed a lawsuit against Belin in South Carolina, died in 1785, shortly after she signed her final will. Despite their legal dispute and the fact that Ann most likely owned very little of value, he traveled to England to settle her estate.

Elizabeth "Betsy" Gwinnett

Even less is known about Elizabeth Gwinnett, Button and Ann's daughter. She was in America in 1777, when her father was killed, and it is believed she lived in Georgia then and moved soon afterward to Charleston to live with a friend of her father's and attend school. While there in 1779, she married Peter Belin, a surveyor, planter and merchant. She was 23 when she died in 1785.

Button Gwinnett's direct descendants

There are none. Button and Ann had only one child, Betsy, who lived to adulthood, but Betsy and her husband had no children. Nor did Button's uncles, William and George. Nor did his brother Samuel or his brother John, who died in 1777, the same year as Button. Nor did his sister, Emilia, who lived into adulthood but never married or bore a child. Button had three other siblings: Anna Maria, Thomas and Robert, who died when they were children. Their father, Samuel Gwinnett, Sr., by the way, died in 1775, 10 years after Anne, his wife and Button's mother.[9]

Samuel Gwinnett Jr.

Button's older brother, Samuel Gwinnett, Jr., an Anglican minister, married Emilia Button, a relative on his mother's side of the family. Emilia inherited a country estate in 1755 and lived there until she died in 1785. Samuel lived there until he died in 1792. He was 59.

Lyman Hall

Lyman Hall, one of Gwinnett's best friends, was a planter, a self-taught doctor, a face of the independence movement in Georgia and a signer of the Declaration of Independence. Refer to the chapters, A Duel to the Death and A Tangled Mess, Part 2, for details of Hall's life after Gwinnett died.

Lachlan McIntosh

After Lachlan McIntosh was run out of Georgia in the fall of 1777, he joined the Central Continental Army under George Washington at Valley Forge, where he commanded several regiments of North Carolina troops. McIntosh served at Fort Pitt in Pittsburgh, Pa., in 1778. He returned to Georgia in the fall of 1779 to fight in the Siege of Savannah, an unsuccessful attempt by American and French troops to oust the British, who had recolonized Georgia, the only one of the 13 American colonies with that dubious distinction. British forces destroyed his plantation, and he never recovered financially. After McIntosh returned to Georgia to fight in the Siege of Savannah, some Georgians were still complaining about his alleged links to the British, but George Washington, as he had previously done, was still defending him. In a 1779 letter, Washington wrote, "The sole reason for appointing General McIntosh to his present command was an opinion of his being in every way qualified for it — and I must observe that while the General was immediately under me his conduct gave the most favourable impression of him in every aspect."[10]

In 1780, McIntosh continued to serve his country, fighting in defense of Charleston, where he was taken prisoner by the British for more than a year. He was exchanged for British Gen. Charles O'Hara on February 9, 1782. McIntosh's critics in Georgia continued to link him to his brother, George, who was suspected of treason. Despite this cloud over his head, state lawmakers chose Lachlan to serve in Congress in 1784, though he didn't attend the session. The next year he served on a commission that led to a treaty with the Cherokee Nation,[11] and in 1787, he played a role in settling a boundary dispute between

Georgia and South Carolina. In May of 1791 — as part of President George Washington's first and only visit to Georgia — McIntosh escorted him around Savannah for four days.

I have read that McIntosh, who owned enslaved people most of his adult life, opposed slavery. This confusion most likely is due to the fact that he presided over and recorded the 1775 St. Andrew's Parish Convention in Darien, where delegates declared their "disapprobation and abhorrence of the unnatural practice of slavery in America."[12] Six months later, McIntosh wrote to a Savannah merchant, asking him to sell two of McIntosh's runaway slaves who ended up in a workhouse in Charleston "to the best advantage & *as soon as possible* to save any further Expence or risque."[13] This was not part of a broader plan by McIntosh to sell his slaves and stop using slave labor. During the 18th and 19th centuries, it was one thing for a slave owner to declare an opposition to slavery and quite another to give enslaved people their freedom. Like virtually every large landowner in America back then, McIntosh depended on slave labor, and when he had underworked slaves, as he did in the 1780s and 1790s, he sometimes leased them to other landowners. At the time of his death in 1806, he owned several parcels of land in coastal Georgia, and in his rambling will, he bequeathed his "house and lot" on Barnard Street in Savannah to his wife, Sarah, and many of his 19 slaves to Charles Harris, a son-in-law.[14]

Tourists in Savannah today sometimes learn of McIntosh while walking past the "Lachlan McIntosh House" on East Oglethorpe Avenue. Despite what the house-mounted plaque states, McIntosh never owned that house or lived in it. If I were asked to write the plaque's inscription, it would read: "Built in 1770, this house is believed to be the oldest brick residence in Georgia, and in January 1784 it was the site of the Georgia legislature's first post-British rule constitutional session." Both of those things are true.

McIntosh County in coastal Georgia was named in honor of his family, who had arrived there from Scotland in 1736 to help defend Georgians from Spaniards in St. Augustine, Fla.

James Wright

James Wright, the royal governor of Georgia from 1760 to 1776 and from 1779 to 1781, had a lot to gain by convincing Parliament to recolonize Georgia after the British were ousted in the winter of 1776. Much of his wealth was in America, where he owned plantations in Georgia and South Carolina and hundreds of enslaved people. After the British lost what is considered the decisive battle of the Revolutionary War in Yorktown, Va., in October 1781, they began to pull out of Georgia. Wright left Savannah on July 11, 1782,[15] and requested transportation to Jamaica for the 2,000 or so enslaved people he owned. More than

1,500 are believed to have made the trip.[16] (For context, Thomas Jefferson owned more enslaved people than any other American Founding Father — about 600 at one time.)

Wright returned to England not long afterward and died in his home in London in 1785, at age 69.[17] He is interred at Westminster Abbey, along with 3,300 other Britons, including Charles Dickens, Isaac Newton, Geoffrey Chaucer, T.S. Eliot, Rudyard Kipling, Stephen Hawking and Laurence Olivier. Wright's ledger stone stands out for being one of the most — if not *the* most— worn grave markers in the 780-year-old church. It's near the visitors entrance, and it's impossible to enter the building without stepping on it.

Wright Square in downtown Savannah is named for him, as is Wrightsboro, Ga., a tiny unincorporated community between Augusta and Athens.

King George III

George III, America's last king, was shrewd and confident, but when it came to his North American colonies, he was too confident. In the years leading up to the Revolutionary War, he underestimated America's desire for independence and never considered granting it. After the war, upon meeting John Adams, he said, "I was the last to consent to the separation." George, who was constitutionally commander-in-chief, worried that the British defeat — "the most serious in which any country was engaged," in his own words — would be "laid at my door."[18] And it was. His biographer Andrew Roberts called it "a colossal disaster, the worst in British history until the loss of India in 1947."[19] Toward the end of the war, this quagmire led the British House of Commons in 1780 to carry a motion that the monarchy's influence "ought to be diminished"[20] — a remarkable rebuke at the time.

Labelled by political essayist Thomas Paine as "the Royal Brute of Great Britain," George III was more accomplished than the loopy, brutal narcissist portrayed in the musical *Hamilton*. He played the flute, harpsicord, piano and organ, and he published an article about crop rotation under a pseudonym in a prestigious agricultural journal. He collected books — 65,000 or so in his lifetime — and more than 40,000 maps,[21] but his curiosity about the world didn't lead to travel. This homebody, who obviously had the means and the opportunity to go anywhere in the world, never visited Scotland, Wales or northern England, let alone any other European nation. He spent the last 14 years of his life within the walls of Windsor Castle, "a place I love best in the world."[22] For most of his life, he suffered from "mania"— what psychiatrists today call bipolar disorder. Dementia, blindness and deafness followed, and pneumonia killed him in 1820, nearly 60 years after he became king. He lived 81 years.

George Walton

George Walton, a Declaration of Independence signer who saw through Button Gwinnett's blind ambition in real time, was censured by the Georgia state legislature for supporting the duel between Gwinnett and Lachlan McIntosh. He became governor in 1779 and was accused of executive overreach, but that didn't slow him down. He returned to Congress in 1780, and served as Georgia's chief justice from 1783 to 1789 and as a U.S. senator from 1795 to 1796. He was 54 when he died in 1804.[23] Forty-four years later, he was reinterred under the Signers Monument — along with fellow signer Lyman Hall — in Augusta. He would be pleased to know that the remains of Gwinnett, who he intensely disliked, are not there. Walton County, in northern Georgia, is named after him.

Arthur Funk

Arthur Funk, the retired public-school educator who put great effort into trying to determine where Button Gwinnett was buried, was very busy in retirement. One year after the historic commission released its report on Gwinnett's burial place in 1959, Funk was elected to the Georgia House of Representatives, representing Chatham County, where his hometown of Savannah is located. Not long afterward, a bill passed in the state House and Senate to provide $5,000 to build a monument for Gwinnett in Colonial Park Cemetery. Funk, who at the time was storing Gwinnett's remains in his guest bedroom, said he had nothing to do with the bill.[24] During his 10 years as a state lawmaker, he made a name for himself as an opponent of what he considered wasteful government spending. Funk died in 1975, five years after he retired from politics.

Sunbury, Georgia

Sunbury, a town about 40 miles southeast of Savannah, was where many of the most passionate revolutionaries in Georgia lived during the 1760s and 1770s. Royal Gov. James Wright was not a fan of these people. One of the first things the British did after recolonizing Georgia in 1779 was torch the town, which once had a port that rivaled Savannah's.[25] Sunbury recovered to a degree after the British left for good in 1782, but was weakened by significant yellow fever outbreaks in 1791, 1805 and 1820, and two powerful hurricanes, in 1804 and 1824. By the time the 1824 hurricane did its damage, Sunbury was in serious decline. Its port ceased operations by 1830, and its post office closed for good on December 8, 1841. Sunbury, which was largely abandoned by the late 1840s, is now a ghost town with three historic markers.

The Gwinnett-McIntosh dueling pistols

The Georgia Historical Society in Savannah says its collection of artifacts includes the dueling pistols used by Button Gwinnett and Lachlan McIntosh on May 16, 1777. Unlike other dueling pistols, these two are not identical. The pistols' donor, Col. Lindsey P. Henderson, received them from the McIntosh family, who told him the stock on one of the pistols had been replaced because "one of the participants — McIntosh or perhaps a second to either duelist — supposedly flung one of the pistols against a tree, fracturing the wooden stock."

That explanation is at odds with the historical record. Here's why:

1. The duel was well documented thanks to two detailed affidavits, one from McIntosh's witness and one from Gwinnett's witness. The affidavits include direct quotes and minute details that have never been challenged, but neither witness mentioned anyone throwing a pistol against a tree for any reason. The pistols belonged to McIntosh, so if anyone purposely damaged one of them, it more than likely would have been him. But why would he do that? Did he feel remorse in the moment — or later that day — for shooting Gwinnett? Was he frustrated that he hadn't killed Gwinnett on the spot? At a time

when letter writing was as common as texting and emailing is today, no letters — to McIntosh, from McIntosh or about McIntosh — make any mention of him damaging one of his dueling pistols for any reason.

2. Not long after Gwinnett died, McIntosh realized that Gwinnett's death had aggravated political tensions in Georgia and that he more than likely was going to stand trial for killing Gwinnett. He went into defense mode and wrote a very long and very self-serving letter, justifying his actions and blaming Gwinnett's doctor for his death. If McIntosh regretted shooting Gwinnett and tried to break the pistol by throwing it against a tree or damaging it in some other way, it would have been expedient for him to include that in the letter. Many Georgians hated McIntosh for shooting Gwinnett, and he would have been wise to say he felt remorse, even if he did not. He couldn't bring himself to write that he did.

3. For those readers who think I prematurely exonerated the witnesses — George Wells for Gwinnett and Joseph Habersham for McIntosh — let's delve into the likelihood that one of them damaged one of the pistols. If that occurred, it would have been on the day of the duel when both men had access to them. Again, the detailed affidavits say nothing like that occurred. Wells

and Habersham were political adversaries, and if one of them damaged a pistol, the other wouldn't have covered that up. What's more, the affidavits state that Gwinnett and McIntosh acted like gentlemen before, during and after the duel. If the duelists acted like gentlemen, would one of their witnesses dishonor his ally and damage one of McIntosh's pistols? Habersham had served under McIntosh in the Battle of the Rice Boats in Savannah in 1776, and remained in the military as a lieutenant colonel for at least another two years. Would a lieutenant colonel damage a brigadier general's pistol? What about Wells? It's safe to assume that he disliked McIntosh, but it's a huge stretch to think that after shots were fired, Wells would leave Gwinnett, who was writhing in pain on the ground and needed help to get to his feet, and throw the pistol that Gwinnett used against a tree or damage it in some other way.

I believe that Col. Henderson told the historical society exactly what the McIntosh family had told him. Remember, according to Henderson, they said *perhaps* McIntosh or one of the seconds damaged the pistol, and one of three *allegedly* flung it against a tree. If the family didn't know for certain who broke the pistol or how it was broken, it's difficult to conclude that they knew for certain *when* it was broken. Maybe one of McIntosh's descendants found the mismatched pair of pistols, wanted to believe they were the ones used in the famous duel and created a story to explain why they don't look the same. This is exactly how family lore becomes fact, and anyone who watches *Antiques Roadshow* knows that happens all the time.

History lovers, myself included, want the historical society's pistols to be the ones used in the Gwinnett-McIntosh duel. But because there is no better provenance to show the pistols' connection to the duel, the historical society should be less definitive about whether they are the real thing.

Georgia's dueling legacy

During the Revolutionary era and well into the 19th century, duels were not rare in Georgia.[26] In fact, someone wrote a 302-page book that focuses on duels that occurred just in Savannah.[27] The 1777 duel between Gwinnett and McIntosh remains the state's best-known duel despite the fact that two Georgia governors, George Wells and David Mitchell, participated in duels of their own. In a fascinating bit of irony, Mitchell, who in 1802 killed a political adversary in a duel, signed a law seven years later banning duels in the state.[28] However, the law wasn't widely enforced, and dueling remained an acceptable — if undesirable — way for men to settle their disputes. Frequent dueling led to the creation on December 30, 1826, of the Savannah Anti-Dueling Association, which reportedly curtailed dueling. The last recorded duel on Georgia soil took place in 1877, a time when Georgia law enforcement officers had become more vigilant about enforcing anti-dueling laws.

In 1889, Georgia railroad executives Patrick Calhoun and J.D. Williamson crossed the state line into Alabama to duel, an event reported on the front page of *The New York Times* on August 11 of that year.[29] Calhoun, general counsel for the West Point Terminal Railway and Warehouse Company, charged Williamson, president of the Chattanooga, Rome and Carrollton Railroad, with "double dealing in railroad matters" at a hearing of the Georgia House of Representatives.[30] Williamson said that was a lie, and the duel was on. Word of it reached law enforcement, but Calhoun and Williamson managed to elude the authorities and settled on a spot for the duel called Hokes Bluff on the Coosa River. (Dueling was also illegal in Alabama at the time.) They agreed to fire five rounds each, if necessary, to settle their dispute.

"They stood game as they faced each other," the *Times* correspondent wrote. "Calhoun's face was white, but he looked determined. Williamson exhibited a flushed face and rather unsteady hand."[31]

At the count of three, they both fired, but Williamson misunderstood the instructions and fired all five of his bullets, one after another, each one missing Calhoun. Calhoun's first and only shot also missed the mark. With no bullets remaining in his gun's chamber,

Williamson decided that the smartest thing to do was to apologize, and Calhoun, being a good sport, accepted the apology and fired his four remaining shots into the air.[32] They returned to Georgia, where Alabama lawmen tracked them down and arrested them for assault and "intent to murder." They were never indicted, and that was the end of that.

And that should be the end of this chapter, but I find Calhoun's post-duel life too fascinating not to share. He became a business financier, investing in street cars and real estate. Years later, he moved to San Francisco, but he was in the wrong place at the wrong time. He lost much of his fortune due to the historic 1906 San Francisco earthquake. Afterward, a regulatory investigation found that he concealed huge losses in a company he owned there to keep the stock price high. That revelation triggered a move to New York City. While there, he lived off of his wife's money. Like Button Gwinnett, whose wife reportedly brought a large dowry to the marriage, Calhoun was not satisfied with that money and tried to repeat his business success, but he never did. After his wife died in 1928, he moved back to California, where he lived with his son. In 1943 — 54 years after five bullets whizzed by him in a duel with J.D. Williamson in Alabama — he was struck outside his son's house by a car involved in a drag race. He died a few hours later and then made his final coast-to-coast trip, resting in the Calhoun family cemetery in Clemson, S.C. He was 87.

Signature Census

"The fame of the man has therefore come to reside largely in the market value of his signature."

— The Savannah-Chatham County Historic Site and Monument Commission Report, released on September 28, 1959

Button Gwinnett, who lived for 42 years and two months, was a student, a grocery store worker, an ironmonger's assistant, a transatlantic merchant, a store owner, a planter, a justice of the peace, a state lawmaker, a congressman, Georgia speaker of the Assembly and the state's interim governor and commander-in-chief. He was also a son, a brother, a godson, a husband, a father and a friend. He lived during a time when letter writing was the predominant form of written communication, so it's safe to say he wrote and signed thousands of letters and notes during his lifetime, but only 51 of his signatures are known to exist, making them extremely valuable today.

In 2022 — during a week when a Thomas Jefferson signature sold for $2,900 on eBay — a collector paid $1.4 million for a one-page document signed by Gwinnett on October 9, 1774.[1]

What happened to the thousands of other Gwinnett-signed documents? That's the $1.4 million question.

Soon after he died on May 19, 1777, the executor of Gwinnett's estate sent appraisers to the plantation where he had lived to compile a list of his assets. It was very detailed, and it contained everything he owned that had any value at all, even old utensils, empty glass bottles and used books.[2] Whatever letters and documents the appraisers may have seen were deemed valueless and were excluded from the inventory. If there were any, Gwinnett's wife, Ann, may have kept some or all of them. If she had any of her husband's signed letters or documents, none have turned up.

Documents signed by Gwinnett may have been destroyed in fires that devastated Savannah in 1796 and again in 1820. The 1820 fire was the most destructive fire on record in the United States at that time, but the 1796 fire, which wiped out nearly half of the city,[3] destroyed a courthouse and the main city government building, where Gwinnett-signed documents may have been located.

His lack of direct descendants also may explain the scarcity of letters and other documents that include his signatures. If any documents or letters signed by Gwinnett surfaced in England or in the United States in the years after he died, would a non-relative have cared enough to keep them? Probably not.

Anyone who may have discarded letters or other documents that Gwinnett signed would have had no way of knowing that his signatures would sell for great sums many years later. That didn't become clear until the 1910s, when deep-pocketed collectors began spending four-figure amounts for Gwinnett's signatures. By the 1920s, the going rate was tens of thousands of dollars for a signed document. A doctor in 1927 paid $51,000 for a document with Gwinnett's signature — the price of seven or eight average-priced houses in America at that time.[4] Major works by Claude Monet were selling for less than Gwinnett-signed documents at that time, even after Monet died in 1926.

After the Roaring Twenties ended and the Great Depression began, prices for Gwinnett signatures dropped, but on July 4, 1943, Georgia Gov. Ellis

Arnall happily announced that a newly discovered Gwinnett-signed document, appraised for $52,000, would be kept in a state treasury vault so it wouldn't "blow away."[5] Arnall said he wanted the state to sell the document to the highest bidder, but that never happened, and it remains in the state archives, the only Gwinnett-signed document there.

Fast forward to 2010, when an unidentified collector paid $722,500 for a letter, written by someone else, that was signed in 1776 by Gwinnett, John Hancock and four others. The $1.4 million sale in 2022 marks the current record for a Gwinnett signature.[6] The next sale almost certainly will exceed that unless someone somewhere finds several other Gwinnett-signed letters or documents. In the unlikely event that the supply increases by more than a few, the value of his signatures may level off or even decrease.

Those who collect signatures from the men who signed the Declaration of Independence especially prize signatures from Gwinnett and South Carolinian Thomas Lynch Jr., who died, along with his wife, at the age of 30 in a shipwreck in the Atlantic Ocean in 1779. There are only 14 known Lynch signatures,[7] but inexplicably, his signatures have sold for considerably less than Gwinnett's. Is it Gwinnett's unique first name? Is it the fact that Gwinnett died in a duel? No one has offered a convincing explanation, except to say that Lynch just doesn't have the same "it" factor as Gwinnett.

Just as curious, signature collectors pay vast sums for Gwinnett signatures despite the fact that most of the surviving documents he signed are so uninteresting. Apart from Congress' "Agreement of Secrecy" document and the Declaration of Independence, about a third of the papers that include Gwinnett's signatures are bonds and mortgages, which reveal nothing more than the negative consequences of excessive borrowing and spending. Other documents record mundane government business. The only existing personal letter he wrote isn't remotely personal. In the two-sentence letter in 1773 to lawyer John Houstoun, the future mayor of Savannah and governor of Georgia, Gwinnett wrote: "Not till this Day, I rec'd y'rs concerning Mrs. Stevens's Demand. I am just going to Chas Town where I will Discharge it."

How fitting that the only surviving personal letter of Gwinnett's involves a debt he owed and promised to repay.

Of his 51 known signatures, four are clipped, meaning the signatures were cut from the documents on which they once appeared. Not having the documents makes it impossible to know when and why Gwinnett signed them, but the most avid collectors still covet his clipped signatures. One sold in 2017 for $319,500.

The 47 other documents, without any additional written documentation to provide context, manage to tell a story of the last 20 years of Gwinnett's life, between 1757 and 1777. These documents alone tell us that Gwinnett was married in England in 1757 at age 22, and his wife, also 22, was described as a "Spinster." His dream of becoming a transatlantic merchant was realized sometime before 1762 because he was doing business in New York City that year. By 1765, he lived in Savannah. Within two years, he received land grants in coastal Georgia, 35 miles or so southeast of Savannah. He was failing as a planter by 1768, and he lost his land on St. Catherines Island to creditors soon afterward. His many creditors hounded him until at least 1775. Between May 20, 1776, and August 2, 1776, he served in the Second Continental Congress and signed at least four documents, including the Declaration of Independence. After he returned to Georgia, he became a state lawmaker and gained political power, eventually serving as Georgia's interim governor and commander-in-chief of the Georgia militia. He wrote his will on March 15, 1777, two months before he died.

That's not a lot, but fortunately, letters written by Gwinnett's contemporaries fill in many of the gaps and help provide a more nuanced and complete picture of the man.

Because Gwinnett's signature is so unique and because there is less known about him than many other Founding Fathers, I wondered what a handwriting analysis would reveal about Gwinnett. Graphology, as it's called, is not an exact science, but certain elements of a signature can reveal interesting, if speculative, insights into someone's personality. Gwinnett's signature is often described as large and bold with confident lettering. Take this for what it's worth, but graphology will have us believe that large, confident lettering suggests someone eager to project authority and importance, and boldness in a signature implies a person who wants to be remembered. Maybe there's something to that because Gwinnett certainly was confident, and after he served in the Second Continental Congress in 1776, his involvement in government affairs makes it clear he wanted to leave a legacy on Georgia as it transitioned from a colony to a state. Gwinnett's legacy is complicated. He is viewed as a patriot and a Founding Father because he signed the Declaration of Independence, but his actions show he put himself before his adopted country, and the historical record highlights little more than his selfishness and his apathy toward American independence.

I want to acknowledge Ryan Speer, who compiled a Gwinnett signature census in 2008, when he worked as a senior archivist at the Georgia Archives. The following census, which updates Speer's work, includes the date of each signature, a description of the document and its current location. Most of these documents can be found on the internet.

1) April 11, 1757 — An application for a marriage license found in the archives of the Church of England. Lambeth Palace Library, London.

2) April 19, 1757 — A marriage registry book at The Collegiate Church of St. Peter, which once tried to sell it. Diocesan officials would not allow it. Staffordshire Records Office, Stafford, England.

3) August 6, 1761 — An account book of the Wolverhampton Bluecoat School, where Gwinnett signed his name as a subscriber. The book and the following three signatures on this list were sold to endow a scholarship. University of Saint Mary of the Lake/Mundelein Seminary, in Mundelein, Illinois, owns the book.

4) September 3, 1761 — The September page of the Wolverhampton Charity School account book. Office of the Historian General, National Society of the Daughters of the American Revolution, Washington, D.C.

5) November 5, 1761 — The November page of the Wolverhampton Charity School account book. Private unknown collection.

6) December 3, 1761 — The December page of the Wolverhampton Charity School account book. Western Reserve Historical Society, Cleveland, Ohio.

7) October 12, 1762 — A receipt for payment of a debt owed to Gwinnett. Yale University, New Haven, Conn.

8) September 14, 1765 — A bill of sale for a boat. Gwinnett signed as a witness. Cornell University, Ithaca, N. Y.

9) June 30, 1767 — Gwinnett signed for a John Barber in a memorial and quit rents book, Georgia Archives, Morrow, Georgia.

10) January 6, 1768 — A bond given to Noble Jones, one of the first Georgia settlers. New York State Library, Albany.

11) October 4, 1768 — A bill for merchandise when Gwinnett owned a dry goods store in Savannah. New York Public Library, New York City.

12) January 2, 1769 — A form that transfers land to a Samuel Farley. Historical Society of Pennsylvania, Philadelphia.

13) April 25, 1769 — A deed of gift, witnessed by Gwinnett, for five acres of land to Henry Yonge. Chicago Historical Society, Chicago, Ill.

14) March 16, 1770 — A bond to pay early Georgia settlers Mordecai and Levi Sheftall. Harvard University, Cambridge, Mass.

15) April 24, 1770 — A mortgage on St. Catherines Island to Edward Mease, an investor in Gwinnett's merchant business. Yale University, New Haven, Conn.

16) April 25, 1770 — A bond given to Mease. Historical Society of Pennsylvania, Philadelphia.

17) April 25, 1770 — A mortgage to Mease. Johns Hopkins University, Baltimore, Md.

18) May 29, 1770 — A will, witnessed by Gwinnett, of someone named Joseph Stanley. Rosenbach Museum and Library. Philadelphia.

19) October 20, 1770 — A receipt for payment of one acre of cedar. Indiana University, Bloomington, Ind.

20) February 5, 1773 — A document regarding debts and obligations to Gwinnett creditors Alexander Rose and Robert Porteous. Library of Congress, Washington, D.C.

21) February 5, 1773 — A document agreeing to sell St. Catherines Island to Porteous. Maine Historical Society, Portland, Maine.

22) February 5, 1773 — A document acknowledging debt owed to Rose and Porteous. Private unknown collection.

23) February 19, 1773 — A receipt for repayment of a debt to Gwinnett. Private unknown collection.

24) February 22, 1773 — A deed transferring livestock from Gwinnett to Rose and Porteous. Harvard University, Cambridge, Mass.

25) February 22, 1773 — An indenture for the sale of St. Catherines Island. Boston Public Library, Boston, Mass.

26) March 11, 1773 — A receipt for land sold to Rose and Porteous. Private unknown collection.

27) May 5, 1773 — The only surviving personal letter written by Gwinnett. The Morgan Library & Museum, New York City.

28) October 18, 1773 — A note written by Savannah lawyer Gray Elliott and endorsed by Gwinnett. Amherst College, Amherst, Mass.

29) March 16, 1774 — A receipt for repayment of a 500-pound loan from Gwinnett to Stephen Drayton. The two had a dispute over land. New York Public Library, New York City.

30) July 8, 1774 — A bond to John Neufville, a South Carolina-based merchant and lender. University of Pennsylvania, Philadelphia.

31) July 8, 1774 — Another bond to Neufville. Princeton University, Princeton, N.J.

32) October 9, 1774 — Another bond to Neufville. This document sold for $1.4 million in 2022 from one unknown private collector to another.

33) June 24, 1775 — The affidavit of a David Rees, signed by Gwinnett in his capacity of a justice of the peace. New York Public Library, New York City.

34) May 20, 1776 — A pledge by members of Congress to keep their proceedings confidential. National Archives, Washington, D.C.

35) July 12, 1776 — A letter signed by Gwinnett, John Hancock and four other members of a Continental Congress committee. It sold for $722,500 in 2010 at an auction in New York City to a private collector.

36) July 22, 1776 — A petition to the Continental Congress on behalf of Joseph Rice. Historical Society of Pennsylvania, Philadelphia.

37) August 2, 1776 — Gwinnett and 48 other congressional delegates signed the Declaration of Independence. (Seven delegates signed after August 2.) National Archives, Washington, D.C.

38) November 26, 1776 — An account paper signed by Gwinnett when he served as speaker of the Georgia Assembly. Yale University Library, New Haven, Conn.

39) December 6, 1776 — A bill to the Georgia leg-islature for mustering of troops. University of Virginia, Charlottesville, Va.

40) December 11, 1776 — An endorsement of a letter to Gwinnett from Continental Army Gen. Robert Howe. Unknown private collection.

41) December 18, 1776 — An order to pay an indi-vidual for his attendance at the constitutional convention. Haverford College, Haverford, Pa.

42) February 22, 1777 — A resolution regarding the exercise of executive powers in the absence of a quorum of the Georgia Executive Council. Private unknown collection.

43) March 4, 1777 — An order to pay a mail carrier named Jacob Linn. Private unknown collection.

44) March 15, 1777 — Gwinnett's will. The Morgan Library & Museum in New York City has had it since 1892.

45) March 16, 1777 — A mortgage for St. Catherines Island to Mordecai and Levi Sheftall. New York Public Library, New York City.

46) March 21, 1777 — A request to exchange $200 in Georgia currency for $200 in "Continental cur-rency" to pay Capt. Clement Nash to continue to recruit soldiers for an upcoming mission, signed,

"Your most humble of servant, Button Gwinnett."
Huntington Library, San Marino, Calif.

47) May 6, 1777 — An order to pay Samuel Stirk, clerk of the Council of Georgia. Wisconsin Historical Society, Madison, Wisc.

48) Unknown date. Clipped signature. Pat and Jerry B. Epstein American History Document Collection, Colonial Williamsburg Foundation, Williamsburg, Va.

49) Unknown date. Clipped signature. Harlan Crow Library, Dallas, Texas.

50) Unknown date. Clipped signature. Private unknown collection.

51) Unknown date. Clipped signature. Private unknown collection.

A careful reader may wonder why this signature census excludes a well-known letter, dated March 28, 1777, that Gwinnett wrote to John Hancock, president of the Second Continental Congress. No one disputes that Gwinnett wrote the letter, which he almost certainly signed, but it has never been found. It is part of the historical record because not long after he wrote the letter, someone copied it, and it ended up with Adam Treutlen, who succeeded Gwinnett as governor of Georgia in May of 1777. Treutlen sent it to Congress along with other documents as evidence against a Georgian accused of treason. Like the original letter, no one disputes the authenticity of the copy, which is stored at the Library of Congress in Washington, D.C., but Gwinnett didn't sign the copy, so it is excluded from this census.

Acknowledgments

William Faulkner described writing as "a solitary job," and I suppose that's true, but I want to thank those who helped me before and after I wrote this book.

Early on, I depended on research librarians who brought me documents and artifacts and pointed me toward information I wouldn't have otherwise seen. Thanks to William Wood and Linda Bridges who work in Savannah's Bull Street Library, and to Rachel Miretti and Meaghan Gray in the Georgia Historical Society's research library. My efforts to determine what Gwinnett looked like, while unsuccessful, were aided by art historian Martha Severens and by Brenna Reilley, associate curator at the Gibbes Museum of Art in Charleston, S.C.

Button Gwinnett's known paper trail is so short that I'm indebted to a handful of his contemporaries: John Adams recorded nearly everything that anyone said during Gwinnett's brief stint in the Second Continental Congress in Philadelphia in 1776. Gwinnett foe Lachlan McIntosh, a prolific letter writer, provided me with valuable information about what Gwinnett was saying and doing, particularly in 1777. Ditto George Walton, one of Georgia's three Declaration of Independence signers, who recognized Gwinnett's political ambition while it was on display during the final year of Gwinnett's life. Ann Gwinnett's correspondence to John Hancock in the summer of 1777, though self-serving, gave me insight into what was bothering her and her husband during this time. James Wright, Georgia's longtime royal governor, wrote many insightful letters to his fellow British dignitaries in England that shed light on the politics and economics in Georgia during the 1760s and 1770s, when Gwinnett lived there.

I leaned on the work of Hugh McCall, who published histories of Georgia in 1811 and 1816, not long after some of those who knew Gwinnett died. Historian Charles C. Jones, Jr., published a multi-volume history of Georgia in 1883 that also contributed to my understanding of the events shaping the state in the 18th century. I decided to write my book after I read *Button Gwinnett: Signer of the Declaration of*

Independence by Charles Francis Jenkins. If you haven't read Jenkins' book — the only other full-length biography of Gwinnett — let's just say he and I interpret the historical record differently when it comes to Gwinnett.

Now onto a couple of modern-day historians: Georgia Southern University historian Solomon K. Smith helped me understand what was happening in America during the latter half of the 18th century. Phillip Hamilton, professor of the American Revolutionary and Early Republican periods at Christopher Newport University in Virginia, provided valuable insight and good advice. Hamilton and Pulitzer Prize-winning journalist Ken Armstrong read an early version of the manuscript and wrote brief reviews that appear on the back cover of the book. Thank you, both.

I'm deeply indebted to my eldest daughter, Rosie, a wonderful wordsmith, who was the book's final editor. Thanks also to my other daughters, Olivia and Sophia, who encouraged me along the way.

Last but not least: My wife and best friend, Jayne, as she's done throughout our many years together, supported me from start to finish. She was the book's first editor and gave me valuable advice that greatly improved the final product. Thank you! You're the best wife and friend anyone could have!

Source Notes

A Land of Opportunity

1   Walter J. Frazer, Savannah in the Old South (University of Georgia Press, 2003) p. 63.

2   Gov. James Wright report to the British Board of Trade, The Colonial Records of the State of Georgia, ed. Allen D. Candler, vol. 28, pt. 2 (Atlanta: State of Georgia, 1916), p. 186.

3   Read and Mossman store ledger, 1765-66, Georgia Historical Society, Savannah, Ga.

4   Ibid

5   Ibid

6   Ibid

7   Ibid

8   Joseph Gaston Baillie Bulloch, A Biographical Sketch of the Hon. Archibald Bulloch, President of Georgia, 1776-77 (Digital Library of Georgia, 1900) p. 15.

9   The Adams Papers, Vol. 4, February–August 1776 (Harvard University Press, 1979,) p. 352-53.

10   Sanika G. Subhash, Phillip Jannotti, Ghatu Subhash, The Impact Response of Coquina: Unlocking the Mystery Behind the Endurance of the Oldest Fort in the United States (Journal of Dynamic Behavior, 2015) p. 397-408.

11   Official letters from Don Manuel de Montiano, Governor of East Florida, to Don Juan Francisco de Guemes y Horcasitas, Captain-General of the Island of Cuba, 1737 Sept. 30 to 1741 Jan. 2, Keith Read, Hargrett Rare Book and Manuscript Library, The University of Georgia Libraries

12   Ibid.

13   Rodney Baine, General James Oglethorpe and the Expedition Against St. Augustine, (The Georgia Historical Quarterly, Summer 2000), p. 197.

14   UK National Archives, Proceedings of the General Court-Martial on Lt. Gen. James Oglethorpe, March 1744, WO 71/57

15   Ibid

16   Ibid, General James Oglethorpe and the Expedition Against St. Augustine

17   Historical Statistics of the United States: Colonial Times to 1970, U.S. Bureau of Census, Part 2, Ser. 481-482, p. 1,192

18   Darold D. Wax, 'New Negroes are Always in Demand:' The Slave Trade in 18th Century Georgia (The Georgia Historical Quarterly, Summer 1984), p. 196.

19 Ibid, p. 197.

20 Intra-American Slave Database, Emory University, Voyage ID 103712

21 Africans in Carolina, Lowcountry History Digital Initiative

22 Paul M. Pressly, Scottish Merchants and the Shaping of Colonial Georgia (The Georgia Historical Quarterly, Vol. XCI, No. 2, Summer 2007), p. 140.

23 Ibid, p. 137.

24 Ibid, Account of the Number of Inhabitants in His Majesty's Colonies in America

25 Trans-Atlantic Slave Database, Emory University, Voyage ID 91133

26 Equiano, Olaudah. The Interesting Narrative of the Life of Olaudah Equiano, or Gustavus Vassa, the African. Written by Himself. London: Printed for and sold by the author, 1789.

27 Gregson v. Gilbert (1783), High Court of Admiralty, in The Annual Register for the Year 1783 (London: J. Dodsley, 1784), pp. 159–160.

28 Ibid, Trans-Atlantic Slave Trade Database

29 Ibid, Liverpool Shipping and Trade

30 Ibid, The Colonial Records of the State of Georgia, Vol. 28, Part II, p. 228.

31 Ibid, Trans-Atlantic Slave Trade Database

32 "State Laws of Georgia, 1755-80," Georgia Board of Regents of the University System

33 Ibid

34   Ibid, Savannah in the Old South, p. 79.

35   Treaty of Paris, 1763, Office of the Historian, Foreign Service Institute, U.S. Department of State

36   Ibid, Savannah in the Old South, p. 58.

37   Ibid

38   Ibid

39   Ibid, p. 61.

40   Ibid

A Man Who Married Well

1   Witchcraft Act of 1735, 9 Geo. 2 c. 5

2   George Hadley, Concerning the cause of the general trade-winds (The Royal Society, Volume 39, Issue 437, June 30, 1735)

3   Gloucestershire Archives, Gloucestershire Church of England Parish Registers, Ref. No. Gdr/V1/109, baptized April 10, 1735

4   gwinnett.me.uk

5   Ibid

6   Great Britain, Parliament, House of Commons, Report and Minutes of Evidence on the State of the Woollen Manufacture of England (1806), B.P.P. 1806, vol. III, Minutes of Evidence, p. 178.

7   Ibid, gwinnett.me.uk

8   Ibid, Button Gwinnett Inventory, Gwinnett Family History

9   Ibid

10   Patrick Wallis, Apprenticeship in Early Modern Europe (Cambridge University Press, 2019)

11   Ibid

12   Donald Jones, Bristol's Sugar Trade and Refining Industry (The Bristol Branch of the Historical Association, 1996), p. 1.

13   Ibid, Trans-Atlantic Slave Trade Database

14   The National Archives of the UK, Board of Stamps, Apprentice Books, Series IR 1, Class IR 1, Piece 21

15   Will dated March 14, 1755, probate records, Glamorgan, Wales

16   Ibid

17   Ibid

18   Extracted Church of England Parish Records, 1538-1839

19   Colin Gwinnett Sharp, Button Gwinnett: Failed Merchant..., (YouCaxton Publications, 2015), p. 23.

20   The Proceedings of the Old Bailey, London's Central Criminal Court, 1674-1913 (The Digital Humanities Institute at the University of Sheffield and the Higher Education Digitisation Service at the University of Herffordshire)

21   Ibid, gwinnett.me.uk

22   Who the Freemen Were and Their Role in the Corporation, Freemen Records, nidirect.gov.uk

23   Ibid, gwinnett.me.uk

24   Staffordshire Record Office, Stafford, Staffordshire, England

25   Ibid

26   Ibid

An Ambitious Merchant

1   William E. Minchinton, Explorations in Enterprise, The Merchants in England in the Eighteenth Century (Harvard University Press, 1965) p.1.

2   Ibid

3   Charles Francis Jenkins, Button Gwinnett: Signer of the Declaration of Independence (Doubleday, Page & Company, 1926), p. 22.

4   History of Morris County, New Jersey, 1739-1882 (W.W. Munsell & Co., 1882) p, 8.

5   Ibid, Signer of the Declaration of Independence, p. 22.

6   Ibid, p. 22-23.

7   Ibid, p. 22.

8   Ibid, p. 23.

9   Ibid, p. 22.

10   A receipt paid to Gwinnett, Oct. 12, 1762, Yale University

11   Register of Collegiate Church, Wolverhampton, England

12   Ibid

13   Peter Razzell and Christine Spence, The History of Infant, Child and Adult Mortality in London, 1550-1850 (London Journal, 2013) p. 271-92.

14   Ibid

15 Commissioner of Records of the County of New York

16 Bill of sale signed by Gwinnett, Sept. 14, 1765, Cornell University

17 Advertisement, Georgia Gazette, Savannah, Ga., Sept. 19 & 26, 1775

18 Ibid, Read and Mossman store ledger

19 Ibid, Georgia Gazette, Oct. 10, 1765, p. 5.

A Major Pivot

1 John D. McDermott, National Register of Historic Places Inventory Nomination Form, St. Catherines Island, July 9, 1969

2 J. Michael Francis, Kathleen M. Kole, David Hurst Thomas, Murder and Martyrdom in Spanish Florida (Anthropological Papers of the American Museum of Natural History, No. 95)

3 Herbert E. Bolton and Mary Ross, The Debatable Land: A Sketch of the Anglo-Spanish Contest for the Georgia Country (University of California Press, 1925)

4 Robert Montgomery, A Discourse Concerning the design'd Establishment Of a New Colony To The South of Carolina, in the Most delightful Country of the Universe (P. Force, 1835) p. 3.

5 Ibid, p. 6-7.

6 Ibid, p. 5.

7 Hugh McCall, History of Georgia (Reprinted by A.B. Caldwell, 1909), p. 24.

8 Ibid, p. 25.

9   Charles C. Jones, Jr., History of Georgia, Vol. 1, p. 384.

10   Andrew K. Frank, Mary Musgrove (New Georgia Encyclopedia, 2002)

11   Ibid, History of Georgia, McCall, p. 150.

12   Ibid, History of Georgia, Jones, p. 384.

13   Unidentified author, Itinerant Observations in America (London Magazine, 1745)

14   Corry, John Pitts, "Some New Light on the Bosomworth Claims," The Georgia Historical Quarterly, Vol. 25, No. 3 (September, 1941), p. 220.

15   Georgia Secretary of State Office, Book B, 375, and Book I, p, 377-378.

16   Ibid., Book C, p. 108.

17   Ibid, Signer of the Declaration of Independence, p. 50.

18   Ibid, p. 45.

19   Kenneth Coleman, The American Revolution in Georgia, 1763-1789 (University of Georgia Press, 1958), p. 8.

20   Ibid, p. 4.

21   Ibid, gwinnett.me.uk

22   "An account of the first settling of the colony of Georgia with a journal of the first embarkation, under the direction of Mr. [James] Oglethorpe," Peter Gordon, Keith Read Collection, Hargrett Rare Book and Manuscript Library, The University of Georgia Libraries

23   Trustees for Establishing the Colony of Georgia in America. "Letters from Georgia, v. 14202, 1736 June-1737 May." 1736-06/1737-05

24 The Colonial Records of the State of Georgia: Letters of the Trustees, 1738–1745, ed. Georgia Historical Society/UGA Press (Manifold digital ed., 2019), letter dated March 25, 1740

25 William Dusinberre, Them Dark Days: Slavery in the American Rice Swamps (University of Georgia Press, 2000), p. 7.

26 Ibid, Appendix C, p. 445-447.

27 Account of the Number of Inhabitants in His Majesty's Colonies in America, Colonial Office Papers, The National Archives (UK), Kew, CO 5/64, ff. 1–12.

28 Georgia: A Brief History, Christopher C. Meyers and David Williams, Mercer University Press, 2012

29 Ibid, gwinnett.me.uk

30 Ibid, Georgia Gazette, Sept. 10, 1766, p. 4, and Sept. 17, 1766, p. 4.

31 Ibid, Georgia Gazette, Jan.14, 1767, p. 3.

32 Adams Papers, Microfilms, Reel No. 197.

33 Lloyd's Register of Shipping, London, 1764, 1768, 1776

34 Colonial Records of Georgia, vol. 18, p. 389.

35 George J. Armelagos and John Toby Woods, "Myth of Button Gwinnett House" (Coastal Courier, July 6, 2009)

36 Lauren B. Sickels-Taves and Michael S. Sheehan, "The Lost Art of Tabby Redefined: Preserving Oglethorpe's Architectural Legacy" (Architectural Conservation Press, 1999)

37 Ibid, Read and Mossman ledger book, 1765-1766

38 Letter from Ann Gwinnett to John Hancock, Aug. 1, 1777, Papers of the Continental Congress, National Archives

39 Ibid, Georgia Gazette, Jan. 20, 1768, p. 2.

40 Franklin Bowditch Dexter, Biographical Sketches of the Graduates of Yale College, May 1745 to May 1763 (Holt, 1896) p. 117.

41 Ibid

42 Ibid

43 Ibid

44 "A good master well served. A brief discourse on the necessary properties & practices of a good servant in every-kind of servitude: and of the methods that should be taken by the heads of a family, to obtain such a servant," Cotton Mather, Evans Early American Imprint Collection, University of Michigan Library Digital Collections

45 William J. Fraser, Savannah in the Old South (University of Georgia Press, 2003), p. 45.

46 Ibid

47 Ibid

48 Allen P. Tankersley, "Midway District: A Study in Puritanism in Colonial Georgia" (The Georgia Historical Society Quarterly, Vol. 32, No. 3, Sept. 1948)

49 Ibid, Them Dark Days, p.7.

50 Ibid, Jones, History of Georgia, p. 52.

51 Ibid

52 Sheftall, John McKay. "Sunbury on the Medway: a selective history of the town, inhabitants, and fortifications [1977]." 1977, p. 19.

53 Ibid, Jones, History of Georgia, Vol. 2 (Houghton, Mifflin and company, 1883), p.167.

54 John McKay Sheftall, "Sunbury on the Medway: a selective history of the town, inhabitants, and fortifications [1977]." 1977, p. 15.

55 Ibid, p. 156.

56 James Wright to the Earl of Halifax, Savannah, Georgia, April 6, 1765, in Colonial Records of the State of Georgia, vol. 28, pt. 2, ed. Allen D. Candler (Atlanta: Franklin Printing and Publishing Co., 1916), p. 50.

57 Ibid, Jones, History of Georgia, Vol. 2, p. 156.

58 Ibid, The dead towns of Georgia, p. 174.

A Judge and a State Lawmaker

1 Swann, Lee Ann Caldwell. "Landgrants to Georgia Women, 1755-1775." The Georgia Historical Quarterly 61, no. 1 (1977): pp. 23–34.

2 "Colonial Records of Georgia," Vol. 9, 699, Vol. 10, 177 and Vol. 11, p. 347.

3 Ibid, The American Revolution in Georgia, 1763 to 1777, p. 8.

4 Memorials and Quit Rents, Georgia Commons House of Assembly, 1767, Georgia Archives

5 Commissioner Book B, 161

6   Ibid, Georgia Gazette, Feb. 24, 1768, p. 2; Georgia Gazette, Feb. 24, 1768, p. 3.

7   Erwin C. Surrency, "The Courts in the American Colonies," (The American Journal of Legal History, Oct. 1967) pp. 347-376.

8   Ibid

9   Ibid

10   Percy Scott Flippin, "The Royal Government in Georgia, 1752-1777, The Judicial System and Administration" (The Georgia Historical Quarterly, Vol. 10, No. 4, Dec. 1926) pp. 251-276.

11   Ibid

12   Lachlan McIntosh Papers in the University of Georgia Libraries, p. 1.

13   Ibid

14   Ibid

15   Harvey Jackson, Lachlan McIntosh and the Politics of Revolutionary Georgia, University of Georgia Press, 1979, p. 2.

16   Ibid

17   Ibid, Lachan McIntosh Papers, p. 2.

18   George White, Historical Collections of Georgia (Pudney & Russell, 1854) p. 334.

19   Ibid, Lachan McIntosh Papers, p. 2.

20   The Papers of Henry Laurens, Vol. 3, Philip Hamer, ed., University of South Carolina Press, 1972,

21   Henry Laurens. A South Carolina protest against slavery: being a letter from Henry Laurens, second

President of the Continental Congress,... G. P. Putnam, New York, 1861.

22 Bartram, William. Travels Through North & South Carolina, Georgia, East & West Florida, Philadelphia: James & Johnson, 1791

23 Ibid, Lachlan McIntosh and the Politics of Revolutionary Georgia, p. 6.

24 Ibid, Lachlan McIntosh Papers, p. 2.

25 Ibid, Georgia Gazette, June 16, 1763, p. 3.

26 Colonial Records of Georgia, vol. 18, p. 389.

27 Journal of the Commons House of Assembly, Jan. 7, 1755-June 16, 1782 (The Franklin-Turner Company, 1907), Nov. 6, 1769

28 Ibid

29 Ibid

30 Ibid

31 Ibid, Journal of the Commons House of Assembly, Feb. 22, 1771

32 William Harden, 1844-1936. "A history of Savannah and South Georgia : volume I." 1913, p. 160.

33 Ibid, Journal of the Commons House of Assembly

A Tangled Mess, Part 1

1 Ibid, McCall, The History of Georgia, Vol. 1, p. 404.

2 A bond given to Noble Jones, Jan. 6, 1768, New York State Library

3   A bill for merchandise, Oct. 4, 1768, New York Public Library

4   A bond to pay the Sheftalls, March 16, 1770, Harvard University

5   Biographical Note, Mordecai Sheftall Papers, Center for Jewish History

6   A mortgage for St. Catherines Island to the Sheftalls, March 16, 1777, New York Public Library

7   Ibid, Georgia Gazette, April 4, 1770, p. 2.

8   A mortgage on St. Catherines Island to Edward Mease, April 24, 1770, Yale University

9   A document regarding debts and obligations to Gwinnett creditors Alexander Rose and Robert Porteous, Library of Congress; a document agreeing to sell St. Catherines Island to Porteous. Maine Historical Society; a document acknowledging debt owed to Rose and Porteous. Private unknown collection.

10 A receipt for land sold to Rose and Porteous. Private unknown collection.

11 Ibid, The Revolutionary Records of the State of Georgia, Vol. 1, p. 613.

12 The first bond, University of Pennsylvania; the second, Princeton University; the third, private unknown collection.

A Revolution Brewing

1   Ibid, The American Revolution in Georgia, 1763-1789, p. 3-5.

2	Charles Lowell Downs, 1936-. "Revolutionary background, 1763-1775 / Charles Downs." University of Georgia Map and Government Information Library, 1974

3	Ibid, Savannah in the Old South, p. 83.

4	Alexander A. Lawrence, James Johnston: Georgia's First Printer, The Pigeonhole Press, 1956

5	Ibid, Georgia Gazette, 1765 October 31, p. 1.

6	Kenneth Coleman and Milton Ready, Colonial Records of the State of Georgia, Vol. 28, Part 2, University of Georgia Press, 1979, p. 133.

7	British War Office Muster Rolls & Pay Lists, War Office Series WO 12/868–873 and WO 4/90–94

8	Ibid, Colonial Records of the State of Georgia, pp. 133-134.

9	Ibid, p. xii.

10	William Harden, A history of Savannah and South Georgia : volume I. 1913, p. 172; David Ramsay, The History of the Revolution of South Carolina (1785), vol. 1, p. 10.

11	Merrill Jensen, The Founding of a Nation: A History of the American Revolution, 1763–1776 (New York: Oxford University Press, 1968), pp. 466–467.

12	The Papers of Thomas Jefferson, Retirement Series, vol. 8, 1 October 1814 to 31 August 1815, ed. J. Jefferson Looney. Princeton: Princeton University Press, 2011, pp. 682–684.

13	Ibid, Georgia Gazette, July 14, 1774, p. 1.

14 Two bonds to John Neufville, dated July 8,1774

15 Sir James Wright. Proclamation, Aug. 5, 1774. CO 5/663 f.156. The National Archives (Kew, London, UK)

16 Gt. Brit. Sovereigns. The King's Speech to both Houses of Parliament, on the 30th of November 1774. Together with their Addresses to His Majesty. Boston: Printed by Mills & Hicks?, 1775. Broadside. Library of Congress.

17 Ibid, The Papers of Thomas Jefferson, Retirement Series

18 "Resolve of a Convention of Georgia," The Pennsylvania Journal, 1775

19 Governor Wright's Speech to the General Assembly, January 18, 1775, American Archives: Consisting of a Collection of Authentick Records..., 4th series, vol. 1, ed. Peter Force (Washington, D.C.: M. St. Clair Clarke and Peter Force, 1837–1846), pp. 1152–1153.

20 Charles C. Jones, Jr., Biographical sketches of the delegates from Georgia to the Continental Congress,"1891

21 Charles C. Jones, Jr., The Dead Towns of Georgia (The Morning News Steam Printing House, 1878), p. 173.

22 "Georgia Historical Collections," Vol. 3, p. 227.

23 Ibid, Journals of the Continental Congress, Vol. 1, p. 45.

24 J.H. Redding, Life and Times of Jonathan Bryan 1708 to 1788 (The Morning News Print, 1901), p. 64.

25 Ibid

26 Sheldon S. Cohen, "The Philippa Affair," (The Georgia Historical Quarterly, Fall 1985), p. 342.

27 Ibid, p. 346.

28   Ibid, p. 347.

29   Ibid, p. 348.

30   Ibid, p. 350.

31   "Proceedings of the first Provincial Congress of Georgia, 1775," Braid & Hutton, 1901, p. 4.

32   Ibid

33   Ibid, p. 5.

34   Ibid, Trans-Atlantic Slave Trade Database, Savannah-bound voyages, 1774-1784

35   Ibid

36   Ibid

37   Ibid, Lachlan McIntosh and the Politics of Revolutionary Georgia, p. 32.

38   "Remarks on a pamphlet, entitled "Strictures on a pamphlet, entitled The Case of George M'Intosh, Esq." (Savannah: Lancaster & Mumford, 1777), p. 15.

39   Ibid, "Proceedings of the first Provincial Congress of Georgia, 1775," p. 7.

40   Ibid, Journal of the Continental Congress, Vol. 2, p. 193.

41   Joel A. Nichols, A Man True to His Principles: John Joachim Zubly and Calvinism (Oxford University Press, 2001), p. 297.

42   Ibid, The American Revolution in Georgia, 1763-1789, p.18.

43   Lilla Mills Hawes, "Journal of the Revd. John Joachim Zubly from March 5, 1770 to 9 April 1781," (The Georgia Historical Society, 1989) p. xii.

44   Ibid

45   Ibid, The Revolutionary Records of the State of Geor-
     gia, Vol. 1, p. 241.

46   Ibid, A Man True to His Principles: John Joachim
     Zubly and Calvinism, p. 297.

47   Royal Gov. James Wright to Lord Dartmouth, July 29,
     1775, Collections, GHS, III, 200-203; South Carolina
     Gazette, Aug. 1, 1775.

48   Ibid

49   Ibid

50   Ibid, "A history of Savannah and South Georgia :
     volume I," p. 187.

51   Ibid

52   Letters of Delegates to Congress: Vol. 2, p.108 & p. 111.

53   John Adams, Notes on Debate, Continental Congress,
     Oct. 12, 1775

54   Ibid

55   Ibid

56   Ibid, Notes on Debate, Oct. 20, 1775

57   John Joachim Zubly,1724-1781. "Journal of the Reve-
     rend John Joachim Zubly A.M., D.D. March 5, 1770
     through June 22, 1781." 1989, p. 108.

58   Ibid

59   Journals of the American Congress: from 1774 to
     1788, vol. 1, From September 5, 1774, to Decem-
     ber 31, 1776, Inclusive (Washington, D.C.: Way and
     Gideon, 1823), p. 7 & p. 55.

60 Georgia Council of Safety meeting minutes, Dec. 19, 1775

61 Ibid, Zubly journal, p. 40.

62 Ibid, The Revolutionary Records of the State of Georgia. Vol. 1, pp. 77-78.

A Reluctant Public Servant

1 Ibid, Journals of the Continental Congress, Vol. 2, Oct. 12, 1775, p. 494.

2 Proceedings of the Georgia Council of Safety, 1775 to 1777, Oct. 7, 1776 meeting minutes (Braid & Hutton Printers and Binders, 1901,) p. 27 & p. 29.

3 Interview with Solomon K. Smith, June 4, 2025

4 Arrest warrant for James Wright, Jan. 18, 1776, Joseph Vallence Bevan Papers

5 Ibid

6 Ibid, "Strictures on a Pamphlet, Entitled, the Case of George M'Intosh, Esq. Published by Order of the Liberty Society," First Series ; No. 15605. p. 15.

7 Archibald Bulloch letter to John Adams, May 1, 1776; John Adams, The Adams Papers, Vol. 4, February–August 1776 (Harvard University Press, 1979,) pp. 158-159.

8 Ibid

9 Ibid, The Adams Papers, pp. 352.

10 James Wright, "Letter to the Georgia Assembly, February 13, 1776." Keith M. Read Collection (MS 921).

Hargrett Rare Book and Manuscript Library, University of Georgia.

11   Ibid, Jones, History of Georgia: Vol. 2, p, 225.

12   Ibid, p. 226.

13   Ibid

14   Letter from Lachlan McIntosh to George Washington, March 8, 1776, White's Historical Collections of Georgia (Pudney & Russel, 1854), pp. 92-93.

15   Ibid

16   Ibid, Jones, History of Georgia, Vo. 2,, p. 226.

17   Ibid, p. 228.

18   Ibid, McIntosh's letter to Washington

19   Mary E. Stakes, "Government and Laws," (New Georgia Encyclopedia, 2004)

20   Proceedings of the Georgia Council of Safety, April 5, 1776, meeting minutes

21   Ibid, Signer of the Declaration of Independence, p.182.

22   "Papers of Lachlan McIntosh, 1774-1779 [sic]." 1957, p. 7.

23   Ibid, Journals of the Continental Congress, Vol. 4, p. 367.

24   Ibid

25   James W. Hall, Lyman Hall: Georgia Patriot, (The Pigeonhole Press, 1959), p. 94.

26   Carl Van Doren, Benjamin Franklin's Autobiographical Writings (New York, 1945), pp. 418–419.

27   Ibid, Journals of the Continental Congress, Vol. 5, p. 425.

28   Ibid

29 Ibid

30 Julian P. Boyd, The Papers of Thomas Jefferson, Vol. 1: 1760 to 1776, (Princeton University Press, 1950) p.44.

31 National Archives, "The Declaration of Independence: How Did It Happen?" last modified July 24, 2023

32 The Writings of Thomas Jefferson, ed. Andrew A. Lipscomb, Vol. 15 (Washington, D.C.: Thomas Jefferson Memorial Association, 1904), p. 491.

33 Ibid

34 Thomas Jefferson, The Life and Morals of Jesus of Nazareth, Smithsonian Institution Press, 1904

35 Ibid, "The Declaration of Independence: How Did It Happen?"

36 Ibid, Journals of the Continental Congress, Vol. 5, p. 433.

37 John Adams, Notes of Debate, Continental Congress, July 26, 1776, Vol. 6, p. 1,077.

38 Ibid, p. 1,078.

39 Ibid, p. 1,077.

40 Ibid, Interview, June 4, 2025

41 Ibid, Journals of the Continental Congress, Vol. 4, p. 346.

42 Ibid

43 Ibid

44 The Papers of Thomas Jefferson, Vol. 1, ed. Julian P. Boyd, Charles T. Cullen, John Catanzariti, Barbara B. Oberg, James P. McClure, and others, Princeton, N.J., 1950, p. 314.

45 Letter from John Adams to Abigail Adams, July 3, 1776, Adams Family Papers: An Electronic Archive

46 National Archives, The Declaration of Independence

An Unworthy Founding Father

1   Ibid, Journals of the Continental Congress, Vol. 5, June 11, 1776, p. 431.

2   "Presidents of the Continental Congresses and Confederation Congress, 1774–1789," History, Art & Archives, U.S. House of Representatives

3   Ibid

4   Ibid, Journals of the Continental Congress, Vol. 5, p. 425.

5   James Wilson (1742-1798), George Washington's Mount Vernon

6   Penn People: George Clymer, Penn Libraries, University of Pennsylvania

7   George Wythe, Thomas Jefferson Encyclopedia

8   Henry Stephens Randall, The Life of Thomas Jefferson, (J. B. Lippincott, 1871), p. 182.

9   John Oller, The Swamp Fox: How Francis Marion Saved the American Revolution, (De Capo Press, 2016), p. 227.

10 Ibid, p. 74.

11 Ibid, pp. 73-74.

12 Letter from Robert Morris to Gen. Horatio Gates, dated Oct. 27, 1776

13 Diary and Autobiography of John Adams, Vol. 2 (Harvard University Press, 1961), p. 156.

14 Ibid, Decision in '76, p. 79.

15 Ibid, Signers of the Declaration of Independence

16 Ibid, Diary and Autobiography of John Adams, Vol. 3, p. 347.

17 Letter from Lyman Hall to Roger Sherman, dated May 16, 1777 and June 1, 1777

18 Ibid, Lachlan McIntosh and the Politics of Revolutionary Georgia, p. 32.

19 Ibid

20 The Papers of George Washington, Revolutionary War Series, vol. 7, 21 October 1776–5 January 1777, ed. Philander D. Chase. Charlottesville: University Press of Virginia, 1997, pp. 309–312.

21 The Selected Papers of John Jay, vol. 1, 1760–1779, ed. Elizabeth M. Nuxoll. Charlottesville: University of Virginia Press, 2010, pp. 437–438.

22 John Sanderson, Sanderson's Biography of the Signers to the Declaration of Independence, ed. Robert T. Conrad (Philadelphia: Thomas, Cowperthwait & Co., 1846), p. 292.

A Hometown Hero

1 Ibid, The Revolutionary Records of the State of Georgia, Vol. 1, pp.174, 194 & p. 280.

2 Ibid, Jones, History of Georgia, Vol. 2, pp. 242-243.

3 Ibid, p. 244.

4   Ibid

5   Ibid, Journals of the Continental Congress, Vol. 5, p. 628.

6   "Letters Colonial and Revolutionary," The Pennsylvania Magazine of History and Biography, Vo. XLII, No. 1, The Historical Society of Pennsylvania, January 1918, p. 78.

7   Ibid, The American Revolution in Georgia, 1763-1789, p. 170.

8   Ibid

9   Ibid, p. 171.

10   Ibid, Journals of the Continental Congress, p. 528.

11   Ibid, p. 470.

12   Ibid, p. 711.

13   Proceedings of the Georgia Council of Safety, 1775 to 1777, Oct. 7, 1776 meeting minutes (Braid & Hutton Printers and Binders, 1901), pp. 103-104.

14   Ibid

15   "Papers of Lachlan McIntosh, 1774-1779," p. 7.

16   Ibid, Interview, June 4, 2025

17   Ibid, The Revolutionary records of the State of Georgia, Vol, 1, p. 281.

18   Ibid, Letters Colonial and Revolutionary, The Pennsylvania Magazine of History and Biography

19   The Papers of Alexander Hamilton, vol. 1, 1768–1778, ed. Harold C. Syrett. New York: Columbia University Press, 1961, p. 231.

20 George Walton to Lachlan McIntosh, April, 18, 1777, extract, Lachlan McIntosh Papers, 1774–1799, Folder 7, Hargrett Rare Book and Manuscript Library, University of Georgia

21 Ibid, Journals of the Continental Congress, p. 761.

22 George Washington Papers, Series 4, General Correspondence: Robert Howe to Archibald Bulloch, General Howe's First Letter to the State of Georgia. 1776

23 Ibid, Proceedings of the First Provincial Congress of Georgia, p. 111.

24 Ibid, Proceedings of the Georgia Council of Safety, 1775 to 1777, Oct. 7, 1776, meeting minutes

25 Ibid, The History of Georgia, Vol. 2, p. 271.

26 Georgia Council of Safety, Minutes of the Council of Safety, 1775–1777, in The Colonial Records of the State of Georgia, vol. 1, comp. Allen D. Candler (Atlanta: Franklin Printing and Publishing Co., 1904), pp. 473–475.

27 Lachlan McIntosh, 1725-1806. "Papers of Lachlan McIntosh, 1774-1779 [sic]." 1957, p. 33.

28 Kenneth Coleman, The American Revolution in Georgia, 1763-1789, University of Georgia Press, 1958, p. 80.

29 The Constitution of the State of Georgia, Georgia Archives, 1777

30 Ibid, History of Georgia, p. 259.

31 Ibid, Constitution;

32 Ibid, Constitution; pp. 254-255, 259.

33 The Parliamentary History of England, vol. 19,Debate of 18 November 1777, House of Lords, (London: T.C. Hansard, 1813), pp. 1027–1028.

34 Ibid, Constitution; p. 253.

35 Ibid, Constitution; p. 256.

36 Ibid

37 Ibid, Constitution; pp. 259-260.

38 Letter from Lyman Hall to Roger Sherman, dated May 16, 1777 and June 1, 1777

39 "Letters of Joseph Clay: Merchant of Savannah 1776-1793 and a list of ships and vessels entered at the port of Savannah for May 1765, 1766, and 1767." Savannah, Ga., The Morning News, Printers, 1913, p. 34.

40 Ibid

41 John Wereat letter to George Walton, Aug. 30, 1777, Lachlan McIntosh Papers, Georgia Historical Society

42 Lachlan McIntosh letter to George Walton, Dec. 15, 1776, Lachlan McIntosh Papers, Georgia Historical Society

43 George White, Historical Collections of Georgia (Pudney & Russell, 1854), pp. 203-204.

44 Ibid, p. 206

45 Ibid

46 Ibid, p. 205.

47 Ibid, p. 206.

48 Ibid, The Revolutionary Records of the State of Georgia, Vol. 1, pp. 120–121.

49   Ibid, p. 225.

50   Ibid

51   U.S. Bureau of the Census, Historical Statistics of the United States: Colonial Times to 1970 (Washington, D.C.: Government Printing Office, 1975)

52   Ann Gwinnett to John Hancock, 1777, Papers of the Continental Congress, 1774–1789, National Archives Microfilm Publication M247, roll 78, item 78, folios 85–88.

53   Ibid, The Revolutionary Records of the State of Georgia, Vol 1, p. 305.

54   Ibid, p. 307.

55   John Hancock to Archibald Bulloch, October 2, 1776, in Letters of Delegates to Congress, 1774–1789, ed. Paul H. Smith, vol. 5, August 16–December 31, 1776 (Washington, D.C.: Library of Congress, 1979), pp. 260–261.

56   Edith Duncan Johnston, The Houstouns of Georgia. Athens: University of Georgia Press, 2021, pp. 343-390.

57   Ibid

58   Ibid

59   Ibid

60   Ibid

61   Ibid

62   Committee Report on George McIntosh, Oct. 9, 1777, Papers of John Adams, Vo. 5, p. 308.

63   Ibid, The Houstouns of Georgia

64 Ibid, Ann Gwinnett to John Hancock, 1777

65 Ibid

66 "The Case of George McIntosh," (The Georgia Historical Quarterly, September 1919), p.132.

67 Button Gwinnett to John Hancock, March 30, 1777, Papers of the Continental Congress, 1774–1789, M247, roll 80, item 68, folder "Georgia, 1777.

68 Ibid

69 Ibid, McCall, History of Georgia, Vol. 2, pp. 192–197.

70 Letters of Delegates to Congress: Vol. 6, April 18, 1777, p. 615.

71 Ibid, Ann Gwinnett to John Hancock, Aug. 1, 1777

72 Button Gwinnett to Gen. Robert Howe, March 28 1777, photocopy, GHS 0336, Georgia Historical Society, Savannah, GA—original at the Library of Congress

73 Ibid

74 The Papers of George Washington, Revolutionary War Series, vol. 3, 1 January 1776–31 March 1776, ed. Philander D. Chase. Charlottesville: University Press of Virginia, 1988, pp. 415–417.

75 John Hancock, letter to the Convention of the State of Georgia, 20 November 1776, Gilder-Lehrman Collection, GLC07853, Gilder-Lehrman Institute, New York.

76 Ibid, Letter to Robert Howe

77 Lachlan Mcintosh to John Lawrence, May 30, 1777, Merion Station, 1937, Portfolio 162, Folder 33, Library of Congress.

78 Ibid, McCall, History of Georgia, p. 332.

79 Ibid, Letters to Delegates, p. 615.

80 Letter from George Walton to Lachlan McIntosh, May 1, 1777, Letters of Delegates to Congress, Vol. 7, pp. 11-12.

81 British Board of Trade population estimate

82 Ibid, McCall, History of Georgia, p. 332.

83 A note from Button Gwinnett, March 21, 1777, Huntington Library, San Marino, California

84 Lachlan McIntosh, Papers Respecting the Augustine Expedition in April 1777, March 25, 1777

85 Ibid, "Papers of Lachlan McIntosh, 1774-1779," p. 43.

86 Ibid, Papers Respecting the Augustine Expedition in April 1777

87 Lyman Hall to Roger Sherman, June 1, 1777, Letters of Delegates to Congress, 1774–1789, Vol. 7, edited by Paul H. Smith, Washington, D.C.: Library of Congress, 1981, pp. 161–162.

88 Ibid

89 Calvin W. Smith, "Mermaids Riding Alligators: Divided Command on the Southern Frontier, 1776-1778," Florida Historical Quarterly, Vol. 54, Number 4, p. 454.

90 Lilla M. Hawes, The Papers of Lachlan McIntosh, 1774-1799, Part III: Letter Book of Lachlan McIntosh, 1776-1777, The Georgia Historical Quarterly, Vol. 38, No. 4 (December, 1954), pp. 367-368.

91 Ibid, Papers Respecting the Augustine Expedition in April 1777

92 Ibid, Revolutionary Records of the State of Georgia, Vol. 1, p. 306.

93 Jim Schmidt, John Adam Treutlen, (New Georgia Encyclopedia, 2018)

94 Ibid

95 Ibid

96 Ibid

97 Ibid, McCall, History of Georgia, p. 333.

98 Ibid, Revolutionary Records of the State of Georgia, p. 306.

99 Ibid, Papers Respecting the Augustine Expedition in April 1777

100 Ibid

101 Ibid, Historical Collections of Georgia, pp. 92-93.

102 Ibid, Letter from Hall to Sherman, May 16 and June 1, 1777

103 Ibid, Ann Gwinnett to John Hancock, 1777

A Duel to the Death

1 "From Benjamin Franklin to Thomas Percival, 17 July 1784," Founders Online, National Archives

2 George Wells affidavit to Lachlan McIntosh, June 1777

3 Ibid

4 Ibid

5 Lyman Hall letter to Roger Sherman, dated May 16, 1777,

6   Ibid

7   Ibid, Wells affidavit

8   Ibid

9   Richard Hopton, Pistols at Dawn: A History of Duelling, (Piatkus Books, 2011), p. 81.

10   Ibid, Wells affidavit

11   Ibid

12   Ibid, Pistols at Dawn, p. 80.

13   Ibid, Wells affidavit

14   Ibid

15   Ibid, Wells affidavit and Hall letter to Sherman

16   Ibid

17   Ibid, Wells affidavit

18   John Hunter, A Treatise on the Blood, Inflammation, and Gun-shot Wounds. George Nicol, London,1794.

19   Ibid

20   Ibid

21   Ibid

22   Ibid, Hall letter to Sherman

23   Ibid, Signer of the Declaration of Independence, p. 155.

24   Lachlan McIntosh letter to John Lawrence, May 30, 1777, Library of Congress

25   Ibid, Ann Gwinnett to John Hancock, 1777

26   Ibid

27   Ibid

28 Gordon S. Wood, The Radicalism of the American Revolution, (New York: Vintage, 1993), p. 31.

29 Ibid, Hall's letter to Sherman

30 Letter from John Wereat to George Walton, Aug. 30, 1777 (Force Georgia Transcripts, Library of Congress)

31 Letter from John Adam Treutlen to John Hancock, June 19, 1777, Library of Congress

32 Ibid

33 Lachlan McIntosh to George Walton, July 14 1777, copy of original in Lachlan McIntosh Papers, Folder 7: "Copies of letters and other papers, 1777–1779," Georgia Historical Society, Savannah, GA

34 Ibid, Journals of the Continental Congress, Vol. 9, pp. 764-765.

35 Letterbook, September 1, 1777, Henry Laurens Papers, South Carolina Historical Society, Charleston, SC., pp. 144-45.

36 Lachlan McIntosh to George Walton, September 14, 1777. Papers of the Continental Congress, National Archives

37 The Papers of George Washington, Revolutionary War Series, Vol. 10, 11 June 1777–18 August 1777 (University Press of Virginia, 2000,) pp. 513-514.

A Tangled Mess, Part 2

1 "Estate of Hon. Button Gwinnett, Esq. Deceased," Court of Ordinary, Chatham County, Ga., Vol. A-B, 1775-1787

2   Ibid, Lyman Hall: Georgia Patriot, p. 95.

3   Ibi, "Estate of Hon. Button Gwinnett…"

4   Ibid, gwinnett.me.uk

5   Ibid

6   Ibid

7   Ibid

8   Ibid

9   Ibid

10 Ibid, Signer of the Declaration of Independence, p. 175.

11 Ibid

12 Ibid

13 Ibid, "Estate of Hon. Button Gwinnett…"

14 Ibid, Letters of Delegates to Congress: Vol. 4, July 12, 1776, pp. 445 & 446.

15 Ibid, Vol. 7, May 1, 1777, pp. 11 & 12.

16 Ibid

17 Ibid, Ann Gwinnett letter to John Hancock, Aug. 1, 1777

18 Ibid, Gwinnett Estate Document

19 Ibid, Signer of the Declaration of Independence, p. 175.

20 Ibid, Ann Gwinnett letter to John Hancock, Aug. 1, 1777

21 Ibid, Signer of the Declaration of Independence, p. 177.

22 James F. Cook, Governors of Georgia, 1754-2004, 3d ed. (Mercer University Press, 2005)

23 Ibid, Signer of the Declaration of Independence, p. 182.

24   Ibid, Governors of Georgia

A Missing Button

1   Savannah-Chatham County Historic Site and Monument Commission, The Burial Place of Button Gwinnett (1959)

2   Ibid

3   Ibid

4   Ibid

5   Ibid

6   Ibid

7   Ibid

8   Ibid

9   Ibid

10   Ibid

11   Ibid

12   Ibid

13   Ibid

14   Ibid

15   Ibid

16   Ibid

17   Ibid

18   Ibid

19   Roger M. Williams, "Who's Got Button's Bones?" American Heritage, February 1966

20 Ibid

21 Ibid

A Final Look Back

1 "University Archives Acquires Record Setting $1.4 million Declaration Signer Set," universityarchives. com, June 29, 2022

2 Ibid, gwinnett.me.uk

3 Letter from Granger Hansell to Margaret Simon Middleton, Sept. 12, 1958, Gibbes Museum of Art archives, Charleston, S.C.

4 Ibid

5 Ibid

6 Interview with Martha Severens, December 13, 2025

7 Ibid, Ann Gwinnett to John Hancock, 1777

8 Ibid, Journals of the Continental Congress, Vol. 9, p. 757.

9 Ibid, gwinnett.me.uk

10 The Papers of George Washington, Revolutionary War Series, Vol. 19, (University of Virginia Press, 2009,) pp. 365–367.

11 Ibid, Lachlan McIntosh Papers, p. 7.

12 Ibid, Revolutionary Records of the State of Georgia, Vol. 1, pp. 38-42.

13 Harvey H., Jackson, III. Lachlan McIntosh Papers in the University of Georgia Libraries. Athens: University of Georgia Press, 2021.

14 Abstracts of Wills, Chatham County, Georgia, 1773–1817, DAR Lachlan McIntosh, Will Book D, pp. 97-98.

15 Ibid, The American Revolution in Georgia, 1763-1789, p. 145

16 Ibid

17 Stan Deaton, "James Wright," New Georgia Encyclopedia, last modified Sep 29, 2020.

18 The Correspondence of King George the Third from 1760 to December 1783, edited by Sir John Fortescue (London: Macmillan, 1927), Vol. 3, p. 300.

19 Andrew Roberts, George III: The Life and Reign of Britain's Most Misunderstood Monarch, Penguin Books Limited, 2021

20 The Parliamentary Register (Almon), Vol. XVII (London, 1780), p. 133.

21 British Library. "King's Topographical Collection." British Library: Collection Guides.

22 Ibid, The Correspondence of King George the Third from 1760 to December 1783, p. 222.

23 Stan Deaton, "George Walton," New Georgia Encyclopedia, last modified Feb 21, 2018.

24 Ibid, "Who's Got Button's Bones?"

25 Ibid, The Dead Towns of Georgia, pp. 195-200.

26 Witt Calloway, "Dueling in Georgia," (New Georgia Encyclopedia, 2018)

27 Thomas Gamble, Savannah Duels and Duelists, 1733-1877 (Review Publishing & Printing Company, 1923)

28   Ibid, Duels and Duelists, pp. 112-113.

29   "Pistols Used in a Duel; Between Patrick Calhoun and J.D. Williamson..." The New York Times, Aug. 11, 1889), p.1.

30   Ibid

31   Ibid

32   Ibid

Signature Census

1   Ibid, "University Archives Acquires..."

2   Ibid, gwinnett.me.uk

3   "Leventhal Map, Savannah, 1796," Marion S. Carson Collection, Library of Congress

4   Historic Census of Housing Tables, U.S. Census Bureau

5   "Arnall to Seek Signature Sale," The Butler (Ga.) Herald, July 8, 1943, p. 6.

6   Ibid, "University Archives Acquires..."

7   Thomas Lynch, Jr., clipped signature sale, christies.com/en/lot/lot-6082882

Name Index

About the Author

Mark Di Vincenzo, an award-winning journalist, made a name for himself as a reporter who exposed abuses and as a writer who made the complicated seem simple.

During the summer of 2007, he left daily journalism to pursue book projects and start a public relations company. In 2009, HarperCollins published his *New York Times* best-seller *Buy Ketchup in May and Fly At Noon: A Guide to the Best Time to Buy This, Do That and Go There.* He also wrote the HarperCollins titles *Your Pinkie Is More Powerful Than Your Thumb* and *Buy Shoes on Wednesday and Tweet at 4:00.*

Born and reared in Cleveland, he lives a few miles south of Richmond, Va., on land once occupied by a Confederate battery that spied on and occasionally attacked Union ships moving up and down the James River.

He and his wife, Jayne, have three adult daughters, Rosie, Olivia and Sophia.

www.ingramcontent.com/pod-product-compliance
Lightning Source LLC
Chambersburg PA
CBHW031245160726
47993CB00001B/25